CLASSROOM CONNECTIONS

CLASSROOM CONNECTIONS

Understanding and Using Cooperative Learning

PHILIP C. ABRAMI
BETTE CHAMBERS
CATHERINE POULSEN
CHRISTINA DE SIMONE
SYLVIA D'APOLLONIA
JAMES HOWDEN

CENTRE FOR THE STUDY OF CLASSROOM PROCESSES
CONCORDIA UNIVERSITY

HARCOURT
BRACE

Harcourt Brace & Company

Toronto Montreal Fort Worth New York Orlando
Philadelphia San Diego London Sydney Tokyo

Canadian Cataloguing in Publication Data

Main entry under title:

Classroom connections

Includes bibliographical references and index.
ISBN 0–7747–3370–5

1 Group work in education. I. Abrami, Philip C.

LB1032.C53 1994   371.3'95   C94–931382–3

Publisher: Heather McWhinney
Editor and Marketing Manager: Joanna Cotton
Projects Coordinator: Laura Paterson Pratt
Director of Publishing Services: Jean Davies
Editorial Manager: Marcel Chiera
Supervising Editor: Semareh Al-Hillal
Production Editor: Sheila Barry
Production Manager: Sue-Ann Becker
Production Supervisor: Carol Tong
Copy Editor: Louise Oborne
Cover and Interior Design: Matthews Communications Design
Cover Photo: Bill Hickey, The Image Bank
Typesetting and Assembly: Impressions, A Division of Edwards Brothers Incorporated
Printing and Binding: Edwards Brothers Incorporated

This book was printed in the United States of America.

1 2 3 4 5   99 98 97 96 95

•••••••••••••••••• *Preface*

Purposes and Goals

Why did we write this book about cooperative learning? First, we were motivated by the enthusiasm our own students displayed when we implemented cooperative learning in our classrooms. Second, in training teachers, we saw how implementing cooperative learning inspired them and renewed their excitement about teaching. Third, we were impressed by the solid bank of research showing that cooperative learning can be a very effective learning strategy. Fourth, we saw some teachers struggle with having their students work in groups and wanted to help them structure their group work more effectively.

We also wrote this book because we searched for several years for a cooperative learning text that spoke to educators in a thoughtful and meaningful way. Mostly, what we found were three categories of books: one that showed practitioners how to use cooperative learning with little explanation of how or why it works; one composed of books replete with specific terminology appropriate for the researcher of cooperative learning; and another that presented cooperative learning from only one theoretical perspective.

Who did we write this book for? This book is intended for educators and students in education looking for both concrete strategies and an understanding of the theory and research supporting cooperative learning. Our book will also interest researchers who want a better appreciation of the breadth of cooperative learning techniques practitioners employ.

We have three aims in this book. First, we offer a broad view of cooperative learning, incorporating many different theoretical and practical approaches. Second, we present an overview of contemporary theory and research related to cooperative learning in a way that practitioners and researchers will appreciate. Third, we provide novices and more sea-

soned cooperative learning users with a description and explanation of cooperative learning elements and methods. This approach will give you a more critical appreciation of cooperative learning techniques and will help you make implementation decisions.

We have taken many steps in writing this book to attain our goals. First, as authors, we come from varied backgrounds; some of us contributed theoretical insights and expertise, while others shared practical experiences and knowledge. We feel this combination of expertise will guide practitioners in implementing cooperative learning. Second, we have taken an eclectic approach, providing several explanations for the effectiveness of cooperative learning. The integration of ideas drawn from a variety of viewpoints can provide the basis for effective cooperative learning instruction. Third, we have included some pedagogical devices to help you learn the concepts presented in this book: (a) advance organizers for each chapter that outline what the chapter contains, (b) scenarios describing classroom situations, (c) illustrative examples of cooperative learning, and (d) reflection activities at the end of each chapter to help you actively process the material presented (try doing them with a partner or in small groups!). These special features make concrete cooperative learning concepts that are sometimes complex and difficult to grasp.

How to Use This Book

This book is organized so that the background you need for *understanding* cooperative learning is presented in Part One, and the elements and specific methods for *using* cooperative learning are presented in Parts Two and Three, respectively. Depending on your needs and learning style, you might follow the order presented below. Or you might begin with the practical issues and choices we describe in Part Two, go on to Part Three, and then return to Part One. Here is a breakdown of the organization of this book.

Part One: Theoretical Foundations addresses the principle explanations of cooperative learning. We begin with an overview of behavioral, cognitive, humanistic, and developmental approaches to learning and motivation and show their relationship to cooperative learning. We continue with an exploration of how the performance of students is affected by working with others, what tasks are appropriate for students to complete when working in groups, and how relations develop over time, including interracial and interethnic relations. We also describe specific motivational and learning explanations of cooperative learning and present an organizational model that you may find useful when making implementation decisions.

Part Two: Implementation differs from Part One in that it places special emphasis on practical concerns. In this part of the book, we address the issues and choices you need to make when you use cooperative learning. We present classbuilding and teambuilding activities that you can use to create group cohesiveness and a positive classroom climate. We discuss the development and maintenance of cooperative groups and show you how to assign students to groups, foster positive interdependence, and encourage students to assume responsibility for their own learning and for helping others to learn. We also show you how important developing interpersonal and cognitive skills is for effective learning in groups, and we examine how self- and peer evaluation and reflection can involve students in their own learning. To help you get started, we offer suggestions for overcoming some of the problems you might encounter in implementing cooperative learning in your classroom.

Part Three: Selected Methods highlights some popular cooperative learning methods: Student Teams-Achievement Divisions (STAD) and Teams-Games-Tournaments (TGT), which use group rewards for individual contributions to a team; Jigsaw, a technique in which every student is accountable for teaching other group members; and Learning Together, which emphasizes group cohesiveness, teaches interpersonal skills, and encourages mastery of academic content. We also present two group project methods—Co-op Co-op and Group Investigation—which give students responsibility for selecting study topics and carrying out group projects. To implement cooperative learning in a flexible and eclectic way, we discuss the structural approach and offer a repertoire of content-free activity structures from which to choose. We also explore cooperative concept mapping and other peer-interaction methods.

Appendix A: Research Evidence presents the seminal findings on the effectiveness of cooperative learning. *Appendix B: Selected Resources* lists print and nonprint materials you may find useful.

ACKNOWLEDGMENTS

The preparation of this book would not have been possible without the assistance of many others. We would like to thank the following individuals for their contributions: Anne Wade, Craig Wright, and Lori Errington, who worked so diligently with us on the preparation of this manuscript; the staff, faculty, and students of the Centre for the Study of Classroom Processes; and, of course, the students and teachers who helped us learn to understand and use cooperative learning. We also wish to thank Mona Farrell, Alexandra Glashan, Kiki Kastelorizios, Jenny Schaeff, Diane Wagner, and Linda Wasserman, who contributed to earlier versions of this book and helped shape our present understanding of cooperative learning.

The comments we received on drafts of the text from Joanna Cotton, Heather McWhinney, and Laura Pratt Paterson at Harcourt Brace were especially useful. We appreciate the care reviewers of earlier drafts took in providing detailed and constructive feedback: Jim Cooper, California State University; Cheryll Duquette, University of Ottawa; Greer Knox, Ottawa Board of Education; Helmutt Lang, University of Regina; and Carol Rolheiser, University of Toronto.

We are grateful to the research funding agencies of Canada (SSHRC) and Quebec (FCAR) that have provided financial assistance for our research on cooperative learning, which significantly shaped the ideas in this book. We also want to thank our colleagues in the International Association for the Study of Cooperation in Education (IASCE). Through its conferences and publications, the IASCE has provided us with opportunities to exchange ideas with others specializing in cooperative learning, and thus helped us to refine our conceptualization of this field.

And finally, we thank our loved ones for their support, encouragement, and understanding.

A Note from the Publisher

Thank you for selecting *Classroom Connections: Understanding and Using Cooperative Learning* by

Philip C. Abrami, Bette Chambers, Catherine Poulsen, Christina De Simone, Sylvia d'Apollonia, and James Howden. The authors and publisher have devoted considerable time to the careful development of this book. We appreciate your recognition of this effort and accomplishment.

We want to hear what you think about *Classroom Connections*. Please take a few minutes to fill in the stamped reply card at the back of the book. Your comments and suggestions will be valuable to us as we prepare new editions and other books.

Contents in Brief

Table of Contents

PART TWO IMPLEMENTATION   45

CHAPTER 4 *Classbuilding and Teambuilding*   47

CHAPTER 5 *Grouping Students*   59

CHAPTER 6 *Fostering Positive Interdependence*   68

• • • • • • • • • • • • • • *Introduction*

Nathan was enrolled in a year-long university course in educational psychology. By midyear, Nathan had done little to distinguish himself in the course. His grades were all right, but both he and the instructor knew that Nathan would learn up to his potential if he committed himself more. But then things changed in the course. As part of a unit on instruction, the class was divided into heterogeneous learning teams and students needed to work together to learn. There were weekly quizzes and teams were recognized for the extent of the individual improvement of team members. Nathan and his teammates were having a terrific time working together to learn. "I never thought learning could be so much fun," explained Nathan. "My teammates and I are having a great time—much better than when we work alone. Why aren't all our courses like this one?"

Nathan is the fictitious name for a real student taught by the first author of this book more than ten years ago. Nathan went on to say that cooperative learning was the single most rewarding experience he had at school and was a major factor in his decision to continue his studies.

Cooperative learning has the potential to enhance students' learning. But it is neither a panacea nor certain to prove effective in every classroom application. Using cooperative learning well requires understanding what makes cooperative learning work. For example, when and how does cooperative learning increase the involvement and excitement of students with learning? Why do students try harder to learn? What makes students who work together learn more? How do students in teams come to understand course material better?

In the next few pages, we will provide you with a brief introduction to cooperative learning. We will define cooperative learning and explain how it differs from other forms of instruction.

Definition: Cooperative Learning

Cooperative learning is an instructional strategy in which students work together in groups that are carefully designed to promote positive interdependence. This positive interdependence is coupled with individual accountability so that students are responsible for learning and contributing to the group task. Cooperative learning has been used successfully at all educational levels, from preschool to postsecondary, and across a broad range of subjects. Current research shows the positive effects of cooperative learning on achievement, interpersonal skills, attitudes toward learning and peers, affect, and self-concept.

Group learning is not a new idea. At the turn of the century, John Dewey recommended that students work collaboratively on projects of relevance to their lives. Since then the developers of cooperative learning have provided methods, structures, and activities to make student groups operate more effectively.

A crucial element in group learning is that all members contribute their fair share to the group. This will happen if the foundations of cooperative learning—positive interdependence and individual accountability—are well established. Whenever the success of one student increases another's chance of success, there is positive interdependence. It is up to each group member to make sure that his or her actions help the group achieve its goal. Demonstrating each individual's responsibility for his or her own learning and for helping team members achieve the group goal is individual accountability.

Why Is Everyone Talking about Cooperative Learning?

Many individualized learning programs and materials have been developed to help teachers meet the unique needs of individual students. Cooperative

1

learning, with its emphasis on teamwork, goes one step farther by considering the social relationships among students and using them to promote learning.

The enjoyment of team sports has led some educators to wonder how teams can be used in classrooms to motivate students in their search for knowledge. The success of multidisciplinary project teams in scientific research has led others to consider the benefits of groups in which students of different talents and abilities work together productively. Group methods are showing business and industry new ways to increase productivity and worker satisfaction. The evolving theories of human resource management and social psychology have demonstrated the importance of social factors in adapting to a rapidly changing society. These phenomena have led to a variety of cooperative learning methods, which you can use successfully in your classroom.

Cooperative Learning versus Other Forms of Instruction

Cooperative learning differs from other types of group work or traditional instruction in several ways. First, in contrast to traditional classrooms, where students usually work individually or sometimes competitively, students are required to function interdependently in cooperatively structured classrooms. Positive interdependence can develop in several ways, including sharing resources (e.g., "Janine, pass me our sheet."), working toward a common learning goal (e.g., "Okay, we better stop talking and get to work on our story."), and depending on one another for acknowledgments and rewards (e.g., "Good idea, Finn!").

Second, in a cooperative structure, students' goals are positively linked. When one student attains a goal, it increases the likelihood that other students will attain the goal, whereas in a competitive structure, goals are negatively linked. When one student attains a goal, it reduces the likelihood that other students will attain the goal. In an individualistic structure, goals are not linked; one student attaining a goal has no effect on the likelihood that other students will attain their goals.

Third, cooperative learning differs from traditional instruction and group work in the degree and quality of interaction. Students in traditional whole-class instruction spend most of their time working by themselves or listening to their teacher, giving them minimal opportunity to interact with their peers. Although traditional group work is more conducive to student-student interactions, the participation of students is often unequal. By contrast, cooperative learning involves all students in purposeful interaction.

Finally, the teacher's role in a classroom using cooperative learning differs from a traditional classroom. With whole-class instruction, the teacher typically spends much of the day conducting direct instruction and managing students. The teacher is responsible for setting the academic objectives and controlling all classroom functions. The students adopt roles as listeners and note takers, and work individually.

In a cooperative learning classroom, the setting of academic and social objectives is often done in conjunction with the students. The teacher still uses direct instruction, but the role of the teacher during group work is one of observer and facilitator, rather than that of an all-knowing expert. Desks are grouped together to allow students to interact and to work together. Students may still spend some time as listeners and note takers, but they also become more active problem solvers and contributors. There is more talk and more noise in the classroom.

Teachers who use cooperative learning become different types of communicators. According to Hertz-Lazarowitz and Shachar (1990) teachers in traditional classrooms engage more in lecturing, presenting information, disciplining, and giving instructions. In contrast, teachers using cooperative learning facilitate communication among students by encouraging, and giving feedback.

Trying new challenges in your classroom brings up both new and old questions about teaching and learning. When you think about using cooperative learning in your classroom, many concerns may influence your choice of cooperative learning methods and design.

Some instructional designers treat teachers as if they were cooks. They provide teachers with recipes and tell them that if they follow the instructions exactly their lessons will succeed. Unfortunately, even though the lessons may be followed exactly, some students may still fail to learn because their needs and tastes were not considered in creating the recipe.

We see teachers more as chefs—people who create their own recipes based on their knowledge of the ingredients and how they interact to create a final product. In this book, we present the essential ingredients of cooperative learning and the various ways these ingredients can be combined to suit your students' unique needs.

As you consider implementing cooperative learning, ask yourself questions such as, How will my students react to cooperative group work? What types of cooperative learning are most consistent with my view of teaching and learning? How will my principal and my students' parents react to cooperative group work? Do I have the skills and resources required to make it work? How will my students be motivated to work together? What type of interaction and learning will be taking place during group work? And, finally, What types of outcomes do I want to encourage or can I anticipate? Such questions reflect some of the factors that are implicated in cooperative learning.

PART ONE

THEORETICAL

FOUNDATIONS

Cathie Archbould

CHAPTER

1

Learning and Motivation

WHAT IS LEARNING?

•

WHAT MOTIVATES STUDENTS TO LEARN?

•

WHAT ARE THE MAJOR THEORETICAL APPROACHES
TO LEARNING AND MOTIVATION?

•

WHAT IS MY APPROACH TO LEARNING AND
MOTIVATION AND HOW MIGHT IT INFLUENCE MY
USE OF COOPERATIVE LEARNING?

Mrs. Sanchez is one of the most effective teachers at Harwood Elementary. When asked about her success, she describes her commitment to the children she teaches and to developing each one to the maximum extent possible. "In my classroom," Mrs. Sanchez reports, "students are encouraged to explore subjects they are curious about. I try not to interfere with this and don't impose too many restrictions, rules, or directions. Instead, I work hard to make sure that each child feels comfortable. I use cooperative learning to help students explore topics of common interest, develop a sense of community and sharing, and encourage feelings of self-worth. When children feel good about themselves and feel at ease in the classroom, they become eager to learn."

Mr. Bille is another strong teacher, but his classroom has a different look and feel to it. When asked about his success, Mr. Bille has a very different philosophy about teaching from Mrs. Sanchez. "In my class, I'm always looking for ways to acknowledge students' success at learning. When I decide on the content to be learned, I first divide it into manageable units so that students have a progression of material to master. I use cooperative learning as a way to further motivate students to learn. The idea of everyone sinking or swimming together helps students encourage each other to achieve. After they master each unit, we celebrate their teams' success with reward certificates and gold stars. I praise them a lot, too, when they succeed."

YOUR APPROACH TO TEACHING

Mrs. Sanchez and Mr. Bille are both excellent teachers, but each approaches teaching differently. Mrs. Sanchez's approach reflects a humanistic philosophy. Mr. Bille's approach, on the other hand, uses many principles from behavioral psychology. This difference in approach illustrates an important point: teachers' beliefs about how students learn and what they should learn help determine how a cooperative learning method is selected and implemented.

It is crucial that you understand both your own teaching philosophy and your teaching situation. As a starting point for you to reflect on your teaching, we have prepared a list of questions for you to think about (see Exhibit 1.1). The first three questions are about basic issues in teaching. The next three questions are specific to cooperative learning. Be careful to differentiate the ideal teaching situation you desire from the real teaching situation you face.

As well as encouraging you to think about your own approach to teaching, this chapter provides overviews of the major theories of learning and motivation, including behavioral, cognitive, humanistic, and developmental approaches. Understanding these approaches should help you (a) differentiate among the cooperative learning methods, (b) understand the theoretical explanations of cooperative learning, and (c) design a cooperative learning approach for your classroom.

What Do You Want Your Students to Learn?

Do you view learning primarily from a product orientation and believe that your main objective is to facilitate the development of primary skills and the acquisition of essential information? If so, you will likely focus on your students' mastery of essential instructional objectives, clearly defining each learning step and rewarding students for their achievement. Or do you view learning from a process orientation and believe that your main objective is to foster individual development and complex skills acquisition? If so, you will likely use guided discovery activities to develop students' problem-solving and higher-order thinking skills.

What Motivates Students to Learn?

Do you believe that students possess a basic curiosity and intrinsic interest in learning? If so, you probably assume a facilitator's role. You allow students more input into what they are to learn, and greater control and active responsibility for when and how they learn it. Or do you believe that students must be provided with clear objectives and incentives for achieving those objectives? If so, you probably assume a more directive role. You determine what students are to learn, when and how they are to learn it, and reward them for learning it.

What Importance Do You Attach to Enhancing Students' Affective Skills?

Do you believe that students learn best if you first develop in them a sense of positive academic self-concept? Or do you believe that positive academic self-concept develops from academic success? If you believe the former, you would probably concentrate on nurturing students' feelings about themselves as learners. If you believe the latter, you would most likely concentrate on having students learn the course material.

What Value Do You, Your School, and Your Society Place on Competition and Cooperation?

Do you believe that competition increases productivity and is an essential skill for success in a free-enterprise society? If so, you may encourage competition among students and reward the top performers. Or do you believe that humans are inherently social and that the vast majority of human interactions require the use of cooperative skills and abilities? If so, you may foster cooperation and social support in your classroom by having students work in groups. Finally, do your fellow teachers, the principal, students, and parents share your values regarding competition and cooperation? If not, you may need to overcome resistance to the approach you adopt.

Is Cooperation a Means to Learning or an End in Itself?

Do you believe that schools need to teach students interpersonal and social skills directly? Or do you believe that cognitive and academic objectives are of far greater importance? If you believe the former, you would probably devote a considerable percentage of class time to teaching students how to inter-

act and learn effectively with others. You would probably see learning course content and learning cooperative skills as two intertwined educational goals. If you believe the latter, you would probably avoid using too much class time either to teach social skills directly or to intervene when student groups experience interpersonal problems. You would see cooperative learning primarily as an instructional strategy to enhance student learning.

Why Do Students Cooperate to Learn?

Do you believe that students are motivated to work with one another because they have both an intrinsic interest in learning and a desire to help one another learn? If so, you would probably allow students greater autonomy in selecting material to learn and would allow the motivation for learning

Exhibit 1.1 **Cooperative Learning and Your Approach to Teaching**

What do you want your students to learn?	
What motivates students to learn?	
What importance do you attach to enhancing students' affective skills?	
What value do you, your school, and your society place on competition and cooperation?	
Is cooperation a means to learning or an end in itself?	
Why do students cooperate to learn?	
My own question:	

to arise from peer encouragement and mutual concern. However, you might believe that students work with one another primarily because doing so is instrumental to achieving a tangible reward, such as a high grade. If so, you would probably feel less need to give students a choice about what they are to learn and would instead provide a team with a meaningful, extrinsic incentive for learning together.

MAJOR THEORETICAL APPROACHES TO LEARNING AND MOTIVATION

How do students learn? What motivates students to learn? These two questions are at the heart of the educational system. Given the importance of these questions, we will briefly review the basic explanations of learning and motivation in classrooms. We focus on four major approaches—behavioral, cognitive, humanistic, and developmental—that differentiate the methods of cooperative learning and the explanations for why and how it works.

Behaviorists view behavior as determined by reinforcements. They seek to explain learning by identifying the cues that elicit behavior as well as the reinforcements that sustain and strengthen it.

Cognitivists view behavior as controlled by thought processes. They concentrate on how people process information and interpret events, giving them meaning and attributing causality. Humanists are concerned with the enhancement of personal development, self-actualization, and the removal of obstacles to personal growth. Finally, developmentalists explore changes in thinking, feeling, and acting over time as children grow and mature. These approaches are summarized in Exhibit 1.2. As you read about these approaches, reflect on which views you have integrated into your own teaching.

What Is Learning?

Learning is the process that results in a relatively permanent change in thinking and behavior that comes from experience and practice. Different kinds of learning occur both in and out of school. Learning changes a newborn baby into a thinking, acting, and feeling adult who can solve differential equations, play a mean game of tennis, build cathedrals, and have respect and compassion for others. While not everyone reaches his or her potential, learning can move us toward it.

Different accounts exist of how learning takes place. Behavioral theorists address the questions, What drives learning? and How can learning be increased by external means? Cognitive psycholo-

············· EXHIBIT 1.2 **Major Theoretical Conceptions of Learning and Motivation** ················

	Learning	Motivation
Behaviorist	change in observable behaviors	positive and negative reinforcement (eg., use of rewards)
Cognitivist	information acquisition, representation, and retrieval	expectations for success and beliefs about causes of success or failure
Humanist	satisfaction of needs and development of human potential	desire to become self-actualized
Developmentalist	interaction with the physical and social environment	desire to resolve cognitive disequilibrium

gists are concerned with the questions, How is information processed? and How is thinking enhanced? Humanists ask, How do students learn to become fully functioning adults? Finally, developmentalists are concerned with the question, How do children learn as they mature?

What Is Motivation?

Most teachers are interested in discovering new ways to encourage students. Teachers motivate students both as a means to foster learning and as an end in itself. For many teachers, motivating students to learn is their daily challenge.

The word motivation comes from the Latin word *movere*, which literally means "to move." Motivation provides the energy for action and directs it toward a specific goal. Energy and direction are at the heart of the definition. Energy is the engine that powers action; direction is the steering wheel that focuses it.

The energy for action has several forms: initiation, intensity, and persistence. What initially causes a person to act? Is John motivated by a desire to understand or a wish to outperform his classmates? What explains the force or intensity with which a person acts? Does Antoinette work hard because she fears the negative consequences of failure, or because she desires the positive consequences of success? What causes people to persist in their efforts? Does Felipe think that greater effort will result in his success next time, or does he think that bad luck caused his poor performance?

Understanding what energizes a student to act does not provide a complete picture of motivation. How the student focuses and directs that energy is also important. Why do students select certain learning objectives and avoid others? For example, is Grazia interested in studying mathematics because of parental encouragement? Or did Mohammed try out for the basketball team to be with his friends?

Behavioral Approach

Jonathan is a new student who sits at the rear of the classroom. He doesn't say much and never causes trouble. He is shy and withdrawn, making little effort to excel at classwork. But his teacher, Mrs. Smith, sees that Jonathan has the potential for much more, both academically and socially. She praises and encourages Jonathan every time he speaks out in class and every time he does well at classwork. Within a few weeks, Jonathan is happily integrated into classroom life, is content to be part of the routine, and is achieving his potential. Mrs. Smith has used some basic principles of behavioral theories to shape Jonathan's behavior and motivate him to learn.

REINFORCEMENT AND PUNISHMENT

According to the behavioral approach (Skinner, 1953), the key to motivating students to learn is to identify reinforcers that will increase the likelihood of desired behaviors. There are two types of reinforcers—positive and negative.

Positive reinforcers, or rewards, affect learning when they follow a desired response. For example, the likelihood of Joshua completing his in-class assignments will be increased if there is a connection between completing the assignments and his teacher's praise (the reinforcer).

You can use several categories of positive reinforcers in the classroom. Social reinforcers include teacher and student praise, smiles, hugs, and attention. Field trips, toys, and games are examples of activity-based reinforcers. Symbolic or token reinforcers include grades, stars, improvement points, and reward certificates. Tangible reinforcers include books, stickers, and felt pens.

In general, reinforcers are external stimuli. Increasingly, however, behaviorists are recognizing that reinforcers may be internal. For example, symbolic stimuli in the form of internal statements (e.g., "Great," says Joshua, "I did a good assignment!") may be the only reinforcers in certain situations, yet they can also strengthen behavior.

Negative reinforcers also strengthen behavior, but they operate differently from positive reinforcers. Negative reinforcers remove something negative or aversive following a desired response. For example, if Joshua completes his in-class assignment satisfactorily, his teacher might release him from doing certain homework assignments. If the homework is seen as an undesirable chore, then release from it will have a reinforcing effect.

Negative reinforcement is not the same as punishment. Negative reinforcement strengthens desirable behavior, while punishment suppresses undesirable behavior. Typical punishments include placing students on "time out" or sending them to the principal.

Using Group Rewards

The behavioral approach to motivation can be readily extended to students learning in small groups. A group reward system exists when the whole group is rewarded based on the actions of the group members. Effective group rewards result in group members encouraging each other to help earn the reward (Hayes, 1976).

To be effective, a group reward needs to be valued and attainable by members of the group. Group rewards may be decided by the teacher. Or students may choose from a reward menu or suggest a reward following a group discussion.

Group rewards can be used to recognize the combined performance of group members (e.g., the average of individual quiz scores), or a single group product (e.g., an essay or term project). When using group products, the contributions of each member should be clearly identified (Slavin a and b, 1983). Otherwise, participation may not be equal, thus adversely affecting student achievement.

Cognitive Approach

Mathieu sits at his desk frustrated. He wants to do well on the upcoming history test, but he is having difficulty understanding the material. He is starting to think that the task is too difficult for him. One of his teammates, Mary, notices Mathieu's frustration and offers to help. She shows Mathieu how to organize the information he has to learn into manageable units. Mary also shows Mathieu how the concepts are related to each other and to previous course content. Mathieu discovers that it is easier to remember and apply the new information once he sees how it fits in with his current understanding. He thanks Mary and redoubles his efforts to learn.

In this scenario, you can see that Mathieu is having problems organizing and processing the information he needs to learn. These difficulties initially lead him to believe that success at learning is not something he can control. Mathieu may want to earn points for his team—the external reward—but his learning and motivation are affected more by his internal thought processes. Cognitive theories of learning and motivation concentrate on understanding thought processes.

KNOWLEDGE ACQUISITION, REPRESENTATION, AND RETRIEVAL

How can learners increase their capacity to acquire and process large amounts of new information? How is information represented in memory, and how is it retrieved and applied in new situations? How does a learner's prior knowledge and experience influence the perception and representation of new information? Cognitive theories address these issues.

Our ability to process large amounts of information can be enhanced by several processes, including automatization, rehearsal, "chunking," and elaboration. For example, consider Mathieu when he is taking notes during a lecture. He must simultaneously attend to a multitude of tasks, including recognizing and understanding the words spoken by the teacher, retrieving relevant prior knowledge from long-term memory and integrating it with the new information, constructing a global understanding of the lecture, deciding what is important to note, and actually noting the information.

Certain of these processes, such as recognizing words and routine components of writing, can become highly developed through extensive practice so that they are carried out automatically (Shiffrin and Schneider, 1977). This automatization increases the attention learners can give to more complex tasks.

If Mathieu has too much information to cope with and time is limited, he may opt to use rehearsal. That is, Mathieu may decide to repeat important terms in his head until he is able to get them down on paper. Though less effective as a strategy for long-term retention, rehearsal is less demanding than deeper, more meaningful processing.

The amount of new information acquired and retrieved can be dramatically increased if the learner structures it. A simple strategy is to group, or "chunk," similar items. For example, while listening to a lecture about the causes of the Second World War, Mathieu is able to retain more if he groups causes as economic, social, and political. Mathieu's teacher could distribute an advance organizer to help students structure and "chunk" information presented in the lecture.

Using elaboration to make information meaningful is another way to ensure long-term retention and retrieval. Elaboration involves the student determining the relationships between concepts and linking new information with prior knowledge. Elaboration occurs, for example, when Mathieu explains the ideas to his classmate, illustrates them with examples, and responds to questions.

Using Groups to Facilitate Meaningful Understanding

From the cognitive perspective, the role of instruction is to have learners work actively with information so that it becomes well integrated and meaningful to them. Cooperative learning techniques can help learners discuss and wrestle with ideas, deepening their understanding of how new concepts relate to one another and to students' prior knowledge. For example, group members may ask each other, What other examples of this volcanic activity do you know? Are earthquakes a characteristic, a cause, or an effect of tectonic plates? How can your idea and my idea both be correct? Such questions may also help students learn by encouraging them to rethink certain concepts. (See Chapter 16: Cooperative Concept Mapping for a cooperative learning method that encourages this type of learning.)

ACHIEVEMENT MOTIVATION THEORY

Timothy, Sasha, and Trina are among the brightest students in Mr. Jona's class. When Mr. Jona asks them to select a project, Timothy elects to complete a small, easy project, one well within his abilities. Sasha elects to complete a project that will challenge him, but with which he has a reasonable chance of success. Trina, however, decides to complete an extremely difficult and challenging project. If successful, her project will be the best in the entire district. But there is only a small chance Trina will succeed.

What explains the project preferences of Timothy, Sasha, and Trina? Why do students of similar abilities work in strikingly different ways? Cognitive approaches to motivation assume that people respond to their own internal interpretations of the learning situation and not to the actual events themselves. One of the most influential cognitive motivational theories of human learning is Atkinson's achievement motivation theory (1964). It explains why, what, and how students strive to achieve.

Atkinson was interested in understanding why some students seek out achievement-oriented tasks, while others avoid them. He speculated that in every individual there are two competing tendencies, approach and avoidance, which are in conflict. A student's actions in an achievement situation depend on which tendency is strongest in that situation.

Three factors influence a student's willingness to engage in an achievement task: the motivation to succeed, the personal expectation of success, and the incentive for success. The combination of these three factors determines the strength of a student's approach tendencies. But understanding these factors alone is insufficient to explain the actions of a student.

Atkinson realized that a second motive was in conflict with the motivation to succeed. He believed that not every student is primarily motivated by the desire for success. Unfortunately, some students are primarily motivated by the desire to avoid failure and the shame, ridicule, and punishment associated with failure.

Three factors influence a student's *unwillingness* to engage in an achievement task: the motivation to avoid failure, the personal expectation of failure, and the negative incentive for failure. The combination of these three factors determines the strength of a student's avoidance tendencies.

Why do students high in achievement motivation choose moderately difficult tasks? They are attempting to maximize both their chances for success and the incentive for success. An easy task leads to success, but there is little incentive value associated with it. A very difficult task has high incentive value, but it is unlikely to be achieved. Consequently, the high-need achievement student, like Sasha, generally selects moderately difficult learning tasks.

In contrast, students highly motivated to avoid failure, like Timothy, either seek out easy tasks to minimize the likelihood of failure, or, like Trina, seek out very difficult tasks in which failure does not have highly punitive consequences. It is not shameful to fail at the impossible; it is shameful to fail at something within your grasp.

Using Groups to Change Expectations

Using small groups for cooperative learning can help facilitate the development of expectations that promote student learning. For example, assigning students to diverse, heterogeneous groups can promote beliefs that every group has an equal probability of success. That is, the same task may be seen as moderately difficult for each group.

Such beliefs are different from those that usually occur in a class that is structured for individual or competitive learning. Under these conditions, only a few students will believe the same task is moderately difficult. Some will see it as too easy; others will see it as too hard.

Students' beliefs about group success affect their individual behavior. Students high in prior achievement might view an individual task as rather easy. For them, a cooperatively structured activity leads to beliefs that the task will be more difficult. In contrast, students low in prior achievement might view an individual task as difficult. For these students, a cooperatively structured activity leads to beliefs that the task will be less difficult. Thus, heterogeneous groups can lead to a uniform expectation that the assigned task is challenging but attainable.

ATTRIBUTION THEORY

Annette's score of 71 on her Calculus 101 test is less than she expected. She immediately begins to wonder why. Was the examination extremely difficult? How did other students do? Didn't she prepare enough for the test? Was she just unlucky because she prepared for material not included in the test this time? She wonders if maybe she just doesn't have the ability to do well in college-level mathematics.

Depending on what belief Annette forms about the causes of her test score, her motivation to learn in Calculus 101 will be affected. If she believes the cause of her low score was her lack of ability, Annette might drop the course. However, if she attributes her low score to lack of effort, Annette will increase the amount of time she devotes to studying.

The attribution theory of motivation (Weiner, 1986) concerns the causal explanations used by students to explain their academic performance. These causal explanations are based on individual, subjective perceptions of learning events. Like achievement motivation theory, attribution theory emphasizes the importance of students' expectations about the subjective probability of success at a learning task. But attribution theory concerns not only what students expect, but why and how they form these expectations.

For example, students with the same expectation for success may have different reasons for their beliefs. John may believe that he will be successful only if he works hard and prepares. Mary may believe that she will be successful without much effort, because she is smart and able to do the task with little preparation. While both expect the same learning outcome, the achievement strivings of John and Mary will be markedly different.

Students use diverse causal factors to explain a learning event or outcome. However, the four most frequently mentioned causal explanations for academic success or failure are ability (high or low), effort (little or much), task difficulty (easy or hard), and luck (good or bad). For example, Joey says he succeeded because he worked hard to understand the material. Di claims she earned her "A" because she's smart. Jamie says he failed because he just wasn't lucky in picking his answers. Jason thinks the teacher made the examination too difficult.

Attribution theory highlights students' causal beliefs as important determinants of subsequent thoughts, feelings, and actions. For example, students who attribute their failure to lack of ability will likely decrease their expectations for future success and, therefore, decrease their subsequent efforts. In contrast, students who attribute their failure to lack of effort, may not change their expectations for success, but may redouble their efforts to succeed.

Using Groups to Enhance Attributions

Cooperative learning provides an excellent opportunity to enhance students' beliefs in the importance of individual effort to succeed at academic tasks. When students believe that their contributions and those of other group members are required to succeed, the amount of individual effort they exert should increase. Group members encourage each other to exert their best efforts and they provide support and assistance when necessary. Such encouragement and support leads group members, even lower-ability ones, to attribute subsequent success to effort. (See Chapter 3: Theories of Cooperative Learning for a more in-depth discussion.) Exhibit 1.3 provides an instrument for measuring your students' beliefs about the importance of individual and teammate contributions to cooperative learning.

Humanistic Approach

Allison is an intelligent teenager. When she was younger, school was an important focus of her life. But recently, Allison is uninterested in school. She admits to both her parents and teachers, "School is boring. It doesn't have any meaning for me." What has changed Allison's attitude toward learning?

Humanistic theories of motivation consider the development of the whole person, cognitively, socially, and affectively. Although all humanists are concerned with developing human potential, they vary in the importance they attach to particular school outcomes. Some humanists argue that education based on humanistic principles enhances the mastery of school subjects and general cognitive performance. Others argue that it is unimportant if humanistic teaching relates to academic performance, since personal development is an important objective of education by itself.

HIERARCHY OF NEEDS

Abraham Maslow (1970) believed that need gratification is the most important principle underlying all human development. He believed that development is the result of a never-ending series of situations offering a choice between the attractions and dangers of safety, and the attractions and dangers of growth.

Maslow saw the individual as motivated by a host of needs that are arranged hierarchically, from the most basic to highly advanced. He identified seven general categories of human needs (see Exhibit 1.4). He further grouped these into two categories—defi-

················· Exhibit 1.3 **Attribution Rating Scale for Cooperative Learning** ·····················

Use the following scale in making your judgments.

(a)   (b)   (c)   (d)   (e)

Strongly disagree   Strongly agree

←————————————————————————————————————→

1. Whether our group does well or poorly depends on the efforts I make.

2. Whether our group does well or poorly depends on my personal ability.

3. Whether our group does well or poorly depends on how easy or difficult the task is.

4. Whether our group does well or poorly depends on whether we are lucky or unlucky.

5. Whether our group does well or poorly depends on the efforts my teammates make.

6. Whether our group does well or poorly depends on the abilities of my teammates.

ciency needs and growth needs. Deficiency needs are critical to physical and psychological well-being and include physiological, safety, belonging, and esteem needs. Growth needs are also important and include intellectual, aesthetic, and self-actualization needs.

Maslow contended that deficiency needs must at least partially be satisfied before an individual can attempt to satisfy growth needs. Certainly, a child cannot come to school hungry or cold and seek knowledge and understanding. Similarly, a child whose feelings of safety are threatened by divorce may have little interest in learning arithmetic.

An important distinction between deficiency needs and growth needs lies in how an individual is motivated to satisfy them. When deficiency needs are not met, an individual's motivation increases to find ways to satisfy them. When deficiency needs are satisfied, the motivation for fulfilling them decreases. In contrast, as growth needs are met, an individual's motivation does not decrease. Instead, meeting growth needs can actually increase the motivation to seek further fulfilment. For example, the more successful an individual's efforts are to know and understand, the more likely that individual will be to seek even greater knowledge and understanding.

Using Groups to Meet Students' Needs

In many traditional classrooms, feelings of belonging and esteem may be actively promoted only by the teacher. Students typically have responsibility only for themselves, are not allowed to help one another, and may compete for grades.

EXHIBIT 1.4 **Maslow's Hierarchy of Needs**

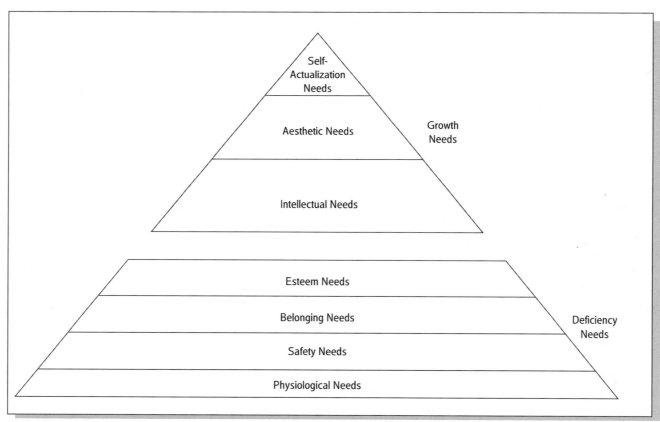

Source: From A. H. Maslow, *Motivation and Personality*, Second Edition. Copyright 1954 by Harper & Row Publishers, Inc. Copyright © 1970 by Abraham H. Maslow. Reprinted by permission of HarperCollins Publishers, Inc.

In classrooms that are structured cooperatively, students learn to value their classmates, and feelings of belonging and esteem are promoted by both the teacher and other students. First, teachers use structures that enhance each student's sense of interdependence (e.g., students may be assigned unique and essential roles within the group). Second, attention to classbuilding and teambuilding, interpersonal skills training, and reflection promotes appreciation for and integration of classmates. Third, teachers may have groups identify and pursue common interests and goals. In addition to increasing group cohesiveness, this helps meet growth needs by encouraging students to be autonomous from the teacher, take personal risks, and be self-directed.

Developmental Approach

Andrew is the only child of highly educated, professional parents. To help Andrew reach his maximum potential, his parents have made significant efforts to prepare him for school. By kindergarten, Andrew has already learned the alphabet, numbers to 100, color recognition, and basic addition and subtraction. However, Andrew's parents are startled to learn that he is progressing at about the same pace as his classmates.

Andrew's development is perfectly understandable. While his parents have concentrated on teaching Andrew to memorize basic facts, his teacher is more interested in Andrew's understanding of the concepts that underlie those facts.

For many years, developmentalists believed in the concept of *tabula rasa*, or the blank slate; that is, a newborn infant starts with nothing and learning is the process of continually acquiring more knowledge. But more recently, human development has been seen not as a quantitative increase in knowledge but as a progression through qualitatively different stages of thought and understanding. This view of development has been influenced extensively by the work of Piaget (1954) and, more recently, by Vygotsky (1978; see also Wertsch, 1985). What separates developmental theories from behavioral, cognitive, and humanistic theories is an emphasis on both the structure of and environmental influences on cognitive growth and development over long periods of time, especially from infancy to adulthood.

INTELLECTUAL DEVELOPMENT THROUGH SOCIAL INTERACTION

According to Piaget (1954), children proceed through a sequence of four stages: sensorimotor, preoperational, concrete operational, and formal operational. As children develop, they move from attempting to understand their environment by physically manipulating it (e.g., playing with a ball), to attempting to understand their environment by mentally manipulating abstract concepts through reasoning (e.g., learning about the laws of motion).

Children manipulate their environment and create cognitive schemes by constructing mental structures of the knowledge they have acquired. Cognitive disequilibrium, which is experienced when learners perceive a discrepancy between reality and their mental schemes, motivates children to refine their understanding by revising their schemes. Children accomplish this through assimilation (integrating new information into existing mental schemes) and accommodation (radically restructuring mental schemes that are inconsistent with reality, or creating new ones). Piaget identified four factors that influence an individual's development of schemes: heredity, physical experience with the world, adaptation of one's mental schemes to fit reality, and social transmission of knowledge through interaction.

Vygotsky (1978; see also Wertsch, 1985) placed greater significance than Piaget on the role of interaction with others. Three aspects of Vygotsky's view of cognitive development stand out: (a) his emphasis on social, cultural, and historical influences; (b) his analysis of the relationship between thought and language; and (c) his account of how learning and instruction advance development.

According to Vygotsky, adults interact with children in order to help them master the language, customs, and tools of their culture. In turn, children internalize these social interactions, which then determine the course of their cognitive development. In other words, cognitive development proceeds from other-regulated behavior (social) to self-regulated behavior (personal).

Children can perform tasks at one level when they are unassisted and at a higher level when they have help. The difference between these two levels of functioning has been referred to as the *zone of proximal development*. To enhance learning, teachers must select classroom activities that fall within this zone and encourage dialogue to bridge this gap. For example, in guiding learners through a problem-solving task, teachers might think aloud about the processes involved in the task to make their reasoning clear.

Using Groups to Promote Development through Peer Interaction

Support for learning does not need to be provided solely by the teacher. Other students in the class can also provide support. Many cooperative learning techniques require group members to wrestle with ideas, challenge views, and resolve conflicts. Children are encouraged to reach consensus and modify their own points of view in order to accommodate varying perspectives. In Piaget's view, children work together to act as a source of feedback for one another, which, in turn, they can use to initiate change in their ways of thinking. In Vygotsky's view, peer talk not only initiates change, but also molds it. That is, cooperative learning encourages the development of a community of learners exhibiting particular historical, cultural, and social characteristics.

SUMMARY

In this chapter, we have invited you to think about your own approach to teaching, learning, and motivation. In addition, you have read about behavioral, cognitive, humanistic, and developmental approaches and how they are reflected in cooperative learning.

Understanding what learning is, how it develops, and what motivates it helps practitioners decide how to use cooperative learning, how to help groups

learn, and how to motivate them to learn. As you read through the remainder of this book, you should be in a better position to determine whether your own approach to teaching is compatible with the particular ideas and methods we have described. Because cooperative learning is not a single method of instruction, you may find many suggestions that fit your approach and others that do not. It's up to you to decide which methods best suit your teaching style.

REFLECTION ACTIVITIES

1. Answer the questions in Exhibit 1.1 concerning your approach to teaching. Interview a colleague using these questions. Compare your answers with your colleague's responses. Ask your students to list the qualities of good teaching and how students learn best. Compare students' responses to your own philosophy and beliefs. (You can give older students copies of Exhibit 1.1 to complete.)

2. Imagine you are to meet the parents of a very bright and motivated student who plans to attend law school. How would you explain your teaching philosophy to these parents?

3. Use the attribution rating scale in Exhibit 1.3 and ask students to rate their beliefs about learning in your class. (If you do not currently have students learning in groups, you will need to modify the statements to read, "Whether *I* do well or poorly . . . .") What cause does the class rate highest? How do the ratings compare with your expectations? What are the implications for your teaching?

4. Allowing students time to construct their own knowledge sounds terrific in theory. Helping students to achieve their full potential also seems like an important goal. But teachers complain that there just isn't enough time in the day to achieve these goals and meet their curriculum objectives. Are there any ways to reconcile these two positions? How does cooperative learning help achieve them?

Cathie Archbould

2

Group Processes and Productivity

How does the nature of the task affect group productivity?

•

How do groups develop?

•

What resource and process factors influence group effectiveness?

•

What strategies can I use to reduce prejudice in groups?

"Jason can be a very helpful student," confides his teacher, Mr. Rheaume, to Jason's parents. "When I approach him privately, he listens attentively and then works diligently on his reading and mathematics assignments. But when Jason is with his friends, he doesn't pay me or his schoolwork much attention. At these times, Jason is more interested in what his buddies think than in improving his reading and mathematics skills."

This scenario illustrates how groups can influence the behavior of individuals. Knowing how individuals function when they work in groups can help you design more effective cooperative activities. In Chapter 1, we examined learning and motivation from the perspective of individual psychology. In this chapter, we will take the perspective of social psychology.

WORKING WITH OTHERS

Initially, social psychologists found that individuals completing simple tasks performed better in the presence of others, whereas performance on difficult tasks was diminished (Zajonc, 1965). Later research on individuals working actively *with* others, cooperating to achieve common goals, revealed many

19

situations in which group work is superior to individual work for both simple and complex material.

When working individually, people's performance depends solely on personal resources, such as skill and effort. When working in groups, their performance depends on personal resources plus the interpersonal processes that determine how these resources are combined. In this chapter, we will consider several factors that influence the effectiveness of working with others: types of interdependence, group development, task demands, resource and process factors, and interracial and interethnic relations.

Types of Interdependence

Maria is taking her first physics course and she is worried about doing well. After seven weeks of physics, her worries are over. "In this class," explains Maria, "our teacher, Dr. Dapple, placed us in groups from the first day. Everything we learn, we learn together. My teammates are interested in helping me learn and I want to help them, too. As Dr. Dapple says, we either sink or swim together."

Dr. Dapple is having students strive to promote each other's learning. This form of interaction is called positive interdependence. When *positive interdependence*, or cooperation, among group members exists, students work together to learn. When students actively collaborate, they are motivated to help themselves and each other achieve. Chapter 6: Fostering Positive Interdependence provides detailed examples of ways teachers can structure positive interdependence. In contrast to positive interdependence, students sometimes interact under conditions of negative interdependence, independence, and dependence.

When *negative interdependence*, or competition, among group members exists, students work against one another. For example, negative interdependence exists when one student's success negatively influences the chances of other students' successes. Marking "on the curve," where there are a limited number of "A's," is based on negative interdependence.

Students' *independence*, or individualism, exists when the success of one student is unrelated to the success of other students. Individualized instruction and mastery learning are examples of student independence. Students neither compete nor cooperate, but work on their own and at their own pace.

Student *dependence*, or reliance, exists when some students rely substantially on others without reciprocity. For example, in some traditional group-learning activities, the brightest or most ambitious student takes responsibility for the group's work. Other students are dependent on the brightest student, but this student does not depend on others.

What are the effects of the various types of interdependence? The substantial literature on cooperative, competitive, and individualistic structures is reviewed in Appendix A: Research Evidence. In general, cooperative structures promote greater learning, productivity, and personal satisfaction compared to competitive and individualistic structures (Johnson and Johnson, 1989a). Establishing positive interdependence among group members is one of the most important elements in establishing effective cooperative learning.

Group Development

Remember how you felt and behaved when you first became part of a group? You probably were somewhat shy and concerned about how you would get along with other group members. But how did you feel about the group after some time had passed? Your initial concern about getting along with others was probably replaced by concern about getting the group task done.

Groups take time to develop. According to Tuckman and Jensen (1977), groups develop according to five stages: forming, storming, norming, performing, and terminating.

- *Forming.* During this stage, interactions tend to be polite, but superficial, as group members get acquainted with one another and seek out similarities that help unite them.

- *Storming.* Teachers are often distressed when initial congeniality is followed by a stage of conflict and confrontation. Individual members strive to assert their individuality, determine their respective status within the group, and influence group decisions. This is both a natural stage of group development and an important learning experience. Students must develop skill in expressing their opinions clearly and in listening to and carefully evaluating the opinions of others.

- *Norming.* As students resolve their conflicts and develop a sense of trust, they grow to appreciate each other's unique qualities. Students enter a stage in which they clarify their group's goals and reestablish and accept responsibility for norms and roles originally defined by the teacher.

- *Performing.* Motives of achievement become dominant in the performing stage, which is characterized by high productivity. Members focus on completing their tasks and achieving the group's goals.

- *Terminating.* The final, terminating stage, is typically short. However, closure is an important component of any activity. Following completion of a group task, students benefit from reflecting on their interpersonal and academic learning. Through reflection, students can celebrate what went well during their time together and set goals to enhance future interaction and learning.

While forming and terminating are clearly at the beginning and end of the group development process, storming, norming, and performing do not always follow a strict progression. Sometimes, groups experience these stages in cycles, passing through storming-norming-performance periods several times.

It is important to keep these stages in mind when you implement cooperative learning. Tuckman's model suggests that immediately breaking up groups when conflict develops may not be advisable. Rather, attention to teambuilding, positive interdependence, interpersonal-skills training, and reflection can help groups progress through the early stages of development and result in greater productivity.

Task Demands

Lionel, a second-year honors student, is enrolled in Chemistry 912 but is having second thoughts. "I have a terrific professor, but I'm not looking forward to the course. Fifty percent of the final grade depends on a group project. I don't like group projects. They take so much extra time and effort. I always feel I would learn more if I just worked on my own."

Using groups for problem solving, decision making, and productivity in industry and government, and more recently in education, is increasingly widespread. Yet, despite their prevalence, groups are criticized as a waste of time. Does the quantity and quality of group performance exceed or fall short of the performance of individuals working alone? How do group accomplishments compare with the performance of the most proficient member of the group?

Steiner's typology of tasks (1972) can help you analyze how task structure and demands influence group productivity in five different dimensions: task divisibility, basis of assessment, collective versus coactive tasks, source of control, and social combination rules. Each dimension relates to a question teachers might ask about tasks assigned to groups:

1. Can the task be broken down into subcomponents or is the division of the task inappropriate? (task divisibility)

2. Which is more important, the quantity produced or the quality of performance? (basis of assessment)

3. Is there a single product or are group members concerned with individual products? (collective versus coactive tasks)

4. Can group members decide how to contribute or are the rules set? (source of control)

5. How are individual inputs related to the group product? (social combination rules)

Steiner's analysis encourages you to examine which group tasks help focus group activity on the appropriate strategy for success. It highlights those tasks that are problematic for groups and may require the extra intervention of the instructor. Note that this analysis focuses attention on the quality and quantity of the final product. You will need to consider whether you wish to emphasize the individual accomplishments of group members in addition to or instead of group products.

Exhibit 2.1 is a useful guide for categorizing tasks and deciding what type of group work is appropriate for your objectives. Note that group products can be either the sum or the average across all contributions of group members. In addition, some tasks may require a single answer, while others may require answers or input from everyone.

The task types in Exhibit 2.1 refer specifically to activities that require the contribution of each group member in developing the product. Cooperative learning practitioners emphasize the importance of individual accountability to ensure that each member contributes meaningfully to the group product. Slavin's summary (1983a) of research suggests that group products without individual accountability do not enhance individual learning. Cohen (1994a) noted that true group tasks require resources that no single individual possesses so that no one is likely to solve the problem without input from others. Such tasks tend to promote interaction

·················· EXHIBIT 2.1 **Task Types and Their Effects on Group Productivity** ··················

Type of Task	Description	Examples	Group Productivity Effect
Additive	Individual inputs are added together.	pulling a rope, stuffing envelopes, shovelling snow	*Better than the best member*: The group exceeds the performance of even the best individual.
Compensatory	Group product is the average of individual inputs.	averaging individuals' estimates of the number of beans in a jar, weight of an object, or room temperature	*Better than most members*: The group exceeds the performance of a substantial number of the individual members.
Disjunctive	The group selects the product from a pool of individual members' judgments.	questions involving yes/no, either/or answers, such as mathematics problems, puzzles, and choices between options	*Eureka problems—equal to the best member*: The group equals the performance of the most capable individual. *Non-eureka problems—less than the best member*: The group sometimes equals the performance of the most capable member but often falls short.
Conjunctive	All group members must contribute to the product.	climbing a mountain, eating a meal, relay races, soldiers marching in file	*Unitary problems—equal to the worst member*: The group equals the performance of the least capable member. *Divisible problems—better than the worst member*: Performance will be superior if subtasks match members' capabilities.

Source: Adapted from I.D. Steiner, *Group Processes and Productivity*, New York: Academic Press, 1972, and D. R. Forsyth, *Group Dynamics*, Second Edition, Pacific Grove, California: Brooks/Cole Publishing Company, pp. 262, 267. Copyright © 1990, 1983 by Wadsworth, Inc. Used by permission of Brooks/Cole Publishing, a division of Wadsworth, Inc.

among teammates and positive interdependence. Cohen cautions against the use of routine tasks that require stronger students to help weaker students. Such tasks tend to promote the dependence of weaker students on stronger ones.

Resource and Process Factors

Everyone knows the old adage, Two heads are better than one. But how much better? Do too many cooks spoil the broth? Ten factors that influence group productivity are summarized in Exhibit 2.2, and are further explained below. Two factors—size and time—concern the resources available to the group. The other eight factors concern the processes through which group members contribute. You can use the table in several ways: to help plan group activities; to monitor group progress; or to give to students to evaluate their group's effectiveness.

GROUP SIZE AND THE RINGELMANN EFFECT

It takes Marvin five hours to stuff, address, and stamp 500 invitations to his school's homecoming dance. For the winter dance, he decides to get a helper, calculating that it will take both of them two and a half hours. However, they take four hours—a total of eight teenager hours. Based on these experiences, Marvin decides to get three helpers for the spring dance, thinking that he now has it right, and it will take them only two hours. However, to Marvin's chagrin, he and his helpers take three hours to prepare the invitations—a total of twelve teenager hours. Marvin has experienced the Ringelmann Effect and has learned the mathematics of groups.

The earliest-known attempts to answer questions about group size and productivity were made by Ringelmann (1913; see also Kravitz and Martin, 1986). In their review of 49 studies, Jackson and Williams (1988) confirmed and extended Ringelmann's findings. In additive tasks (summing up individual contributions to make the group product), they found a curvilinear relationship between group size and productivity losses. The change in group size from individuals to pairs to triads caused overall productivity to increase a great deal, although it was not double or triple that of individuals working alone. However, an increase in group size from ten upward tended to have a minimal effect on overall productivity.

Ringelmann speculated that there were two reasons why a group of people working on an additive task do not maximize their productivity: (1) individuals have difficulty combining and coordinating their efforts to reach their full productive potential and (2) people sometimes work harder by themselves than when they join others.

SOCIAL LOAFING

Carrie is considered by her peers to be a hard worker. When Ms. Elliot tells her students to form teams to paint a mural, Ronnie, George, and Mary, who are not hard working, ask Carrie to join them. Carrie does most of the work for the first two weeks, then she stops working hard.

Social psychologists have investigated the productivity losses in groups first identified by Ringelmann. Latane, Williams, and Harkins (1979) called the reduction of effort by individuals when working in groups "social loafing." Several factors affect the effort of group members, and either increase or decrease the operation of social loafing: equality of effort, identifiability, responsibility, redundancy, and involvement.

Equality of Efforts

Kerr (1983) noted that for some group tasks, members share equally in the group's rewards regardless of the amount of individual effort exerted by each member to achieve the group goal. For example, four students assigned to write a group essay will each get the same grade whether they contribute equally to the essay or not. In such instances, harder-working members may perceive that others in the group are getting a "free ride." Like Carrie, they don't want to look like "suckers" by working harder than the others, so they sometimes reduce their efforts to match the level of effort they believe other group members are expending. Individuals maximize their own efforts when they believe their teammates are also working hard.

Identifiability

The effects of social loafing can also be reduced when each member's contribution to the group can be clearly identified (Harkins, 1987). Group members try harder when they know that their own contributions can be singled out and may be evaluated.

Responsibility

Latane and Darley (1970) discovered that when individuals join groups, their feelings of personal responsibility sometimes decrease. If students be-

lieve that they play a very small part in the group, perhaps as Ronnie, George, and Mary did, then they may not feel responsible and they will expend less effort. If students believe their efforts will have an impact on the final group product, they are likely to work hard.

Redundancy

Team members do not try as hard when they believe that their efforts are not essential to the team's success, especially if they duplicate the efforts of other

·············· EXHIBIT 2.2 **Resource and Process Factors That Affect Group Productivity** ··············

Factor	Effective Groups Have:	Ineffective Groups Have:
Size	• enough members to complete the task	• too many (or too few) members to complete the task
Equality of Efforts	• members who share equally both in the work and in the reward for group productivity	• members who share unequally in the work but equally in the reward (work avoiders are termed free riders; hard workers are termed suckers)
Identifiability	• member contributions that are clearly identified	• contributions that cannot be clearly attributed to any one individual
Responsibility	• members who believe their efforts will be used toward the group product	• members who are uncertain about whether their efforts will make a contribution
Redundancy	• members who believe their contributions are unique	• members who believe their efforts are redundant and duplicate the work of others
Involvement	• tasks that are interesting, challenging, or involving	• tasks that are boring, easy, or uninvolving
Cohesiveness	• members who are committed to each other and the group	• members who are uncommitted to each other and to the group
Goals	• homogeneous group goals; everyone shares the same group objectives	• heterogeneous group goals; members disagree about group objectives
Heterogeneity	• members who have a mixture of skills, abilities, and perspectives	• members who have a narrow range of skills, abilities, and perspectives
Time	• sufficient time to express ideas, to interact, and to integrate viewpoints	• insufficient time to work together

team members (Harkins and Petty, 1982). For example, students will not work as hard to solve math problems if other members are also attempting to solve the same problems, and evaluation is based on correct group solutions. In contrast, students who believe their contribution is unique and important to team success do work hard.

Involvement

Brickner, Harkins, and Ostram (1986) asked college students to generate arguments for or against a plan to make all seniors pass a comprehensive examination before graduation. Students who were led to believe that the plan was being considered for their own university generated more ideas. In general, evidence suggests that students exert greater effort when their groups are working on relevant, interesting, challenging, or involving tasks. Irrelevant, boring, easy, or uninvolving tasks tend to heighten the effects of social loafing.

An Integrated Explanation

More recently, Shepperd (1993) reviewed the literature on social loafing and identified three sources of low productivity in groups that incorporate the five factors described above. Group members will reduce their individual efforts if they feel contributing is (1) not worth it or there is no equality of effort (e.g., the task is not intrinsically interesting or contributions are not rewarded), (2) not necessary (which involves identifiability, responsibility, or redundancy) (e.g., other group members can do all the work), or (3) too costly in terms of involvement (e.g., participating in the group task is perceived as too demanding). See Chapter 7: Encouraging Individual Accountability for applications of Shepperd's explanation to cooperative learning.

OTHER FACTORS

In addition to group size and the five factors of social loafing, other factors influence group productivity: group cohesiveness, group goals, group heterogeneity, and time.

Group Cohesiveness

Cohesive groups are ones that have reasons for staying together. Group cohesiveness is affected most strongly by the extent to which each group member is committed to achieving the group goal, and by the attraction among group members and group pride (Mullen and Cooper, 1994).

Cartwright (1968) indicated that cohesiveness has several consequences. Cohesive groups tend to:

- keep their members, which increases the likelihood that group goals will be achieved
- have greater participation among group members
- reduce anxiety, heighten self-esteem, and thus be a source of security for group members
- show greater understanding, acceptance, and intimacy
- allow greater development, expression, and resolution of conflict

There has been considerable research on the nature and extent of the relationship between group cohesiveness and performance. Mullen and Cooper (1994) reviewed 49 studies and concluded that while cohesiveness somewhat affected performance, performance had a much stronger effect on group cohesiveness. Groups that experience success show significantly higher levels of cohesiveness than groups that experience failure.

How can you help your students work in cohesive groups? First, use teambuilding activities (see Chapter 4: Classbuilding and Teambuilding). These activities are designed to increase group cohesiveness by getting new groups off to a good start and by helping them decide on and commit to goals. Second, encourage group reflection (see Chapter 9: Evaluating and Reflecting). This can also help groups maintain cohesiveness by keeping members aware of their interactions with teammates. Finally, and perhaps most importantly, try to ensure team success by assigning groups tasks that are challenging but achievable. You may also wish to monitor unsuccessful groups more carefully and intervene when necessary.

Group Goals

Group members sometimes disagree about their group's goals or the degree to which they are committed to achieving them. In some instances, group members hold different goals for themselves and the group. These different individual orientations can interfere with the productivity of the group.

The most extensive studies of variation of group goals are those dealing with cooperative, competitive, and individualistic goal structures. These studies (e.g., Johnson and Johnson, 1989a) are reviewed more completely in Appendix A: Research Evidence. In general, the research shows that group productivity is greater when group members share a common, cooperative goal than when individuals compete to achieve their goals.

Group Heterogeneity

According to Shaw (1983), enhanced performance results when a group working on a complex task is composed of individuals having a relevant diversity of skills, information, and viewpoints. The effects of diverse personalities, attitudes, and demographics are less clear. While some evidence suggests that a range of personalities can enhance group performance, other evidence suggests that personal diversity may impair the development of cohesiveness and thus reduce subsequent group performance.

Time

If tasks are not additive, the superiority of groups compared to individuals may depend on having sufficient time (Fox and Lorge, 1962). A long work period allows group members to attain Tuckman's performing stage; that is, having enough time helps students adjust to one another, set norms, express ideas, assimilate each other's contributions, interact, criticize, and integrate viewpoints. Under severe time constraints, group members may not discover how best to coordinate their efforts or bother to help each other. Sometimes, for expediency, more able members may simply take over completion of group tasks.

Interracial and Interethnic Relations

Mr. Graham is walking around his grade-two class, observing how his students are working in small groups. He notices that at the science activity center, Patricia, Sacha, and Theo are eagerly leaning over the materials and elbowing out their fourth

team member, Mohammed. Mohammed, who is an African-American, is hovering at the edges of the group, offering suggestions that are ignored, and trying to experiment with a magnet. Finally, he walks away, causes a disturbance, and is labeled a troublemaker.

Children absorb the status distinctions based on social class, race, ethnic group, and gender that are prevalent in our society. These prejudices and stereotypes subsequently affect the way in which they interact with others. The ideal school is a place where students feel encouraged to learn and to explore; where students encourage others to do their best; and where there is an atmosphere of trust, respect, kindness, and mutual concern. Unfortunately, schools are sometimes far from this vision. Instead of all schools being safe havens for learning and growing, some schools are dangerous places, where students verbally abuse or physically attack classmates and teachers.

In all social organizations, including countries, businesses, or classrooms, people categorize themselves and others into "us" (the in-group) and "them" (the out-group). Social psychologists have developed several theories to explain how prejudice develops and is maintained within groups and organizations. These theories are relevant here, since both interracial and interethnic relations can influence the effectiveness of cooperative learning, and inappropriate uses of cooperative learning can reinforce prejudice. If these issues are addressed when they arise within cooperative learning groups, the reduction of racial, ethnic, and gender prejudice can be one of the major benefits of cooperative learning.

Miller and Harrington (1990) described seven explanations of how prejudices and stereotypes may arise and how they affect the interactions between people of different ethnic groups. They also suggested ways to reduce the impact of prejudice in the multiethnic, multiracial classroom using cooperative learning. These explanations and interventions are summarized below and in Exhibit 2.3.

REALISTIC CONFLICT THEORY

Realistic conflict theory suggests that the basis for prejudice and conflict between ethnic groups lies in the struggle for existence or the struggle for access to limited resources. This conflict produces cooperation and feelings of loyalty *within* an individual's own group, but produces competition and feelings of contempt toward outsiders. Using between-group cooperation or developing superordinate goals that require groups to work together to achieve common objectives eliminates conflict between groups and reduces the tendency for ethnic prejudice to develop.

REINFORCEMENT THEORY

According to reinforcement theory, people like those who reward them. Rewards are given for being similar to the in-group, adopting their values, and cooperating in attaining group goals. In the reinforcement view, the perceived likelihood of success in obtaining the group reward determines the cohesion among group members.

SIMILARITY-ATTRACTION HYPOTHESIS

Research on interpersonal attraction has shown that people prefer to associate with others who share their interests, values, and personal traits. Furthermore, friendships are often formed with people who are in close proximity, such as those with whom we live or work. Proximity allows for more frequent contact and a greater opportunity to perceive similarities. According to the similarity-attraction hypothesis, cooperation fosters contact among group members, increasing the likelihood of discovering similar interests, values, and attitudes.

CONTACT HYPOTHESIS

According to the contact hypothesis, interaction among individuals results in familiarity and attraction. When contact does not occur, groups that are segregated from each other will display avoidance and assume that they are dissimilar. In contrast,

·········· EXHIBIT 2.3 **Seven Theoretical Approaches to Interethnic and Interracial Relations** ··········

Theoretical Approach	Causal Antecedent of Prejudice	Key Feature(s) for an Intervention	Mediator of Reduced Prejudice
Realistic Conflict	Competition for resources	Cooperative means	Superordinate goal
Reinforcement	Absence of outgroup reward	Cooperative reward structure	Intergroup success
Similarity-Attraction	Perceived dissimilarity	Interaction	Increased similarity
Contact Hypothesis	Isolation of groups	Equal status contact	Disconfirmed stereotypes
Ignorance Model	Lack of familiarity	Increased familiarity	Reduced anxiety
Expectation States	Negative expectations	Retrained outgroup	Reversed expectations
Situational Identity	Social categorization: Undifferentiated outgroup; Depersonalized members; Competitive social comparison	Decategorization: Differentiation of outgroup; Personalization of member(s); Differentiation of self from ingroup; Personalization of self vis a vis outgroup member	Low situational salience of category boundaries

Source: N. Miller and H.J. Harrington, A Situational Identity Perspective on Cultural Diversity and Teamwork in the Classroom. In S. Sharan (ed.), *Cooperative Learning: Theory and Research*, New York: Praeger Publishers, an imprint of Greenwood Publishing Group, Inc., Westport, Connecticut, p. 45. Copyright © 1990 by Shlomo Sharan. Reprinted with permission.

relations between group members who have not previously interacted will improve following direct contact. Unlike the similarity-attraction hypothesis, which emphasizes the role of contact in discovering interpersonal similarities, the contact hypothesis suggests that the role of contact is to create similarities. In particular, contact among individuals promotes positive attitudes and acceptance when the setting allows for the equal status of the participants.

IGNORANCE MODEL

The ignorance model of intergroup relations emphasizes the negative effects of ethnic and racial stereotyping that stem from a lack of knowledge and familiarity with out-group members. The ignorance model stresses the role of anxiety as it affects intergroup relations. Anxiety is aroused by the prospect of interacting with strangers and must be reduced before positive affect develops. In order to reduce anxiety, individuals must first be educated to relinquish their negative stereotypes.

EXPECTATION STATES THEORY

Society ascribes esteem, privilege, and desirability based on numerous status characteristics, including gender, race, and physical attractiveness. Furthermore, high status produces broad, generalized expectations of competence in a wide range of areas, even when the status characteristic is not logically related to the task to be accomplished. Reversing low-status perceptions requires modifying the perceptions and expectations of both high- and low-status members, the latter being more difficult to modify. This can be achieved by advanced preparation and by using multiple-ability tasks that emphasize the contribution of each group member through their skills and abilities (see Chapter 17: Other Peer Interaction Methods).

SITUATIONAL IDENTITY THEORY

Situational identity theory is based on several basic assumptions. First, people have a basic need to establish and maintain a positive identity. Second, a person's identity includes both social and personal components. That is, the image people have of themselves and of others is based on characteristics of the group to which they belong, and not only on personal features. For example, Billy's teacher believed that he should be smart because he is Chinese. "But I'm average," Billy complained. "People never see me as I really am." Third, people make comparative judgments on both social and personal features, such as, "Jenny's handwriting is nicer than Shlomo's because girls are better than boys at penmanship." Fourth, there is an evaluative and affective dimension to an individual's identity. Identity can have positive or negative components, and strong or weak attributes.

Reducing Prejudice in Groups

According to situational identity theory, two processes are responsible for the development of negative intergroup relations and prejudice: a social rather than a personal *categorization* of individuals and a competitive rather than a cooperative social *comparison* process. Consequently, Miller and Harrington (1992) recommended four principles to guide the way teachers structure cooperative learning in their classrooms.

1. *Minimize the salience of social categories.* Teachers sometimes inadvertently reinforce minority status by ensuring that minority-group members are represented in all cooperative groups. This can create the impression that minority status is a salient characteristic. By periodically rotating group membership or by creating different teams for different subjects, you can help students become familiar with all their classmates. You could also group students by categories that are independent of race, ethnicity, or gender (e.g., group them according to course-topic interests).

2. *Minimize threats to identity.* Peer tutoring among team members can threaten personal identity when certain individuals are always the tutors and others are always the tutees. To minimize threats to identity, use cooperative learning methods that encourage each student to become an expert in his or her area, able to teach the whole group. Or have students take on unique and important roles of equal status within the group.

Having team members contribute individual improvement scores to create a team score can promote positive personal identity. When using interteam competition, be sure that each individual has an equal opportunity to contribute, otherwise low-status members may be blamed for the failure of the losing team.

3. *Provide opportunities for personalization.* Exchanging personal information is an important part of forming close relationships. You can facilitate this process in at least two ways. First, when group tasks can be divided, have students work in heterogeneous pairs. Second, use teambuilding activities to provide opportunities for members to develop an awareness and appreciation of their teammates.

4. *Develop students' interpersonal competencies.* While students may have the will to cooperate, they may lack the ability to do so. Students may need to acquire the interpersonal skills or competencies to learn with others (see Chapter 8: Developing Interpersonal and Cognitive Skills).

SUMMARY

This chapter has taken a social psychological view of groups. Initially, work in the area of groups began with an examination of how an individual's behavior was influenced by the presence of others. Later, social psychologists examined how people work together in groups and how groups develop. We introduced you to a number of factors that influence group processes and productivity. We also briefly reviewed seven explanations of interracial and interethnic relations and strategies for reducing prejudice in groups. Examining group processes is important to a theoretical understanding of the complexity of groups and to a practical understanding of how best to use cooperative groups in the classroom.

REFLECTION ACTIVITIES

1. Some students who work in groups complain that they do most of the work. What type of relationship among group members does this reflect? What are some ways of preventing this type of group structure from continuing?

2. Discuss the concept of social loafing with your students. How important do they judge each of the following factors to be: equality of effort, identifiability, responsibility, redundancy, and involvement? (Be careful to put these concepts in terms your students will understand.)

3. Teachers often use peer tutoring as a way for knowledgeable students to assist students who are having difficulties. What would you do to avoid having peer tutoring reinforce status differences, prejudices, and stereotypes?

Cathie Archbould

Theories of Cooperative Learning

How does cooperative learning increase
students' involvement and excitement
in learning?

•

Why do students try harder to learn when
they are in teams?

•

What makes students who work together
learn more?

•

How do students in teams come to
understand course material better?

In the previous two chapters, you were introduced to some important, basic approaches to
learning and motivation and to group processes
and productivity. This chapter is designed to take
you one step further. It focuses on specific explanations of how cooperative learning operates to promote classroom learning and interaction in small
groups.

We have organized the theories into two broad
categories: motivational explanations and learning
explanations. Motivational explanations are useful
in understanding what increases your students'
interest in, involvement with, and persistence at
learning. But increasing your students' motivation
is not a guarantee that students will learn more.
Cooperative learning can also influence the acquisition, representation, and retrieval of information.

MOTIVATIONAL EXPLANATIONS

In Chapter 2: Group Processes and Productivity, we
introduced you to the concept of interdependence
among team members. Motivational explanations
of cooperative learning concentrate on understanding the impact of interdependence on students.
These explanations include cooperative incentives,
social interdependence, morality-based motivation,

and social cohesion, student empowerment, novelty, and teacher enthusiasm.

Depending on their underlying assumptions, the different motivational explanations emphasize different ways of structuring positive interdependence among students. For example, the theory of cooperative incentives draws on behavioral theories to explain how group rewards increase motivation. In contrast, the theory of social interdependence draws on cognitive theories to explain increased motivation primarily in terms of group goals.

Cooperative Incentives for Learning

Mrs. Jabal placed her grade-eight students in heterogeneous teams to learn geometry. At the end of each week, students were individually quizzed and their relative improvement scores were added to create team scores. Team scores were published in a weekly newsletter. At the end of the term, each member of high-scoring teams was to be recognized with a certificate of merit. The certificates were anticipated with great excitement by the students and motivated them to work hard to improve. Tim, a student who had previously done little to learn mathematics, saw the opportunity to experience success. "Boy, this is great," he said. "My parents would be so happy if I brought one of these home!"

COOPERATIVE INCENTIVES AND COOPERATIVE TASKS

Mrs. Jabal's class illustrates how rewards can be powerful incentives for learning in groups. Slavin (1983b, 1992) made an important distinction between cooperative incentive structures and cooperative task structures. His model is illustrated in Exhibit 3.1.

A cooperative *incentive*, or reward, structure exists when individuals in a group are rewarded equally. A cooperative *task* structure exists when individuals in a group can or must work together, but may or may not receive rewards or recognition based on their group's performance. Both cooperative incentive and cooperative task structures increase performance by increasing encouragement among group members to perform the group task and to help one another in

doing so. However, cooperative incentive structures are also likely to increase the diffusion of responsibility among group members if individual members who have not contributed are rewarded on the basis of the group's performance. Increasing the visibility of individual contributions can counteract these negative effects (see Chapter 7: Encouraging Individual Accountability).

Slavin concluded that work that employs group rewards or group goals in conjunction with individual accountability is most successful in promoting individual learning. In contrast to competitive incentive structures, students receive the benefits of cooperation, such as help and encouragement, but still maintain individual responsibility. Research supporting this conclusion is summarized in Appendix A: Research Evidence.

DO EXTRINSIC REWARDS REDUCE SUBSEQUENT STUDENT INTEREST?

Cooperative learning experts have debated the use of extrinsic rewards to motivate students when they work in groups (cf., Kohn, 1991a, 1991b, 1993; Slavin, 1991a). Most participants in the debate agree that the use of extrinsic rewards can be justified when a concept or skill cannot be presented in a manner that is interesting to the students. What they disagree about is how frequently extrinsic rewards are necessary.

To some, extrinsic rewards interfere with the intrinsic interest generated by the learning task and the positive group environment. Kohn (1991a) believed that student teams too quickly become accustomed to learning for a reward and not for the sake of learning itself.

In contrast, Slavin (1991a) believed that without some form of extrinsic reward, students will avoid learning what they need to learn. Furthermore, outstanding achievement always produces extrinsic rewards of some kind. How else, Slavin wondered, do outstanding achievers maintain their motivation?

Graves (1991) took a conciliatory position midway between these extreme positions. He described the conditions under which a teacher might use extrinsic rewards in the classroom and the conditions under which they would not be appropriate (see Exhibit 3.2.)

Theory of Social Interdependence

Mr. Lapierre decides to experiment with cooperative learning. He dutifully arranges students into groups and gives them ample time to work together. He is pleased to see several groups busily talking and working on class activities. But much to his disappointment, not every group appears to be working together and on task.

Mr. Lapierre decides to spend a little time with each group to discuss his observations with them. When he meets with an especially communicative and cohesive group, members make it clear that they find helping their teammates to learn encourages them to learn, and contributes to achieving the group goal. However, when Mr. Lapierre meets with the members of the quiet and unproductive group, their remarks are quite different. These students don't see the relationship between helping their teammates and their own learning. Nor do they seem especially aware of the group having a goal or purpose.

When group members perceive that they are positively interdependent, students become motivated to work together to achieve mutual goals. The theory of social interdependence (Johnson and Johnson, 1989a, 1992a, 1992b, 1994) suggests that positive interdependence, or cooperation, results in individuals interacting in ways that promote each other's successes. This leads to higher productivity and achievement, more positive relationships among individuals, and greater psychological health and well-being. In contrast, negative interdependence, or competition, results in individuals obstructing each other's success. This leads to lower productivity, more negative relationships, and diminished psychological health. Exhibit 3.3 illustrates these interrelationships.

The promotive interactions encouraged by positive interdependence include communicating ideas effectively, providing mutual help and assistance, building trust, and managing conflict constructively. The relationship between interdependence and interactions is bidirectional. For example, cooperation promotes trust, trust promotes greater cooperation, greater cooperation results in greater trust, and so forth.

The educational outcomes are also interrelated. For example, joint efforts to achieve mutual goals tend to foster caring and committed relationships. In turn, these committed relationships promote joint efforts to achieve. Joint efforts to achieve also tend to increase participants' psychological health, while psychological health tends to increase the productivity of cooperative efforts.

Morality-Based Motivation of Cooperation

Nancy is preparing for the first calculus test she has ever taken. She is nervous about doing well and

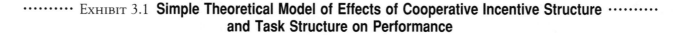

·········· EXHIBIT 3.1 **Simple Theoretical Model of Effects of Cooperative Incentive Structure** ··········
and Task Structure on Performance

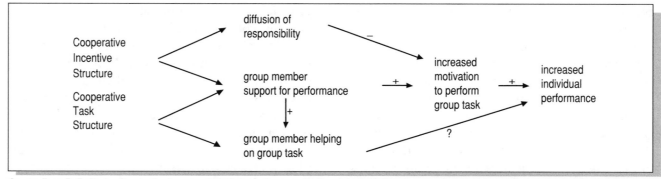

Source: From R. E. Slavin, *Cooperative Learning*, New York: Longman, p. 15. Copyright © 1983 by Longman Inc. Used by permission of Robert E. Slavin.

···················· EXHIBIT 3.2 **Using Extrinsic Rewards for Cooperative Learning** ······················

Avoid using extrinsic rewards:

1. When students would be willing to engage in the activities without the use of the rewards.

2. When the rewards may be seen by students as attempts to manipulate and control their behaviour or as "payoffs" for their performance.

Consider using extrinsic rewards:

1. When the learning task is one students would be unwilling to do on their own.

2. When the rewards are symbolic in form, attempting to inform students how well they are doing and to communicate their teacher's pride in their accomplishments.

3. When the rewards are social rather than tangible.

4. When the rewards are unanticipated.

5. When the rewards are given for successfully completing a task rather than for merely engaging in it.

6. When the rewards are valued by all members of the group.

Source: Adapted from T. Graves, "The Controversy Over Group Rewards in the Classroom," in *Educational Leadership*, 1991, Volume 48, pp. 77–79. Copyright © 1991 by the Association for Supervision and Curriculum Development. Used by permission of Theodore Graves.

············ EXHIBIT 3.3 **Outcomes of Cooperation: The Interrelationships among Positive** ············
Interdependence, Promotive Interactions, and Outcomes

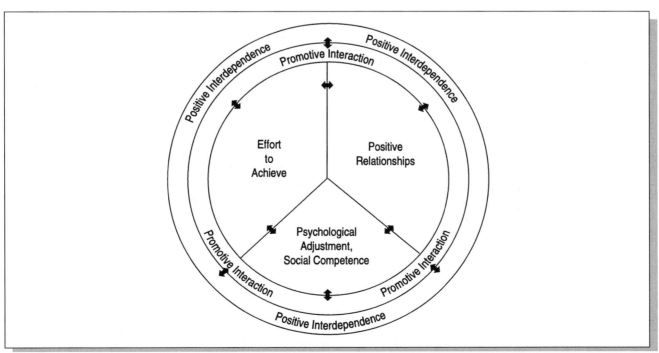

Source: From D. W. Johnson and R. T. Johnson, *Cooperation and Competition: Theory and Research,* Edina, Minnesota: Interaction Book Company, p. 6. Copyright © 1989 by David W. Johnson. Used by permission.

sleeps poorly the night before the exam. Several days after the test, the results are posted outside her teacher's door. Nancy didn't do as well as she had hoped. "Oh well," she exclaims, "I guess calculus just isn't my subject."

Dorothy is also preparing for her first calculus test. Unlike Nancy, Dorothy is working with three other students to learn. Their individual examination results will be combined to give a group grade worth one-third of their overall mark. When the results are posted, Dorothy is disappointed with the results. "I guess we will have to work harder," she says, "to make sure everyone understands how to get the answers."

Given the importance that has been attached to students' attributions (Weiner, 1986), exploring the effect of different classroom goal structures on the causal beliefs of students is interesting. Cooperative, competitive, and individualistic goal structures have different effects on the way students attribute

success or failure to effort, ability, luck, and task difficulty. In many situations, cooperative goal structures are best at encouraging students to attribute their successes to effort.

Ames (1984) proposed a model that explores the effects of cooperative, competitive, and individualistic classroom goal structures on student causal beliefs and affect. Her model highlights the different types of motivation that underlie each classroom goal structure. These different types of motivation, along with situational cues (e.g., whether the group succeeded or failed), combine to influence student causal beliefs, which, in turn, influence students' feelings (e.g., pride or guilt). Ames's model (see Exhibit 3.4) suggests that competitive goal structures result in students believing that learning outcomes are primarily a function of personal ability, while cooperative goal structures result in students attributing learning outcomes to effort.

EXHIBIT 3.4 **Goal Structure Influences on Motivation**

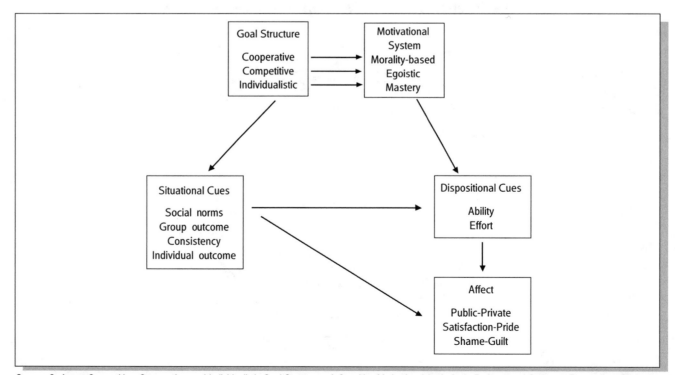

Source: C. Ames, Competitive, Cooperative, and Individualistic Goal Structures: A Cognitive-Motivational Analysis. In R. Ames and C. Ames, *Research on Motivation in Education: Student Motivation*, Volume 1, Orlando, Florida: Academic Press, 1984, p. 189. Copyright © 1984 by Academic Press, Inc. Used by permission.

Ames described the motivational system underlying competitive goal structures as an egoistic motivational system; that is, students are motivated by the desire to win in order to enhance or protect their self-perceptions and self-worth. As a consequence of the exaggerated value of winning in a competitive structure, students attribute learning outcomes to ability—the presence of ability when one wins and the absence of ability when one loses.

A mastery-oriented motivational system underlies individualistic goal structures, that is, students are motivated by the desire to achieve some standard of excellence. However, individualistic goal structures may operate in either of two ways—ability-based or effort-based. Such individualized structures as mastery learning may emphasize self-generated cues for evaluating one's achievement and lead students to attribute learning outcomes to effort. However, in practice, students may actively compare themselves to others (e.g., relative to others in terms of how much material was covered or how difficult the task was). In this case, individualistic structures may promote attributions to ability.

A morality-based motivational system underlies cooperative goal structures. Students are motivated by the desire to help others in order to increase the probability of a successful group outcome. When the focus is on helping and contributing to the group product, teammates place special emphasis on individual and group efforts to achieve. As in moral situations, judgment is based on the intention of the participants, that is, whether individuals make the *effort* to help appears to be a more important factor than their *ability* to help. Harsh judgments are reserved for those who avoid helping, while praise is given to those who try, even if they lack the skills to contribute effectively.

ATTRIBUTIONS IN FAILING TEAMS

Ames (1981) found that when groups fail, the question of responsibility becomes important, and the group member who has contributed the least is judged negatively and may be punished by teammates. This is especially debilitating for low-performing students who carry their own negative beliefs, which become validated by teammates.

Will effort be perceived as the most important element in team learning and be unaffected by group outcome after students have multiple success and failure experiences learning in teams? Chambers and Abrami (1991) and Abrami, Chambers, d'Apollonia, Farrell, and De Simone (1992) corroborated and extended the findings of Ames. Overall, regardless of group outcome, students rated effort as the most important determinant of their successes or failures. However, students also felt that ability and luck contributed somewhat to group outcome. Furthermore, low-ability students from teams that failed rated ability as more important than did low-ability students from teams that succeeded. In the future, these students may come to see effort as increasingly futile.

You can use at least two strategies to reduce the negative effects of team failure. First, avoid cooperative learning methods that employ competition between teams. Have groups work either independently or cooperatively (see Chapter 6: Fostering Positive Interdependence). Second, recognize and modify ineffective group work through regular group reflection and goal setting. Recognize students' attempts to improve the work of their groups by using group improvement points to augment individual improvement points (see Chapter 11: Student Team Learning Methods).

Social Cohesion

Audrey is one hour late coming home from school. Her worried mother meets her at the door. "I'm sorry I didn't phone, Mom," Audrey says, "but one of my teammates was having a problem with an assignment and I wanted to go over it with her. We got talking and lost track of time. We got the answer though!"

Social cohesion explanations (Cohen, 1986, 1994a; Sharan and Sharan, 1976, 1992) contend that the effects of cooperative learning on achievement are strongly mediated by the cohesiveness of the group. (See Chapter 2: Group Processes and Productivity for a review of research on the effects of group cohesiveness.) In the social cohesion view, students help their teammates learn because they care about the group and group members, not simply because it is in their own interests to do so.

The social cohesion perspective emphasizes teambuilding activities that unite groups and build trust and group reflection during and after team activities. Group rewards and individual accountability are downplayed. Instead, other forms of interdependence are stressed, especially identity, task, and role interdependence. For example, students are encouraged to reach consensus on a group name or to subdivide the learning task and then share their specialized information with teammates. Cohen (1994a) has argued that social cohesion increases when group tasks require the contribution of team members and draw upon varied student abilities.

In cohesive groups, members are encouraged to conform to group norms to unite their efforts and achieve their goals. While peer encouragement normally provides support and motivation, it can become too great and can be perceived as peer pressure. You may want to monitor groups to ensure that students do not unduly pressure their teammates to conform to the group norm. Tolerance for individual differences should also be fostered.

Student Empowerment

When asked about effective classroom management, many teachers say their greatest concern is losing control over a class. However, using cooperative learning often means that students take greater control and responsibility for their learning. Providing students with these opportunities increases their sense of empowerment, which motivates them to engage in academic tasks. Especially when students experience success, the increased autonomy and responsibility awakens beliefs in self-efficacy, and enhances students' self-esteem and self-concept. Students come to feel more like "origins" than "pawns" (de Charms, 1976).

When students are empowered to learn, teachers act more as facilitators of learning than as authority figures. They help to create a nonthreatening atmosphere for learning, where students' involvement, independence, creativity, and self-reliance are promoted.

Some cooperative learning methods encourage students to take great responsibility not only for how they learn but for what they learn. Proponents of these methods (e.g., Pradl, 1991) want to restructure the power relationships in schools, making them more egalitarian. They advocate a more democratic process, giving students more power than in traditional instruction. Such learning freedom and autonomy require that students accept the responsibility for learning, and have the interest and the academic and social skills to succeed. Success is also more likely when students have had prior experience with more structured forms of group work.

Novelty and Teacher Enthusiasm

Mrs. Dewhurst attends a series of workshops on cooperative learning and decides to implement it in her grade-six class. At first, she is enthusiastic, spending extra time preparing for each day's activities. She is especially pleased with the changes in her classroom during these first weeks of the school year. For example, the students don't hesitate to form groups, and they are constantly talking about and working on their assignments. But as the weeks pass, Mrs. Dewhurst begins to lose some of her enthusiasm. She doesn't spend as much time preparing, and begins to notice that some students are having difficulty working with others or keeping to the pace she needs to set.

Most educational innovations meet with initial enthusiasm and success. Current research and practical experience may partly reflect the positive effects of the novelty of using cooperative learning. The effects of novelty also underscore the important role that commitment has in successfully implementing cooperative learning. If a teacher is knowledgeable, confident, and enthusiastic about cooperative learning, the likelihood of an effective and enjoyable experience for both teacher and students is greater. If commitment is not present, then cooperative learning will be only a passing fad.

As the teacher, you are a key element in cooperative learning. Therefore, when you consider implementing cooperative learning in your classroom for the first time, think about the suggestions in Exhibit 3.5.

LEARNING EXPLANATIONS

Increasing student motivation to learn is only one part of the cooperative learning puzzle. Researchers have also focused on how the interactions that occur when students learn together in small groups affect the understanding and cognitive processing of team members. With this in mind, we will review several learning explanations: cognitive elaboration, promotive interactions and student thinking, cognitive development, practice, time-on-task, and classroom organization.

Cognitive Elaboration

Audrey and Erica are partners during science class. As they prepare to replicate a chemistry experiment, Audrey is uncertain about why they are following certain procedures. She turns to Erica and asks for help. "I followed this at the beginning, but I don't understand why we need to do steps four and five." As Erica explains the procedure to Audrey, they both realize something new about the nature of the experiment. Both finish the lab with a sense of accomplishment.

Cognitive-elaboration perspectives (Dansereau, 1985; Webb, 1989) suggest that the learner must engage in some sort of cognitive restructuring if information is to be retained and related to infor-

mation already in memory. One form of restructuring is elaboration of the concepts. And one of the most effective means of elaboration is explaining the material to someone else.

Webb (1992) proposed a model of peer interaction and learning in small groups that emphasizes the importance of providing appropriate help (see Exhibit 3.6). Webb described three conditions for help to be effective. First, help must be relevant to the particular misunderstanding of the student. Second, help must be given close to the time of the student's error or question. Third, the level of elaboration must correspond to the level of help requested.

Webb's research (1989) on peer help-giving and -receiving indicates that for students experiencing substantial difficulty in problem solving, the only effective assistance from the group is to provide high-level elaboration; that is, to give explanations that describe in detail how to solve the problem. For students requiring specific information, effective assistance may consist of low-level elaborations; that is, answers to problems, simple procedural information, or other information without explanations. In either case, the student must understand the explanation received. In addition, the student must actually apply the help given to solve the problem.

Webb also synthesized the results of studies that examined the relationship between help-giving and learning. Most of the studies found that giving high-

---

·············· EXHIBIT 3.5 **Strategies Teachers Can Use to Establish and Maintain Student** ··············
Enthusiasm for Cooperative Learning

1. Convey confidence and enthusiasm to your students. Students may be sensitive to your uncertainty, which can affect their involvement.

2. Start small but think big. Slowly integrate cooperative learning into your teaching. Try for a few small successes at first, then increase your use of cooperative learning as you become comfortable with and knowledgeable about group work.

3. Appreciate students' willingness to experiment. Most students will be eager to try new ways of learning in moderation. A gradual introduction to cooperative learning will take advantage of their eagerness to try something new but won't enlarge their fears that team work will not succeed.

4. Only use cooperative learning some of the time. After all, students may need to learn and practice competitive and individualistic skills, too.

5. Find colleagues to work with. You will find implementation to be more effective and enjoyable if you have a peer with whom you can share your experiences.

level, elaborated explanations was positively related to the achievement of the help-giver. In contrast, help-givers who provided only low-level elaborations did not benefit. The Roman philosopher Seneca may have captured the essence of Webb's findings when he said: *"Qui docet, discit."* ("Whoever teaches, learns.")

A number of processes may account for these findings. First, to give a highly elaborated explanation, the help-giver must clarify, organize, and possibly reorganize the material. Doing so may reveal gaps in the help-giver's understanding, which may cause him or her to search for new information, resolve inconsistencies, and learn the material better. Second, the help-giver may have to formulate the answer in new or different ways if the original explanation is not understood. This may include using different vocabulary, generating new examples, linking examples to the recipient's experiences, and so forth. All of these activities are likely to expand and solidify the help-giver's understanding of the material. On the other hand, giving only the correct answer or a low-level explanation will do little to clarify or reorganize the help-giver's own thinking.

High-ability students sometimes object to working in groups, a concern that is occasionally echoed by parents and by teachers who are new to cooperative learning. Webb's work suggests that the learning of high-ability students can be facilitated when they engage in a meaningful dialogue with teammates and attempt explanations. When understanding the material is emphasized more than getting the correct solution, cooperative learning can enhance the learning of both students who give help and students who receive it.

Promotive Interactions and Student Thinking

In their group, Ted and Brenda are debating how to give a presentation on the American Civil War. Ted wants to illustrate some of the important issues by presenting them through the eyes of a runaway slave. Brenda thinks this approach is too one-sided. She is in favor of a more comprehensive explanation, using charts and photographs. After a while, their teammates join in the discussion. Eventually, group members decide on a compromise. They will give a brief overview of the major points of the Civil

·········· EXHIBIT 3.6 **Sequences of Experiences Leading to Positive Learning Outcomes** ··········
for Students Who Express a Need for Help

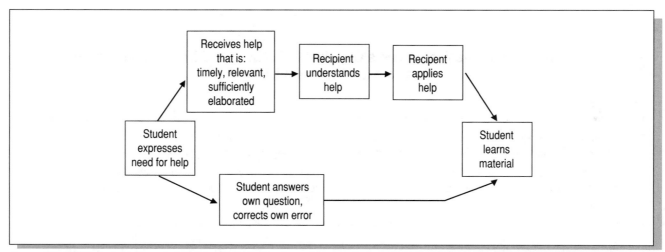

Source: N.M. Webb, Testing a Theoretical Model of Student Interaction and Learning in Small Groups. In R. Hertz-Lazarowitz and N. Miller (eds.), *Interaction in Cooperative Groups: The Theoretical Anatomy of Group Learning.* New York: Cambridge University Press, p. 105. Copyright © by Cambridge University Press 1992. Reprinted with permission of Cambridge University Press.

War with a handout. Then they will have a presentation featuring the perspectives of both a runaway slave and a plantation owner. Anyone who believes that using cooperative learning means an end to student disagreements is in for a surprise. Fortunately, student discussions often reflect involvement and engagement with the material to be learned.

Johnson and Johnson (1989a, 1992a, 1992b, 1994) believe the key to enhanced cognitive processing and higher-level reasoning lies first in establishing positive interdependence among teammates. Once positive interdependence exists, then group members are motivated to engage in promotive interactions, such as helping one another learn and resolving disagreements and controversies. Johnson and Johnson (1992a) give seven reasons why cooperative learning promotes the cognitive and metacognitive activity required to learn.

1. *Instructional expectations.* Students appear to conceptualize material and organize it cognitively in a different way when they expect to summarize, explain, and teach to teammates.

2. *Oral rehearsal.* The discussions that often occur within cooperative learning groups promote more frequent oral summarizing, elaborating, and explaining. This appears to influence the encoding of information into memory, facilitating long-term retention and retrieval.

3. *Heterogenous groups.* When groups are composed of a broad mix of students, group members must deal with different perspectives, strategies, and approaches to completing the learning task. This stimulates divergent and creative thinking.

4. *Perspective-taking.* Interaction with group members who bring different perspectives and information to bear on the content promotes greater "perspective-taking" than does competitive or individualistic learning. Perspective-taking results in better understanding and retention of the information, reasoning, and perspectives presented by others.

5. *Peer monitoring.* Group members develop their meta-cognitive skills as they call on each other

to explain and justify their thinking and reasoning.

6. *Feedback.* Throughout the learning process, group members give each other timely, formative feedback concerning ways to improve and the quality and relevance of individual contributions.

7. *Controversy.* Conflicts over ideas, opinions, conclusions, theories, and information among group members promote controversy, which may function as a mediator of cognitive activity.

Cognitive Development

Andrew watches intently as Julia sits next to him at the computer and activates a learning game. After watching for several minutes, Andrew is ready for his turn. He follows the steps that he observed Julia use. After a while, Julia and Andrew take turns and help each other discover new ways to play the game.

Some researchers who have investigated cooperative learning with children have emphasized cognitive-developmental perspectives (Damon, 1984). These views grew out of those of Piaget and Vygotsky concerning the nature of cognitive growth (see Chapter 1: Learning and Motivation). The fundamental assumption is that interaction among children around appropriate tasks increases the mastery of critical concepts.

Damon (1984, 335) proposed four elements as the foundation of peer-based education.

1. Through mutual feedback and debate, peers motivate one another to abandon misconceptions and search for better solutions.

2. The experience of peer communication can help a student master social processes, such as participation and argumentation, and cognitive processes, such as verification and criticism.

3. Collaboration between peers can provide a forum for discovery learning and can encourage creative thinking.

4. Peer interaction can introduce students to the process of generating ideas.

Other Explanations

Nancy and her teammates are studying together for a math test. They each take turns asking each other problem questions from their textbooks. At first, the answers come slowly and each teammate makes mistakes. But as time progresses, each student develops a good mastery of the material. They finish studying, confident that they will do well on the upcoming test.

The *practice* explanation (Rosenshine and Stevens, 1986) contends that cooperative learning increases opportunities to practice material until it is mastered. For example, students who take turns quizzing one another may find it more effective than studying alone.

Students' *time-on-task* can also increase when they learn in groups. It is more difficult for students to daydream or wander off task when they are working toward a common goal with classmates. Time-on-task is a significant predictor of student achievement, according to Fisher and Berliner (1985) and to others who reason that students cannot master what they do not attend to.

Finally, the *classroom organization* explanation (Slavin, 1989a) suggests that one important benefit of cooperative learning is that students take responsibility for managing themselves in groups. This frees the teacher to attend to more essential tasks, such as helping individuals or groups to learn. Because the class is better organized and classroom management chores are minimized, the teacher is able to devote greater time and energy to instruction.

An Organizational Model of Cooperative Learning

Is there some way to organize all these explanations to make them useful? The model in Exhibit 3.7 takes into account the diversity of cooperative learning methods, their motivational and learning influences, and the broad range of effects they have on students' academic and nonacademic outcomes. The model also recognizes that the effectiveness of cooperative learning depends on a number of contextual influences, such as the teacher's experience and enthusiasm, the attitudes and abilities of students, and the support and encouragement provided by fellow teachers and the school's administration. Furthermore, it recognizes that the effectiveness of cooperative learning is multifaceted. Some educators may select cooperative learning to promote the achievement of basic learning objectives, while others may use cooperative learning to foster the development of interpersonal skills or feelings of self-esteem. As you read about, reflect on, and implement cooperative learning, you may find it useful to consider the influence of these factors in your own situation.

Context

In order to implement cooperative learning successfully, you must consider the context in which students learn, including the qualities of students, teachers, and administrators that affect the classroom environment. Cooperative learning, or any other instructional strategy, is never implemented in identical contexts. What may work for one teacher with one group of students at a particular school and in a particular subject may be less successful, sometimes even a complete failure, if any one of these contextual factors changes. For cooperative learning to succeed, you need to select the approach most appropriate to your own situation, taking into account your students, yourself as the teacher, your school's culture, and your curriculum. We will briefly discuss these four factors.

STUDENT

Students have many characteristics, skills, and qualities that affect how they learn and interact in small groups. Students differ most clearly in their academic, cognitive, interpersonal, and language skills. They differ in gender, age, ethnicity, race, and socioeconomic status. They also differ in personality and self-perceptions. These variables take on a new dimension in cooperative learning and are particularly important to consider when assigning students to groups (see Chapter 5: Grouping Students). Students may also differ in their interest in learning particular subject matter, which can affect how you structure your classroom and your decision to use extrinsic rewards. Finally, students' experiences with and attitudes toward group work can also influence their reactions to cooperative learning and the types of activities you select.

TEACHER

No less important are your own characteristics as a teacher. Chapter 1: Learning and Motivation asked you to consider your beliefs about teaching and learning. Your skill and training in cooperative learning, your enthusiasm, and your attitudes will

·················· EXHIBIT 3.7 **Organizational Model of Cooperative Learning** ·······················

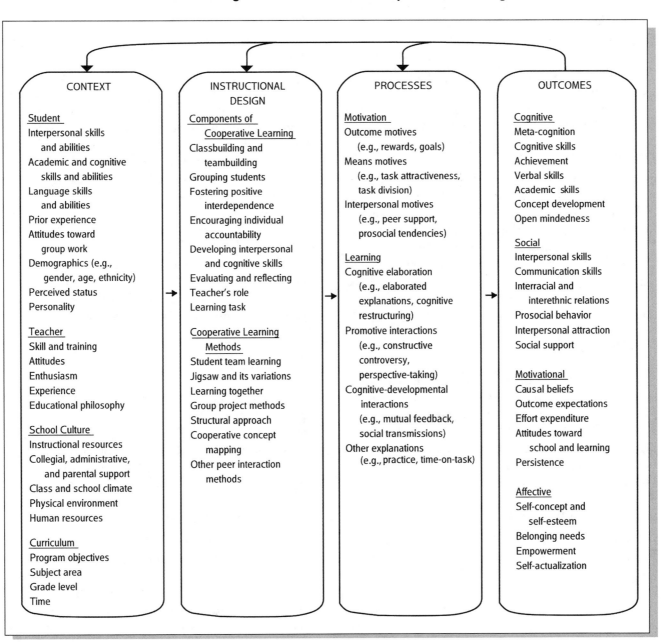

CONTEXT	INSTRUCTIONAL DESIGN	PROCESSES	OUTCOMES
Student	**Components of**	**Motivation**	**Cognitive**
Interpersonal skills	**Cooperative Learning**	Outcome motives	Meta-cognition
and abilities	Classbuilding and	(e.g., rewards, goals)	Cognitive skills
Academic and cognitive	teambuilding	Means motives	Achievement
skills and abilities	Grouping students	(e.g., task attractiveness,	Verbal skills
Language skills	Fostering positive	task division)	Academic skills
and abilities	interdependence	Interpersonal motives	Concept development
Prior experience	Encouraging individual	(e.g., peer support,	Open mindedness
Attitudes toward	accountability	prosocial tendencies)	
group work	Developing interpersonal		**Social**
Demographics (e.g.,	and cognitive skills	**Learning**	Interpersonal skills
gender, age, ethnicity)	Evaluating and reflecting	Cognitive elaboration	Communication skills
Perceived status	Teacher's role	(e.g., elaborated	Interracial and
Personality	Learning task	explanations, cognitive	interethnic relations
		restructuring)	Prosocial behavior
Teacher	**Cooperative Learning**	Promotive interactions	Interpersonal attraction
Skill and training	**Methods**	(e.g., constructive	Social support
Attitudes	Student team learning	controversy,	
Enthusiasm	Jigsaw and its variations	perspective-taking)	**Motivational**
Experience	Learning together	Cognitive-developmental	Causal beliefs
Educational philosophy	Group project methods	interactions	Outcome expectations
	Structural approach	(e.g., mutual feedback,	Effort expenditure
School Culture	Cooperative concept	social transmissions)	Attitudes toward
Instructional resources	mapping	Other explanations	school and learning
Collegial, administrative,	Other peer interaction	(e.g., practice, time-on-task)	Persistence
and parental support	methods		
Class and school climate			**Affective**
Physical environment			Self-concept and
Human resources			self-esteem
			Belonging needs
Curriculum			Empowerment
Program objectives			Self-actualization
Subject area			
Grade level			
Time			

also influence your selection of cooperative learning methods and your success in implementing them.

SCHOOL CULTURE

Attempting a new strategy is easier when there is collegial, administrative, and parental support. In addition, available resources and the physical environment may influence both your method and application of cooperative learning. For example, some cooperative learning methods require specially prepared curriculum materials. If these are not available, you may choose a method you can implement more easily with your own materials. As well, if your class and school climate has been primarily individualistic or competitive, you may decide to devote more time to developing a cooperative climate, as described in Chapter 4: Classbuilding and Teambuilding.

CURRICULUM

Most often, teachers have only limited flexibility in curriculum objectives and coverage. Typically, you have little control over the grade level of your students, the subject, its global program objectives, and the timetable. Consequently, the emphasis you give to decisions such as cognitive or interpersonal skill training, type of task, and type of grading will be influenced by these curriculum issues.

Instructional Design

Many options are open to you in implementing cooperative learning. A thorough understanding of the major components of cooperative learning allows you to design a customized method for your own context and instructional objectives, or to select a cooperative learning method that is suitable for your classroom.

CUSTOMIZED METHODS

Part Two: Implementation presents the major components of cooperative learning and the options available to you when you design a cooperative activity. As you have read so far, the decisions you make about whether and how you promote classbuilding and teambuilding, how you group your students, and what structure you use to promote positive interdependence and individual accountability are extremely important. Whether and how you develop your students' interpersonal and cognitive skills, how you evaluate and reward their learning, how you define your role in the classroom, and, finally, how you structure the group task can also affect your students' motivations, interaction patterns, behaviors, and outcomes.

COOPERATIVE LEARNING METHODS

The cooperative learning methods that have already been developed (see Part Three: Selected Methods) differ dramatically in the motivational and learning processes they activate. For example, Student Team Learning methods (Chapter 11) rely on group rewards based on individual improvement points, along with peer tutoring and basic skills practice. The Learning Together method (Chapter 13) emphasizes peer support and constructive controversy. Group Investigation and Co-op Co-op methods (Chapter 14) seek to stimulate task attractiveness and intrinsic motivation. And Cooperative Concept Mapping (Chapter 16) stresses the role of cognitive elaboration.

The various methods also differ in intended outcomes. Some methods are designed for acquiring basic skills, others stress higher-level cognitive skills, and others improve interpersonal skills.

Processes

Cooperative learning operates by two interrelated processes—students' motivation and students' learning processes. These processes operate differently depending on the context of instruction and the method selected. Both have been discussed in detail in this and earlier chapters of Part One.

MOTIVATION PROCESSES

The desire to learn cooperatively is affected by three broad and interrelated motive categories: outcome motives, means motives, and interpersonal motives. Outcome motives encourage learning together through rewards, recognition, and goal achievement. These processes have an impact on feelings of self-actualization, personal efficacy, and expectations of success. They also affect beliefs about effort-outcome covariation. Means motives encourage learning together through task attractiveness (e.g., intrinsic interest), task novelty (e.g., curiosity), and task structure (e.g., scope, complexity, resources, and division). Interpersonal motives encourage learning together through peer support (e.g., help-receiving), prosocial tendencies (e.g., help-giving), and affiliative need (e.g., belonging).

The explanations presented in this and earlier chapters illustrate one or more of these motives. For example, Slavin's Cooperative Incentives theory (1991a) stresses the role of rewards, an outcome motive; Steiner's task typology (1972) considers the effect of task structure, a means motive.

LEARNING PROCESSES

Learning through cooperative group work can be explained by the activation of one or more global learning processes: cognitive elaboration, promotive interactions, cognitive-developmental explanations, and practice, time-on-task, and enhanced classroom organization explanations.

As with motivation processes, learning processes involved in cooperative learning can also be viewed from a behavioral, cognitive, developmental, or humanistic approach. As discussed in Chapter 1: Learning and Motivation, behaviorists would explain learning in interaction with others through the immediate feedback students receive from their peers and through the benefits of increased practice. Cognitivists would stress the importance of students elaborating and verbalizing their understanding. Developmentalists would emphasize the process of peer modeling. And humanists would suggest learning is enhanced by responding to students' natural curiosity.

Outcomes

The results of learning in cooperative groups are classified in four domains: cognitive, social, motivational, and affective. (Appendix A: Research Evidence reviews the research literature on the effects of cooperative learning on several major outcomes, some academic and some nonacademic.) In addi-

tion, theories of cooperative learning make a number of predictions regarding outcomes, which are included in this model. These outcomes affect one another. For example, a student's academic learning (cognitive outcome) promotes feelings of self-worth (affective outcome). They also affect, in a cyclical fashion, context characteristics (e.g., by affecting students' attitudes to group work or by changing the class climate).

COGNITIVE OUTCOMES

Research has found that academic achievement can be significantly enhanced through cooperative learning. By increasing students' verbalization of their understanding, and providing each other with elaborated explanations, cooperative learning has the potential to improve verbal skills, academic skills, and cognitive skills.

SOCIAL OUTCOMES

Cooperative learning methods, such as Learning Together, are designed primarily to enhance social outcomes. Interpersonal and communication skills and prosocial behavior are developed and reinforced through effective group interactions. These social benefits also serve to improve interracial and interethnic relations.

MOTIVATIONAL OUTCOMES

Successful learning in groups promotes expectations that success in the future is attainable (outcome expectations), and the belief that success is due to effort, rather than ability or luck (causal beliefs). Some methods reinforce persistence and effort expenditure by rewarding improvement, thus giving lower-ability members an equal opportunity to experience successful contributions to their team.

AFFECTIVE OUTCOMES

The emphases on creating a cooperative, supportive climate for learning, reducing competition, and encouraging the development of interpersonal skills are all designed to have a positive effect on students' self-concept and self-esteem. Students develop a sense of belonging among their peers. By giving students increased responsibility for their learning and decision making, cooperative learning seeks to empower students and satisfy their need for self-actualization.

SUMMARY

Is there a single factor that best describes the mechanisms underlying cooperative learning? So far in this book, we have summarized many explanations. Each is not necessarily exclusive of others. In other words, cooperative learning has multiple determinants.

In this chapter, you have seen how students may be motivated to engage in cooperative activities for a number of reasons. They may desire tangible group rewards for assisting their teammates (cooperative incentives explanation). They may care about the group and its accomplishments (social interdependence explanation). They may believe personal effort affects learning (morality-based motivation explanation) and that their expectations for success are enhanced (achievement need explanation). They may desire to help others (social cohesion explanation). You have also seen that students actively involved in a nonthreatening environment that fosters independence, creativity, and self-reliance may be affected positively (student empowerment explanation). And you have explored how the novelty of a new learning situation and teacher enthusiasm can have an impact on cooperative learning.

We have discussed how cooperative learning may affect students' learning in a variety of ways. Cognitive elaboration explanations contend that cognitive restructuring is promoted when students explain and elaborate upon new information. The promotive interactions explanation provides seven reasons why cooperative learning promotes the cognitive and meta-cognitive activity required to learn. Cognitive-developmental explanations claim that interactions among children around appropriate tasks enhances their understanding. Increased practice, time-on-task, and better classroom organization may also be responsible for student-learning gains in small groups.

Finally, we have presented an organizational model of cooperative learning that encourages you to consider four broad areas and how they may affect your implementation: context (student, teacher, school culture, and curriculum); instructional design (customized and cooperative learning methods); processes (motivation and learning); and outcomes (cognitive, social, motivational, and affective).

REFLECTION ACTIVITIES

1. Ames (1981) found that team failure has debilitating consequences for group members. What might you do to avoid these negative consequences?

2. It sometimes seems as though learning in small groups is not very efficient. High-ability students also complain that they are being "held up" by their teammates. When and to what extent are these concerns legitimate? In what ways might you deal with them?

3. Using the model of cooperative learning, describe your current teaching context. How do you think it might influence your decisions regarding cooperative learning implementation in your classroom?

PART

TWO

IMPLEMENTATION

Cathie Archbould

CHAPTER

4

Classbuilding and Teambuilding

How will I develop a climate of mutual acceptance, openness, and commitment?

•

How will I help my students get to know each other?

•

How will I help my students appreciate their similarities and learn to value the richness of each other's differences?

•

How will I help my students set positive goals and norms for group work?

As educators, we strive to maximize the learning of our students. Accordingly, we work hard to ensure that the curriculum and course are well designed, the content is covered, and high-quality resources and facilities are provided. All these are necessary, but far from sufficient, ingredients for successful learning.

Consideration of the students' preparedness for learning is also critically important. As first outlined by Maslow (see Chapter 1: Learning and Motivation), if students' basic needs have not been met, their ability to assimilate and process new information will be considerably diminished. Among these, individuals' need for affiliation, power, and achievement—that is, their need to feel wanted, influential, and capable—operate in all classrooms. It is natural for students to be concerned over such questions as, Will the teachers and other students like me? Will I have anything in common with the other students? Will they listen to and respect my opinions? Will I learn what is interesting and meaningful to me? Will I be successful? The quality of subsequent classroom interactions and experiences will provide responses to these questions. A competitive experience may lead to feelings of alienation, powerlessness, and incompetence, particularly for less able students. A cooperative experience, on the other hand, develops in students feelings of inclusion, empowerment, and competence (see Exhibit 4.1).

Satisfaction of these important psychological and social needs is closely related to the development of positive self-esteem and, subsequently, achievement. A student with low self-esteem, who feels rejected and incompetent, is not likely to achieve. Classbuilders and teambuilders are activities designed to break down these psychological and social barriers to learning, and help learners develop the trust and confidence they need to explore new ideas, overcome challenges, and pursue their goals. Devoting time and energy to creating a positive classroom and small-group climate does not detract from learning; it fosters the conditions under which learning will flourish. As you will discover, creating a positive learning environment does not need to take substantial time away from content coverage, and can form an integral part of content-based lesson plans.

In this chapter, we discuss the rationale behind the use of classbuilding and teambuilding, and provide numerous examples of activities you can use to enhance your classroom and small-group learning

· EXHIBIT 4.1 **Individual Needs and Classroom Experience** ·

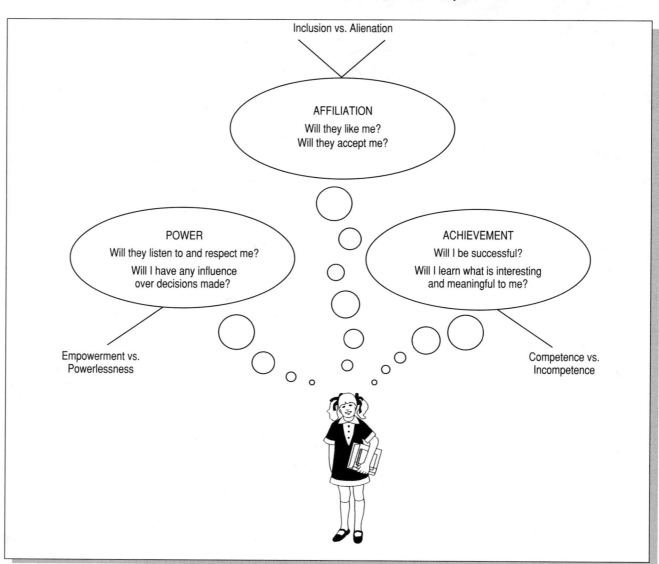

environment. The activities are all designed to promote a climate of mutual acceptance, openness, and commitment, and to recognize and respond positively to students' need for affiliation, power, and achievement. As explained in Appendix A: Research Evidence, cooperative learning has produced consistent gains in attitudinal, affective, and achievement outcomes when compared to competitive or individualistic classroom environments. However, even the best-designed course and cooperative group activities may not live up to their potential if students are not able to perform because of low esteem for and trust in themselves and their peers.

GROUPS AND THEIR DEVELOPMENT

On the first day of the term, your classroom gradually fills with students. Although physically present in the same room, this assembly of individuals cannot yet be considered a group. What is a group, and how can you facilitate the development of a group from a composite of individuals with individual personalities, strengths, weaknesses, and motives?

As outlined in Chapter 2: Group Processes and Productivity, Tuckman's revised model of group development (Tuckman and Jensen, 1977) listed five typical stages: forming, storming, norming, performing, and terminating. These stages are most pronounced in small groups, but the class as a whole experiences similar concerns as a sense of community and interdependence among all students develops. Ideally, groups progress quickly through issues of forming, storming, and norming, and devote most time and energy to performing. Often, however, groups need assistance in the early stages and in managing group interactions. Classbuilding and teambuilding activities focus on the first three stages of group development and, in conjunction with interpersonal skill development, help to make group work a productive, enriching, and enjoyable experience.

Classbuilding creates a supportive, nonthreatening climate in the class as a whole, and helps define expectations for positive interaction among students. When assigned to small-group work, however, students often experience a stronger sense of interdependence and engage in more intense interaction. Consequently, relationships among students are amplified and must be redefined within the context of the small group. Teambuilding, therefore, is equally important. While classbuilding and teambuilding share similar concerns and goals, each responds to a different context and neither should be neglected.

To summarize, classbuilding and teambuilding have as their goal to facilitate learning by:

- responding positively to students' need for affiliation, power, and achievement
- facilitating progression of the class or group through the stages of forming, storming, and norming

To accomplish these goals, classbuilding and teambuilding must:

- create a climate of mutual acceptance, openness, and commitment
- develop in each student feelings of inclusion, empowerment, and competence
- develop in each student trust and confidence in themselves and in their classmates and fellow group members

CLASSBUILDING AND TEAMBUILDING ACTIVITIES

Specific activities have been developed to enhance both classbuilding and teambuilding. These can be nonacademic activities designed to relieve tension and help students get to know each other on a more personal level, or academic activities related to the content the group is studying. Effective classbuilding or teambuilding activities are *inclusive*, that is, they require active interaction, equal recognition, and participation of all group members. It's important that *all* members are able to contribute meaningfully and successfully to the completion of the activity. Designing activities that require a unique, personalized contribution from each group member is one way of ensuring inclusivity. You should take particular care when designing academically based classbuilding or teambuilding activities, since differences in prior ability and knowledge make equal participation more difficult to achieve. Through classbuilding and teambuilding activities, students should experience the enjoyment and benefits of working together cooperatively. Such positive group experiences will strengthen members' commitment to the group and increase their motivation to work together to achieve their learning goals.

Not all methods of small-group learning consider specialized classbuilding and teambuilding activities necessary. Collaborative learning assumes a positive climate will develop naturally without careful attention, and leaves each teacher to decide whether groups are functioning well and if some type of intervention is needed. Slavin (1990b) believed that common goals and rewards, plus the success of achieving group goals, are usually sufficient to encourage students to work together and classbuilding and teambuilding are rarely necessary. Group-work for Multiple Abilities (Cohen, 1994a), used student facilitators who were trained to help the group work together effectively rather than activities for whole-group participation. Other coopera-tive learning methods, however, such as those developed by Kagan (1992) and Johnson, Johnson, and Johnson Holubec (1993), do consider class-building and teambuilding to be essential in the development of groups that function effectively.

One often-expressed concern is that classbuild-ing and teambuilding activities will take time that teachers might prefer to spend on reaching specific curriculum objectives. Some of the sample activities here will take time; others less so. However, many teachers, like the university professor in Exhibit 4.2, have found that it is time well spent.

Ideally, a cooperative climate should be initiated right from the first day of class and should continue to develop throughout the year. Classbuilding and teambuilding activities should be conducted as soon as possible in order to set the stage for cooperative learning, but they should be considered in the design of *all* learning activities in the cooperative classroom. This is not something that happens only on the first day of class or the first time a group works together; it becomes part of the process of learning through interpersonal interaction.

The classbuilding and teambuilding activities in this book are classified according to their primary function or goal. *Icebreaker* activities facilitate initial contact among students. *Appreciation and trust* activities help develop mutual understanding and

···················· EXHIBIT 4.2 **An Instructor's Experience with Teambuilding** ····················

One summer I was teaching an intensive six-week course on Issues in Early Childhood Education. I assigned the students to four-member groups and had them doing cooperative activities almost daily. I was fairly new to cooperative learning and was not convinced about the value of teambuilding. I had a great deal of content to cover and did not want to waste time with frivolous activities. However, I did some teambuilding at the beginning of the course, so the students could get to know each other and because it was advised by many proponents of cooperative learning.

A few weeks into the term, there happened to be two students absent from each of two groups, so when it came time for the cooperative activity, I put the two pairs together to make a new group of four. It was amazing how much less efficiently this group worked in compar-ison to the other groups, who by that time had developed a group identity and the group members had learned to trust one another. The new group members were tentative in putting forth their ideas as they did not know each other well and were not sure that their ideas would be accepted. I believe that the teambuilding activities contributed to a feeling of acceptance and trust among the members of the other groups. I now view teambuild-ing as an investment; you invest some time, but the dividends come in the form of more efficient groups.

University Professor

trust, and invite students both to celebrate their similarities and to value each other's differences. *Goal- and norm-setting* activities involve students in setting common objectives and formulating guidelines for achieving those objectives cooperatively.

Icebreaker Activities

The first day of class is exciting, but stressful, for both teachers and students. As we are confronted with a sea of new faces, we are also confronted with accompanying fears and concerns. Will they like me? Will they even talk to me? What should I say? Will I fit in? We've all known classrooms where, even well into the first semester, some students still don't know each other's names or have almost never spoken to each other. A basic, but essential, component of classbuilding is learning and using names. Being addressed by your name activates feelings of recognition and belonging. The first step in building a cooperative classroom climate, therefore, is to help your students break the ice and meet each other. In many classrooms, teachers attempt this by asking students to introduce themselves in turn. No matter how innocuous such an activity appears, it can strike fear in many students.

Similar concerns are experienced when students are assigned to small-group work. Whenever a small group is assembled for the first time, there are awkward moments as people struggle with how to get started. This is particularly true of teacher-selected heterogeneous groups, which are often made up of students who would not normally mix together. You can use icebreakers to help groups get a good start before they have to deal with difficulties that may arise during academic group work.

Whether used for classbuilding or teambuilding, icebreakers should be fun, nonthreatening activities designed to put people at ease and help them make initial contact. You should take care neither to put anyone "on the spot" nor to require skills or knowledge that some of your students may not possess. Since one-on-one interactions are least intimidating, many icebreakers, such as Name Cards (Activity 4.1) and People Search (Activity 4.2) add a game element that helps to alleviate some stress.

You can also assign your students a simple, fun, cooperative task. By moving the focus of attention away from individuals and onto concrete materials, these tasks ease the students into contact while relieving self-consciousness. Whole-class icebreakers that require physical movement, such as People Search (Activity 4.2), reduce tension and isolation by getting your students out of their seats and interacting with their classmates. Small-group icebreakers may also develop out of an activity or topics used to assign your students to groups. For example, the Category Cards activity (see Chapter 5: Grouping Students) can be extended into a teambuilder by asking group members to use the words (or pictures) on their category cards to create a story based on a theme you assign. This provides continuity from one activity to the next and saves time by allowing each group to start "breaking the ice" immediately.

For various reasons, such as prior classroom experience, expectations about academic environments, or issues of time and content coverage, some teachers and students may feel uncomfortable engaging in nonacademic icebreaker activities, thus defeating their purpose. Many teachers will ask their students to relate the content they are studying to their own experiences. For example, Karl Smith asked his engineering students to: "Describe something you've built, something tangible you've constructed" (cited in Graves, 1993, 15).

Incorporating subject matter into an activity such as Communication Cube (Activity 4.3) or into a corner item in Name Cards (Activity 4.1) allows you to create fun, nonthreatening, *content-based* icebreakers. Remember, however, that specialized prior knowledge or skills should not be required. Some useful topics for content-based icebreakers are expectations about the course or upcoming small-group activities, questions students wish to explore or seek answers to during the course or group work, and examples of careers or everyday activities requiring course-related skills.

Appreciation and Trust Activities

Knowing the names and superficial characteristics of classmates is a start, but it does not guarantee a willingness to work together. Many students feel more comfortable with those they already know well and sometimes prejudices interfere with the ability to get along with others. This struggle between the individual and the collective, the need for influence and the need for affiliation, contributes to conflicts experienced during the storming phases of group development.

Appreciation activities respond to both these concerns. They strengthen students' sense of belonging and group identity by recognizing and celebrating the similarities that unite them. They also help students to acknowledge their own and their classmates' individuality and to value the richness such diversity can bring to learning. Uncommon Commonalities (Activity 4.4) and Star Discoveries (Activity 4.5) are designed for these purposes.

Trust activities, such as Developing Trust (Activity 4.6) and Dear Inge Nilsson (Activity 4.7),

go one step further in actively building students' confidence in themselves and their group members. Johnson (1993) distinguished between two types of behavior necessary for a climate of trust among group members—trusting behavior and trustworthy behavior. Group members exhibit trusting behavior when they take the risk of contributing their ideas and expressing their feelings. They exhibit trustworthy behavior when they express acceptance and support for other group members' ideas and feelings. Gibb (1978) considered the formation of trust critical to effective group work. When trust is low, fear predominates and communication remains guarded, superficial, and manipulative. High trust among group members promotes openness, acceptance, flexibility, concern for congruence between individual goals and group goals, and effective coordination of efforts.

As with icebreakers, you can design or adapt appreciation and trust activities to incorporate

---

ACTIVITY 4.1 NAME CARDS

In the centre of a 3 × 5 index card, each student writes his or her name. In each of the four corners, the student writes personalized information that corresponds to categories set by the teacher. This information is meant to be shared with others, so students are encouraged not to specify something they don't wish to discuss. Some appropriate categories might be the place you were born, personality traits, a place you like to be, favorite hobbies, a person you admire, a quality you admire in a person, a memorable event, and so on.

These name tags are worn by the students. The information can be shared in various ways, such as walking around, then pairing up with another student on cue and asking one question about the information on the tag; or as an icebreaker within small groups. This could be conducted in the following manner.

1. Assign students to groups of four. Specify a category for the group members to share (e.g., a person you admire).

2. Assign four rotating roles, one to each member: Speaker (shares the information); Prober (asks questions to discover underlying characteristics of the response or reasons for the speaker's response);

Recorder (jots down notes on the group's record sheet); Timekeeper (indicates when it's time to rotate roles)

3. Inform groups of the time limit per speaker, including probing (e.g., four minutes). After the first speaker's four minutes are up, the timekeeper tells the group to rotate roles so each member has a new role and the new speaker begins.

4. After four rotations, the group's record sheet is complete with notes about each member's responses. The group then explores the commonalities in the answers and comes to a consensus on a name for their group representing these commonalities.

5. Each group then presents its group name and introduces its members to the rest of the class.

Montreal		tennis
		SPCA
		antiques
	ANNE	
generous		Brome Lake
conscientious		

ACTIVITY 4.2 PEOPLE SEARCH

Students are given lists of attributes and circulate in the classroom finding classmates who correspond to a characteristic. They then enter that person's name next to the corresponding item on the sheet. They cannot ask the same person more than one question in a row and cannot enter that person's name more than once on their sheet. The content of the search can vary depending on the grade level, subject matter, interests, and linguistic skills of the students. It can also be customized for specific topics. Below is an excerpt from a People Search for a biology class.

Find someone who . . .

has lived on a farm. _____

has been scuba diving or snorkelling. _____

has visited a zoo. _____

has a vegetable garden. _____

has an unusual pet. _____

has a microscope at home. _____

has grown a plant from seed. _____

has had a job working with animals. _____

has had a job working with plants. _____

Variations

1. Have students generate the questions based on their interests (i.e., I hope I find someone who . . .).

2. Assign categories (e.g., favorite food) and have students search for someone who gave the same or a similar response.

3. Assign each group a different category and ask them to conduct a survey of the class and report the results at the end of the activity. This report could include the most frequent response, the most unusual response, and the response of each of their group members.

ACTIVITY 4.3 COMMUNICATION CUBE

Choose six discussion topics, questions, or pictures that are appropriate to the age level of the class (these may cover a topic or unit students are studying). Write or glue these cues onto the sides of a cube. Divide the class into groups and give one cube to each. Each group chooses one person to start who tosses the cube and talks about the item that turns up. Group members should actively listen to their teammates and ask for clarifications and elaborations.

Afterwards, have the listeners tell each speaker one interesting thing they learned from him or her during the activity (e.g., "I found it particularly interesting to learn that . . ."). Then, students should discuss their feelings during the experience and the kinds of questions asked by the listeners and other behaviors that encouraged the speaker. Finally, allow two or three minutes for the groups to determine what feelings they had in common.

Variation

Materials preparation for this structure can be simplified by using regular dice and having corresponding questions (or pictures) on a sheet of paper or the board. For example, if the number 6 is thrown on the dice, the student who rolled the die would talk about or respond to the sixth question (or picture).

ACTIVITY 4.4 UNCOMMON COMMONALITIES

Uncommon commonalities is a simple activity used for exploring team diversity and building team identity.

1. Teammates brainstorm topics or categories to discover things they have in common.

2. Once they have found a general category, teammates are urged to discover an even "tighter connection."

Variations on Uncommon Commonalities
Groups can be given initial topics for discussion. Teammates then brainstorm subcategories of the topic given. Some ideas for initial topics are family, sports, food, and hobbies. This also can be used for content instruction.

Examples

1. Group 1 members all love to watch sports. After further discussion, they discover they all love hockey and soon realize they like the same team and dislike the goalie!

2. In a language arts class, students brainstorm fairytales to discover the "tightest" connection. For example, they list characters they identify with.

Source: Adapted from S. Kagan, *Cooperative Learning: Resources for Teachers,* San Juan Capistrano, California: Resources for Teachers, 1990. Copyright © 1990 by Spencer Kagan. Used by permission.

ACTIVITY 4.5 STAR DISCOVERIES

Prepare a Star Discoveries sheet consisting of a large star below the activity title. Make enough copies for the class and put the name of one student on each sheet. Distribute the sheets at random to members of the class. (They cannot change sheets unless they have received their own name.) In the next fifteen minutes, students may ask questions of anyone except the student named on their sheet. The object is to find five reasons (e.g., academic, sports, social) why that person deserves recognition and to write one reason on each point of the star. The teacher can suggest questions or prompt if necessary to make sure everyone finds five reasons. At the end of the fifteen minutes, the stars are presented to each student and posted on their desks or the wall.

ACTIVITY 4.6 DEVELOPING TRUST

The objectives of this activity, designed by Johnson (1993), are for the members of the group to arrive at a summary statement concerning the ways in which trust can be built in a relationship. The procedure for the exercise is:

1. Divide into groups of four.
2. Individually, arrive at the ten most important things a person can do to develop trust in a relationship. Take twenty minutes for this.
3. Share the results across the group.

4. As a whole, rank the ten most important aspects of developing trust from the most important to the least important.

After the activity, have the students reflect on whether their list included any of the following: progressively disclosing yourself to the other person; making sure your behavior regarding the other person is consistent; following through on your commitments to the other person; expressing warmth and acceptance to the other person; avoiding being judgmental of the other person; being trustworthy; being honest.

Source: Adapted from D. W. Johnson, *Reaching Out: Interpersonal Effectiveness and Self-Actualization,* Second Edition, Englewood Cliffs, New Jersey: Prentice-Hall, p. 69. © 1981, 1972 by Prentice-Hall, Inc., Englewood Cliffs, New Jersey. Used by permission of David W. Johnson.

academic content. Building mutual understanding and trust on course-related aspects may be most beneficial, since students will ultimately need to work cooperatively toward the completion of academic tasks. It is important that students build beliefs in their own and others' willingness and ability to contribute to the task at hand.

Goal- and Norm-Setting Activities

When groups work together for a considerable length of time, they should establish a common frame of reference so that all group members have agreement on goals and objectives, a vision of the ideal climate for achieving these objectives, and a shared commitment to successful completion of the group task.

Students' involvement in the planning stages of group projects promotes more active participation from the members. When groups are at the exploratory stage, a visioning process will help them establish common objectives and areas of interest. Once the group has decided which topic to focus on, goal-setting activities will ensure agreement on priorities, and hence encourage productive use of time and resources.

Deciding on common goals and setting behavioral norms for achieving those goals are important steps in becoming a cohesive, cooperative group. In setting their own goals, your students also take on more responsibility and a more active role in their own learning. When they are motivated to work together toward a clearly defined goal, their commitment and involvement in the task is heightened. They become more appreciative of each other's efforts and contributions, and less tolerant of off-task behavior that interferes with achieving their objectives.

In addition to strengthening students' sense of affiliation and control over their learning, such a process also considers students' need for achievement. Your students must have a clear understanding of their learning objectives, feel a personal commitment to those objectives, and believe that they can achieve them. When students subsequently achieve these objectives, feelings of pride in their accomplishment and self-competence are enhanced.

Involving your students in setting their own class and small-group goals and behavior norms are all part of the transition from traditional teaching, where all decisions about learning are made by you, to the cooperative classroom where students' opinions are welcomed. Setting their own goals and behavioral norms can motivate your students by giving them responsibility for their learning and can inform you of additional aspects to consider when preparing to teach a particular class. Depending on the duration of the group and complexity of the task, whole-class and small-group goals and norms may need to be revised several times in the course of an activity or semester.

There are certain behaviors that promote a positive classroom environment and respect for self and others, such as listening actively and attentively to each other and helping each other and the teacher. Norm-setting activities, such as Class Contract (Activity 4.8), involve students in the process of generating guidelines for such behaviors. In doing so, students develop a sense of ownership

---

ACTIVITY 4.7 DEAR INGE NILSSON

Select an assortment of letters from the newspaper-advice column, choosing topics suitable to the age and interests of the students. Divide the class into groups. Distribute copies of one letter and answer to each group. After reading the letter, each person in the group tells whether he or she feels the answer would be helpful and why. As a group, students change the answer to make it more useful to the person seeking advice. Each group reads its answer to the class.

If groups have different answers, discuss what influenced them and why everyone did not think the same way. Continue with other letters as time and interest permit.

and commitment to them. Over time, these guidelines become internalized, and students think of them simply as, "the way we do things in our class."

Norm-setting activities may also be used to set behaviors for achieving specific class or small-group goals, such as Goal Setting (Activity 4.9). In this case, goal-setting activities would precede the setting of norms.

Class goals are best elicited by activities that give all students in the class the opportunity to express their ideas. Think-Pair-Share (Activity

---

ACTIVITY 4.8 CLASS CONTRACT

This exercise is designed to help students write a contract that will encourage high standards of behavior. Follow this procedure, informing the class when time limits are up.

1. Individually list three or more things others do in class that make it more difficult to learn. (several minutes)

2. Individually list three or more things others do in class that make it easier to learn. (several minutes)

3. Find a partner, then compare and discuss the items on your list. (10 minutes)

4. Join another pair to make a group of four. Make a list of class behaviors that will help everyone get maximum benefit from the course. Choose a reporter to read the list to the class.

5. The teacher notes down the suggestions on the board to outline a contract.

6. When everyone has agreed on the terms, each student copies down the agreed-upon contract. This contract should be a series of "We will . . ." statements. One official contract should be signed by everyone and posted on the wall.

Source: Adapted from G. Gibbs, S. Habeshaw, and T. Habeshaw, *53 Interesting Ways of Helping Your Students to Study*, Bristol, England: Technical and Educational Services Limited, 1989, p. 133. Used by permission.

ACTIVITY 4.9 GOAL SETTING

Classes that have some prior familiarity with an upcoming topic of study can engage in a group goal-setting process that will encourage commitment and reduce conflict. This process consists of a series of steps adjusted to the group's task and time limits. Younger students will need help in evaluating the feasibility of their goals and designing a timetable for accomplishing them.

Steps in Goal Setting

1. Without consulting other group members, list the goals you would like to accomplish while working on (topic, unit, course) during the coming (lesson, unit, term, six months).

2. Individually, number your items in order of priority, putting number 1 beside the most important.

3. Each student reads his or her list to the group, while a recorder collates the information on a large sheet of newsprint (chart paper) or bristol board.

4. Use lines to connect similar items or different colored markers to circle similar items in order to determine common objectives.

5. Discuss and set group, subgroup, and individual priorities. Decide which items will be worked on by the whole group, which will be worked on by pairs or smaller subgroups, which will be done by individuals, and which will be dropped.

6. Plan a timetable, making sure items are in a logical sequence so that the accomplishment of each goal contributes to subsequent ones.

7. Finally, decide how members will help each other achieve both common and individual goals.

Brainstorming can replace the first step in the goal-setting process if individuals have not decided on any personal priorities. Eliminate impossible or impractical suggestions prior to this, if necessary. Once the plan has been accepted, conferences should be scheduled with groups to see how well they are implementing it.

4.10) and Cooperative Graffiti (Activity 4.11) are ideal for this. Goals may include both academic objectives (e.g., helping every student achieve some minimum grade on a test), and nonacademic objectives (e.g., helping everyone feel at home in the classroom). You should encourage your students to set goals or subgoals that can be realized in the short term. Shared goals become more powerful classbuilders when students experience success in achieving them. Long-term goals may seem overwhelming and too distant to unite students. Once the ideas are elicited, your students must decide which ones they will work toward and how they will go about it. If not all students are committed to the goals, the result may be divisive rather than unifying. Sometimes, a multistep process allows for greater participation in the decision process (see Chapter 5: Grouping Students).

SUMMARY

When using cooperative learning in the classroom, the initial few weeks are crucial. Establishing an atmosphere where your students feel part of a risk-free learning environment is important. You should reinforce this environment throughout the duration of the course or school year. Along with interpersonal-skills training, classbuilders and teambuilders help promote a climate for learning, cooperation, and positive esteem for self and peers.

In this chapter, we have presented several types of classbuilding and teambuilding activities that will help your students get to know each other, develop an appreciation for both their similarities and differences, and set common goals and norms for effective learning through interaction. By responding positively to their need for affiliation,

---

ACTIVITY 4.10 THINK-PAIR-SHARE

Think-Pair-Share is a useful structure for eliciting students' opinions on and experience with a particular topic. Think-Pair-Share offers *all* students an opportunity to express their responses to a question. In a typical classroom, the teacher asks a question, and only one or two students raise their hands to answer. Using Think-Pair-Share, the teacher asks a question, the students are given some "private" time to think about their responses, and then they share their responses with their partners. This allows all students to respond to the question, receive feedback, and engage in a brief discussion of their ideas. Students are then invited to share their responses with the whole class. Since students are able to "test out" their ideas before sharing them with the class, this method is also likely to improve the quality of the subsequent whole-class discussion.

Choose a Topic

1. Choose something that interests your students.
2. Choose something they have probably experienced.
3. Choose something that has many aspects or involves many opinions.

Ask Students to Do the Following

1. *Think* about your response to the following . . . (topic/question).
2. *Pair* up with the person next to you and share the ideas you have been thinking about. (When time is up, or conversations seem to lag, ask for the class's attention.)
3. *Share* your ideas with the class. (Note the ideas on the board or on the chart paper.)

Variation: Think-*Note*-Pair-Share

After students have taken some time to think about the assigned question or topic (step 1), ask them to make some *brief* notes on their ideas before sharing them with their partners. This variation increases the individual accountability and contribution component of this structure. It also helps students consolidate their individual thoughts on a topic, thereby reducing the risk of shy students being overpowered by more assertive ones.

Source: Adapted from S. Kagan, *Cooperative Learning: Resources for Teachers,* San Juan Capistrano, California: Resources for Teachers, 1990. © 1990 by Spencer Kagan. Used by permission.

ACTIVITY 4.11 COOPERATIVE GRAFFITI

Cooperative Graffiti is a simple structure ideal for group members to brainstorm aspects of a topic simultaneously. It can be used effectively as a teambuilding or classbuilding activity, and for eliciting prior knowledge or opinions on topics related to academic material.

1. On a single large sheet of paper, each team member simultaneously writes down as many ideas on a given topic as possible, using a different colored pen.

2. After a predetermined time, group members put down their pens and work together to categorize their ideas, looking for similarities, differences, and relationships among them. Roles such as Reader, Checker, and Recorder could be assigned to encourage participation of all members in this phase.

Variation: *Rotational* Graffiti

To give all groups in the class an opportunity to contribute ideas on each of several topics, rotational graffiti can be used. Each group is assigned a topic, which is written on a large sheet of paper. Allow each group to write graffiti about their topic as described in step 1. After a short time, tell students to put down their pens and rotate the sheets to the next group in a clockwise direction. Each group then checks the topic on the sheet passed to them and begins immediately to add to the graffiti on this topic. Repetition of ideas is not a problem. Encourage students to write as many ideas as possible, without taking time to read those of others at this stage. This procedure continues until all groups have written graffiti on each topic and are passed back the sheet they started with. Each group then works together to categorize the ideas expressed by *all* the groups as in step 2. Finally, each group presents a summary of their findings to the class.

---

power, and achievement, such activities facilitate and enhance learning, group interaction, and personal growth. In guiding your students through the group development process, the activities reduce the time spent struggling with initial contact, storming over issues of control, and negotiating goals and norms. Thus, they help the group focus on performing effectively together.

Both classbuilders and teambuilders can be content free or reflect the curriculum objectives. Although teachers may sometimes view teambuilders as games or unstructured activities, they are purposeful and respecting their underlying rationale and objectives is important. Group members should experience mutual support in completing activities and satisfaction in having made a contribution.

REFLECTION ACTIVITIES

1. Think about concerns you have felt on the first day of class or when assigned peers with whom you must complete a group project. Make a quick list of the questions or concerns that were on your mind. Then, try to categorize them as questions relating to affiliation, power, or achievement needs. How did your subsequent classroom experiences affect your concerns? Did you look forward to, or feel reluctant about, returning to class? Brainstorm ways you could help assuage similar concerns felt by your own students.

2. Referring to Chapter 2: Group Processes and Productivity, explore how the use of classbuilding and teambuilding can help transform the classroom into a community of learners working with others. Which activities would you use with your students to achieve this goal?

3. Working with a colleague who is interested in the same subject matter as you, create a teambuilding activity that incorporates academic content. Explain how it employs the principles of teambuilding.

5

Grouping Students

How many students per group
should there be?

•

What characteristics of my students should
I consider when assigning them to groups?

•

Will I use heterogeneous or
homogeneous groups?

•

What techniques will I use
to group students?

•

How long should students work
in the same group?

Teachers who attempt to use cooperative learning have new decisions to make when they structure learning activities. One of the first decisions teachers must make to implement cooperative learning concerns the grouping of students; that is, teachers must decide on the size of the groups, the length of time students should stay together (duration), how groups should be composed and organized, and how students should be assigned to them.

In this chapter, we will discuss the factors influencing these decisions and present examples of ways to assign students to groups.

The types of groups that you form will depend on many factors, such as the age of your students, their level of interpersonal skills, the goals of instruction, the length and complexity of the activity, the climate of trust that exists in the class, and so on. Your beliefs about what is important for students to learn is also an important factor. A grade-four social studies teacher who wants students to learn to relate well with racially different peers will assign students to groups differently from a grade-nine teacher who wants to drill them on their knowledge of geometry.

Group Size and Duration

Cooperative learning groups typically range in size from two to six; there is no perfect size for a cooperative learning team. Group size depends on the subject matter being taught, the desired interaction, the length of the teaching unit, students' skills and experience with cooperative learning, and the physical limitations of each classroom.

Teachers and students who are new to cooperative learning usually start with pairs or small groups for short periods of time. Smaller groups require less sophisticated interpersonal skills. The larger the group, the more complex communication becomes, and the more difficult it is to promote equal participation, interpersonal skill development, and, possibly, learning. Very small groups maximize the amount of interaction that occurs. In pairs, students are always involved in the task. In triads, the interaction may be less intense but may bring an additional perspective to the task. Groups of four are appropriate for more complex tasks. For most tasks, you should ensure that each group is about the same size. If groups vary in size too much, they will likely take considerably different lengths of time to complete the task.

How long groups stay together depends on a host of factors. Groups can be formed for periods of a few minutes, for students to check their understanding of a newly taught concept with their neighbors, or for a whole year as a support group. Teachers usually change groups periodically to avoid boredom and to encourage students to experience working with a variety of their peers. Changing groups can be done effectively, but it takes time, so you will probably not want to change them after every activity. Also, changing groups frequently does not give group members time to develop a sense of trust or a team identity.

Assigning Students to Groups

There are many ways to create learning groups. Your students may choose their own groups on the basis of topic interest or friendship. Or you can form groups randomly or on the basis of students' characteristics, such as ability, gender, and ethnicity. At first, students may feel awkward about getting into groups and it may take them a while; but once they get used to relocating, the process should take only a few minutes.

Student-Initiated Groups

As the year progresses, and depending on your students' developmental level, you may give your students opportunities to form their own groups. The more mature they are, the better able they will be to choose appropriate teammates. More mature students may be more sensitive to others' feelings and, therefore, be less likely to blatantly reject a student. You may also choose to employ student-initiated groups if your objectives include encouraging student autonomy and developing your students' ability to recognize the value of diversity in creating their groups. However, student-initiated groups should be used only if you are certain that no students will feel rejected in the process. Exhibit 5.1 is an example of how one teacher's experiences as a student influenced how she forms groups with her students. Broadly speaking, there are two types of student-initiated groups—friendship groups and interest groups.

FRIENDSHIP GROUPS

Friendship groups are those that students form on the basis of common social interests. When teachers ask students to work together, these are often the groups that form first and are met with enthusiasm. However, friendship groups can divide students in undesirable ways. High-ability students may group together or homogeneous groups may form according to race or gender. Such groups may not experience the advantages provided by a diversity of skills and personalities. Some students may be left out entirely if they are newcomers, shy, or have not established friendships. Furthermore, friends often discover that they do not always make effective teammates for learning.

INTEREST GROUPS

Interest groups are those that students form, sometimes with the teacher's assistance, on the basis of common academic interests. For example, in a primary science classroom, students who want to learn about *Tyrannosaurus rex* would work together at the same time as another group of students investigating *Brontosaurus*. Each group would prepare a project on their particular dinosaur.

Interest groups are used primarily for content that does not have to be mastered by all students before progressing to the next topic. This type of grouping is suitable if students' interests are evenly divided and groups can be about equal in size. Your students may complain if they are first given a choice and then have to change topics to even out the groups.

Teacher-Initiated Groups

Under most circumstances, you should assign your students to groups. Learning to work with others, even with those who are very different, is a valuable skill that students need to practice. There are several ways in which you can form groups. Students may be grouped quite casually (and briefly) by proximity, or quite deliberately according to significant characteristics, such as ability.

PROXIMITY GROUPS

Proximity groups are formed by simply having your students work with others who are seated near them. You could say: "Turn to your neighbor and discuss three ways to solve this problem." This will result in an informal grouping that may occur frequently during the day. It often takes some time and

noise to have students reorganize themselves into structured groups, while turning to a neighbor only takes a second. To avoid the possibility of leaving students out, ask students sitting in adjacent rows to pair up. This way, everyone ends up with a partner.

SPONTANEOUS GROUPS

You may assign students to groups in a random or spontaneous fashion using a variety of techniques. Spontaneous groups ensure that each student gets practice working with a diversity of peers. You may want to try forming spontaneous groups at the beginning of the year, before you know your students well, and, perhaps, before they know each other well. This way, new or unpopular students will not be left out, and your students will have a chance to get to know one another and feel that the classroom is a safe, comfortable place. Used throughout the year, spontaneous grouping provides variety as long as you vary the methods of grouping.

One way to assign students to spontaneous groups is to simply count off and assemble all students with the same number. For example, if you have a class of 32 students and you want eight groups of four, have your students count off four times from one to eight. Or, if you use colors, have students read aloud in order from a list of colors on the board. All the students who read "blue" would form a group, and so on.

Another way to form spontaneous groups is to use one of a variety of students' characteristics. For example, ask students to form groups of four with

················ EXHIBIT 5.1 **One Teacher's Experience with Student Groups** ·····················

When I was in grade seven, I went to a four-room school with no gym or physical education specialist. For physical education, the teacher took us out to the baseball diamond, chose the two most athletic children in the class, and had them choose teams for softball. As I was a plump, unathletic child who ran like a sloth, I was one of the last children chosen. On the rare occasion when I actually hit the ball, I almost never made it to first base. This was a humiliating experience for me. These experiences have profoundly influenced how I organize my students into groups. I do not want students in my classes to experience this rejection and embarrassment, so I almost always assign students to groups. I make it clear from the beginning that throughout the year each student will work with every other student in the class.

classmates who have about the same length of hair or who were born in the same season. Be careful to avoid characteristics that students might feel self-conscious about (e.g., shoe size or age).

A third technique for spontaneous grouping is to use a deck of playing cards. For example, if you want eight groups of four, select eight numbers from each of four suits; for ten groups of three, select ten numbers from each of three suits. Then, deal out one playing card randomly to each student and have those with the same number form groups. Alternatively, Activity 5.1 describes more elaborate category cards you can create.

One of the advantages of spontaneous grouping is that students will less likely feel left out because they are not chosen by others. Spontaneous groups take less time to form than groups students choose themselves because there is less discussion about who is going to be in which group.

For any cooperative activity, each group must be able to complete the assigned task, so spontaneous grouping is inappropriate for complex tasks because some groups may be composed of only low-ability students. For short activities, such as reviewing material or brainstorming, spontaneous groups are ideal. Once you have had a chance to observe how your students interact when they work in various spontaneous groups, you will have a better idea about which students work well together and which do not.

HETEROGENEOUS GROUPS

When people enter the workforce they do not usually have a choice about the people they work with. Therefore, in school, students should get plenty of practice working with a diversity of people. Students need to learn to work effectively with others of different gender, races, cultures, abilities, and interests. This is particularly important in multicultural areas, where students need to understand and appreciate different values and customs.

Some authors (Johnson, Johnson, and Johnson Holubec, 1988; Kagan, 1990; Slavin, 1986) claim that students learn best, both academically and socially, in heterogeneous groups. They recommend that teachers assign students to groups so that *within* each group students are as different as possible, while abilities *between* each group are as similar as possible.

When you assign groups yourself, you should make it clear that one of your objectives is to have students learn to work effectively with others. You may want to inform your class that throughout the year each student will work with every other stu-

---

ACTIVITY 5.1 AN EXAMPLE OF SPONTANEOUS GROUPING

CATEGORY CARDS

Objective: To group students heterogeneously
Materials: Category cards
Grade level: Kindergarten to adult
Duration: 5 to 10 minutes.
Procedure:

1. Create categories and write a number of items within each category corresponding to your desired group size in each section of a rectangular strip. Cut the strips into Jigsaw sections and randomly distribute them. Alternatively, you can subtly "structure" the grouping in order to break up cliques or mix the ability levels by handing certain students certain cards (e.g., give more able students the first item in each category).
   Examples of categories and items:
      Adjectives: pretty, small, wet, cold

   Verbs: run, fall, find, wash
   Sports: figure skating, racket ball, skiing, hockey
   Math symbols: %, $\geq$, Σ, $\approx$

2. Students ask each other questions as they "roam the room" looking for students holding another item in their category.

3. Students verify the items by fitting the four parts together. (It should form a rectangle.)

4. Students can then brainstorm other items in their category, create a story with the words, or complete another task based on their words or category.

Variation

For students who cannot read, use pictures of the category items.

dent in the class. This helps prevent complaints about having to work with a particular student.

Heterogeneous-Ability Groups

Ability or prior achievement is the most salient characteristic for heterogeneous grouping. One benefit of learning in heterogeneous-ability groups is that the more able students take on the role of tutors, teaching lower-ability students material that they have not grasped. Less able students are exposed to and model the learning strategies of their more able teammates. Also, through teaching the content, the tutors come to learn the material better.

Some techniques of assigning students to heterogeneous ability groups, such as Slavin's technique (1986), are very structured (see Chapter 11: Student Team Learning Methods). Such techniques ensure that there is a variety of ability levels within each group, but that all teams are as equal in ability as possible.

The range of ability within each group is one of the factors that influences successful cooperative learning. Research by Webb (1989) suggests that extremely varied teams did not work as well as only somewhat varied teams. In groups composed of high-ability students and low-ability students, the high-ability students may resent spending so much time teaching others, and low-ability students may feel singled out for needing special attention. If there is a wide range of abilities in your class, we suggest you create teams that contain a moderate range of abilities. That is, group high- and average-ability students together and average- and low-ability students, but do not assign high- and low-ability students to the same group.

Other Characteristics to Consider

Learning in groups teaches students important attitudes and values, including the understanding of and tolerance for others, especially those who are racially, culturally, or otherwise different. If these goals are included in your objectives, you may consider assigning your students to teams based primarily on nonacademic factors, such as gender, race, ethnicity, language, status, learning styles, and personality traits.

Status Problems

Assigning students to heterogeneous groups often results in the creation of status differences among group members. For example, Cohen (1994a) pointed out that students who have limited proficiency in the language of instruction, or who are functioning below grade level, often adopt a non-participatory role and are neglected as group members. Imagine the grief of a student with limited knowledge of the language of instruction, who attempts to contribute, only to have his or her ideas and suggestions ignored. Such behavior in a group illustrates what Cohen refers to as status problems.

There are expectations of all participants within any group. Unfortunately, low-status students may have low expectations of themselves. In addition, the teacher and other students may also expect little and act accordingly toward these students. It is the responsibility of the group, not solely of the individual, to change these perceptions and behaviors. To deal with this problem, Cohen (1994a) suggested that teachers design multi-ability tasks that draw on a wider range of skills and abilities than do traditional curricula (see Chapter 17: Other Peer Interaction Methods).

HOMOGENEOUS GROUPS

Students can be grouped homogeneously based on many variables. Homogeneous-ability groups are most common and are discussed below, but other characteristics may also be considered. For instance, if your students are expected to work together on a project outside school, grouping them with others that live nearby might be a good idea. Activity 5.2 presents a way to get students into groups with others who live near them.

Occasionally, you can group students together who share a first language other than English. This frees the students to explore a topic more deeply than their limited English skills might permit and allows them to grapple with complex concepts in their first language. You should *not* do this consistently, because these students need to practice their English and remain integrated with the class.

When assigning students to homogeneous groups on the basis of a given characteristic, be careful not to segregate them on another related, but undesired, characteristic. For example, forming groups based on common neighborhoods might also group students along unintended socioeconomic or racial lines.

Homogeneous-Ability Groups

In the reality of mixed-ability classes, structuring activities and lessons that meet the needs of all students is important. Judicious use of homogeneous groups can encourage your students to work to their potential. For example, some students working in heterogeneous-ability teams may not feel challenged, and may need the opportunity to interact with more advanced material. At the same time, special-needs students may need to work on specific skills already mastered by higher-ability students.

One drawback to homogeneous-ability groups is that polarization may occur. Students who are in the most able group may not regard their other classmates as equals, while students who are in the less able group may become discouraged. Homogeneous-ability grouping can also lead teachers to lower their expectations of students in low-ability groups to such an extent that the students no longer feel challenged.

GROUP FORMATS AND THEIR PURPOSES

Once you have decided whether to let your students choose their own groups or to assign them yourself, there are a variety of group formats to consider. Each teacher must decide which group format best reflects the objectives of the lesson, and then struc-

ture the learning activity to maximize the strengths of the format chosen. The categorization of group formats described here is adapted from Clarke, Wideman, and Eadie (1990). It is not exhaustive, but it should serve as both a guide and a springboard for creating your own format.

Stable Groups

Stable groups are those in which the same students stay together for an entire group process. This process may consist of a single activity lasting only a few minutes (informal groups), a group project lasting several weeks (project groups), or a support network lasting up to a whole year (base groups). However long they stay together, these groups are called stable, since they work independently of other groups in the class.

INFORMAL GROUPS

Informal groups can meet at any time during the learning experience. At the beginning of a lesson, your students can brainstorm ideas, prepare for a discussion, or activate prior knowledge to enhance learning. During the lesson, you can ask a few strategic questions to stimulate thought or to check for comprehension. For example, you can use informal groups each time you teach a new concept when you ask students to get together with two students near them to work on problems. In concluding a lesson, informal groups can generate questions for further discussion and provide closure. The size of these groups can vary from two to four. Larger groups tend to be less suited for informal groupings.

PROJECT GROUPS

You can use stable groups when students work to complete projects. While the group often subdivides

---

ACTIVITY 5.2	**AN EXAMPLE OF HOMOGENEOUS GROUPING**

NEIGHBORHOOD GROUPS

This example of a teacher-initiated homogeneous grouping is useful for getting students into groups if they are going to work together outside of school. Designate the center of the room as the classroom and indicate north, south, east, and west. Have stu-

dents place themselves in the room according to where they live in relation to the school. Then assign students to groups with two or three others who live close to them. Being in groups with other students from the same area makes it easier for them to get together to work on their projects.

the task so that each member is responsible for a part of it, the group assembles their individual contributions into a common project. Co-op Co-op is an example of a group project method in which students work primarily within a stable group (see Chapter 14: Group Project Methods).

BASE GROUPS

You can also use stable groups as base groups to provide a social support network for students. Base groups typically stay together for an extended period of time (e.g., an entire term). They usually consist of three or four students, formed by the teacher after an initial period of observation of students' interactions. In forming base groups, you should try to break up preestablished cliques, but at the same time avoid assigning students who clearly will not get along to the same group.

The initial five or ten minutes of a class or day can be spent with students working in their base groups. You can immediately get the groups on task if you specify their task during this time. For instance, you could ask groups to check on how each of their members is feeling, discuss their views on an assigned topic, review their homework, or respond to a question that previews upcoming course content. During the last five minutes of a class or day, base-group members can check their homework, chat about the day, or reflect on a specific skill taught by the teacher. Since base groups remain stable over an extended time period, many teachers devote particular attention to building group cohesion and identity. Activity 5.3 is designed to help group members get to know one another better.

Combined Groups

You can create combined groups by putting the students from two or more small working groups together. One purpose of combining small working groups is to provide a forum for larger group discussion without involving the entire class. Other reasons for combining groups are to increase consultation between groups, to establish consensus on any given topic, to discuss the procedures of a learning task, and to give feedback. You may want to combine different groups at different times using proximity, rotation, or random selection as criteria.

Reconstituted Groups

Reconstituted grouping occurs when students are assigned to one group initially (sharing group),

---

ACTIVITY 5.3 BASE GROUP GRIDS

Students can get to know each other in their base groups by structuring a guided interview. Questions are asked on a daily or biweekly basis. Each person has a copy of the grid. As Bettina responds to the question, Cathy, Filipo, and Andrée jot down notes next to her name. This continues until each person has had the opportunity to react to the topic or answer the question.

	BETTINA	CATHY	FILIPO	ANDRÉE
What is your favorite color?				
What book have you enjoyed reading?				
What do you like doing?				
What's a fun experience you've had?				

regroup to work with other students (exploration group), and then return to the sharing group. Reconstituted groups are appropriate to use when it is not essential for each student to master all of the material equally. When students return to their sharing group, it is often to teach their original group members some material they learned while in the exploration group. The various forms of Jigsaw are examples of reconstituted groups (see Chapter 12: Jigsaw and Its Variations).

Reconstituted groups are useful for group projects. For example, each sharing group might be doing a social studies project on a different country in Africa. Each group member might have a different aspect of the country to research, such as food, customs, manufacturing, politics, history, or education. Students from each group who are researching the same aspect (e.g., politics) of different countries get together to discuss where to find information, share resources, and so on. Students then return to their sharing groups to synthesize the information each individual has gathered into a common project.

Students are individually accountable to their sharing groups for accurately obtaining and transmitting the information on their subtopic; and they get help and support in doing so from their exploration groups. It is essential that all students have the abilities necessary to complete their tasks, otherwise more able students in the group might come to resent those students who do an inadequate job of communicating information. However, using reconstituted groups can also help you accommodate some ability differences by allowing you to assign students to homogeneous exploration groups and adjust the difficulty of the materials they use during exploration.

Teachers should use reconstituted groups cautiously. Your students will likely learn the content they have personally investigated and taught to their peers more thoroughly than the content their peers teach to them. Therefore, reconstituted groups are *not* appropriate to use when it is essential for each student to master all of the material equally, or when the content is hierarchically structured.

Representative Reporting Groups

A representative reporting group consists of one member from every working group in the class. These representatives can be selected by you, selected at random, or selected by students. Your role is to be a facilitator or a chairperson. The steps involved in using a representative reporting group are as follows:

- Students are given a topic for discussion or exploration.

- Students develop, explore, and discuss their topic in small working groups.

- Each working group selects a representative.

- A panel is formed at the front of the class consisting of one chairperson from each working group. Two additional chairs are included in the configuration: one for the teacher and one empty chair that can be used by anyone in the class who wants to ask a question or request clarification.

- Each representative gives his or her presentation to the entire class. The teacher can comment, add, or clarify at any time during the presentation.

You can use a representative reporting group at any stage of the learning process. One purpose of a representative reporting group is to provide a forum for discussion on the working groups' progress within the class. Quick sessions for feedback can also be used for formative course evaluation so that you can realign your teaching, objectives, or expectations.

SUMMARY

Organizing a classroom to facilitate effective cooperative learning is a complex endeavor. One of the first decisions you must make concerns the grouping of students. Be prepared for some groups to be successful, for others to be less successful, and, occasionally, for some not to work at all. We have presented ideas and suggestions throughout this chapter to help you be more methodical and practical in developing effective small groups. Generally, we recommend that you assign students to groups rather than allow them to choose their own group members. In this chapter, we have discussed strategies you can use when you assign students to proximity, spontaneous, heterogeneous, and homogeneous groups. We have also explored how you can use different group formats, such as stable, combined, reconstituted, and representative reporting groups, and we have discussed the contexts in which each is appropriate.

REFLECTION ACTIVITIES

1. Think back to your childhood experiences. Was there a time when you felt excluded from a group? How did this make you feel? What can you do to avoid having your students experience rejection in a group?

2. Do a Round Table activity in which the members of each small group pass around a paper and brainstorm characteristics that can be used to group students. Compile the separate lists of characteristics into one large list and post it where it can easily be seen. That way you will have a variety of characteristics on hand and can quickly choose one. Using a variety of characteristics ensures that each student works with many different peers. To give students more responsibility, have them take turns selecting a characteristic on which to be grouped.

3. Which of your students' characteristics would you consider to be important when assigning your students to groups? Compare your response with that of a colleague.

6

Fostering Positive Interdependence

Cathie Archbould

How will I structure the activity to require active participation of *all* students?

•

Will I use group rewards to motivate students to work together?

•

Will I divide the task or assign roles?

•

Will I have students share materials?

•

How will I encourage students to recognize the benefits of cooperating?

Mrs. Singh is a grade-seven teacher who wants her students to learn the different components of an ecosystem. In a *competitive classroom structure*, students would demonstrate their learning in comparison to their classmates' learning—a system that guarantees "winners" and "losers." Mrs. Singh might award the top students gold stars, the medium-high achievers silver stars, and the average achievers red stickers. Some students might not receive any formal recognition for their efforts, even though they may have learned about ecosystems.

If Mrs. Singh used an *individualistic classroom structure*, she would recognize students' learning independently of how well classmates performed. For example, students who obtained 85 to 100 percent on a test would receive gold stars, those who obtained 70 to 84 percent would receive silver stars, and those who obtained 55 to 69 percent would receive red stickers. If all students learned the material well, each student would earn a gold star.

Using a *cooperative classroom structure*, Mrs. Singh might have students study the material in heterogeneous groups of four. Each student would contribute the number of points he or she earned on an individual test to his or her group. These scores would then be averaged to create a team score. Students in teams whose group score was between 85 and 100 percent would receive a gold star. Teams with a group score between 70 and 84 percent would receive a silver star, and those with a group score between 55 and 69 percent would earn a red sticker. In this way, the success of individual students is linked to the success of their teammates. Students who perceive the link among their teammates, and who value learning and the recognition of positive achievements, will support and encourage their classmates.

These three classroom structures lead to very different interaction patterns and may influence students' achievement, relationships to other students, self-concept, attitudes, cognitive skills, and interpersonal skills. (For further information about the relationships that exist between students in various classroom structures see Chapter 2: Group Processes and Productivity.) Appendix A: Research Evidence shows that cooperative classroom structures are generally superior to competitive and individualistic ones. Consequently, our purpose in this chapter is to show you different ways of structuring your lessons cooperatively so that when students engage in group work, they work together to learn the material, rather than compete with one another or ignore others and work individually.

Cooperative learning is not simply group learning. One of the primary differences between group learning and cooperative learning is the degree to which the learning of group members depends on students working together. This key to cooperative learning is referred to as positive interdependence. Traditional group learning activities may have positive student interdependence; cooperative learning activities *must* have it. Positive interdependence should not be confused with student dependence, where some students rely on others to do most of the work. In positive interdependence, there is reciprocity among group members, and all contribute toward completion of the group task. In this chapter, we provide a definition and framework for understanding positive interdependence and its development. Then, in addition to describing various ways you can encourage interdependence, we elaborate a classification scheme that helps clarify the nature of interdependence.

DEFINITION: WHAT IS POSITIVE INTERDEPENDENCE?

When positive interdependence or cooperation among group members exists, students work together to learn. When students actively collaborate, they are motivated to help one another and themselves to achieve. Thus, positive interdependence among students provides the energy for students to cooperate and directs it toward a specific learning goal. Positive interdependence exists when one student's success positively influences the chances of other students' successes.

Positive interdependence can be viewed both as a structure that you can employ to ensure your students work together and as a collaborative ethos that permeates a classroom where students care about and work to enhance their own learning and the learning of their peers. The less this ethos exists, the more necessary it is for you to structure interdependence. Hence, positive interdependence usually needs to be structured more at the beginning of the school year, when a competitive culture exists in the school, or when students do not possess very good interpersonal skills or the intrinsic motivation to collaborate.

Sometimes positive interdependence arises naturally in a classroom, as when students ask their teacher if they can work together on a project and decide for themselves how to divide up the work. However, more often you need to begin by structuring the positive interdependence and teaching students how to behave in this type of structure.

THE DEVELOPMENT OF POSITIVE INTERDEPENDENCE

Positive interdependence has several components that typically follow a developmental progression: teacher-imposed structures, student perceptions, student behaviors, and student values (see Exhibit 6.1).

Initially, students may not have the desire to act cooperatively toward others to help them learn.

Therefore, you can begin by imposing a structure of positive interdependence to foster the perception that working with others has a meaningful, positive influence on learning. Once students perceive the importance of interdependence, they should act in ways consistent with this belief. Eventually, students come to internalize the value of cooperation and act autonomously to help others to learn.

Positive Interdependence As a Teacher-Imposed Structure

Broadly speaking, positive interdependence can be structured by ensuring one or more of the following occurs: (a) the learning outcomes of students are positively related; (b) the means for achieving learning outcomes are positively related among students; and/or (c) the interpersonal relations among students are structured to create group cohesiveness. Usually, these structures are established by you in the creation of a cooperative learning activity.

You need to structure positive interdependence carefully so that your students will encourage each other to work but will not pressure individuals beyond their abilities. Students should encourage one another to learn but not badger, intimidate, or pressure other students to comply.

Positive Interdependence As a Student Perception

The teacher who merely imposes a structure of positive interdependence may not succeed unless students also perceive interdependence as important for their learning. That is, students should come to believe that the participation of all group members is necessary for the group to accomplish the learning task. These perceptions of positive interdependence should, therefore, motivate students to act cooperatively.

To encourage the transfer from a teacher-imposed structure of positive interdependence to students' perceptions of positive interdependence, you must communicate clearly to your students that they are capable of working together and that they are expected to do so. The reasons for working cooperatively and the benefits of doing so must be understood by all students. For example, after a cooperative activity, you might ask students to reflect on how each member contributed to the group achieving its goal. The reflection should help students become more aware of what positive interdependence means.

Positive Interdependence As a Student Behavior

Once students are made aware of how positive interdependence works to the advantage of everyone in the group, they are more likely to engage in cooperative behaviors. Students must be given opportunities for cooperative actions and may also need to learn how to interact cooperatively.

For example, if you structure positive interdependence through the use of rewards, such as per-

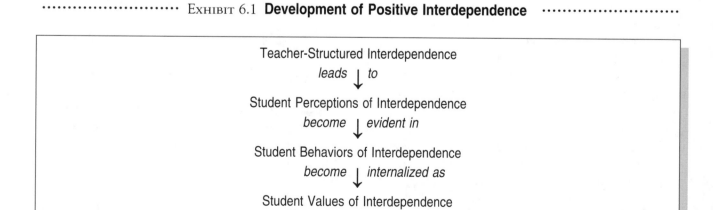

··········· Exhibit 6.1 **Development of Positive Interdependence** ···········

Teacher-Structured Interdependence

leads ↓ *to*

Student Perceptions of Interdependence

become ↓ *evident in*

Student Behaviors of Interdependence

become ↓ *internalized as*

Student Values of Interdependence

formance certificates, it will succeed only if your students value the rewards, perceive working together as the means to obtain them, and behave in ways to earn the rewards. This means that you must take great care to create group tasks that each member can contribute to, or have group goals that can be attained only by input from each student. Otherwise, some members will go along for a free ride, and others will be stuck with all the work and feel that they have been taken advantage of. If your students believe that they must work collaboratively for the group to reach its goal, and they value that goal, then they will behave in ways that will help the group succeed.

Positive Interdependence As a Student Value

Some teachers believe that positive interdependence exists only when students internalize the concept, value it, and become intrinsically motivated by the desire to act cooperatively toward others. For these teachers, true interdependence exists only when students want to contribute to their group's efforts without the need of a teacher-imposed structure. In this view of interdependence, students come to value both the worth of others and of themselves as important for learning.

Some of your students may already have incorporated the value of interdependence, and will automatically think of working collaboratively with others when they are assigned a group task. For others, appreciating the value of interdependence may take a great deal of experience in small groups, with teacher-imposed structures of interdependence, and reflection on how group members depend on one another to successfully complete the task. Even if students do value positive interdependence, if a class is structured competitively, students will begin to behave competitively and will develop competitive values as well.

WAYS OF STRUCTURING POSITIVE INTERDEPENDENCE

There are many ways that you can structure students' learning so that they become positively interdependent (see Exhibit 6.2). You can structure learning so that:

- students' goals are interdependent (outcome interdependence)
- each student is responsible for completing part of the task (means interdependence)

··················· EXHIBIT 6.2 **Types of Positive Interdependence** ···················

OUTCOME INTERDEPENDENCE
    Goal Interdependence
    Reward Interdependence
    Outside Force Interdependence

MEANS INTERDEPENDENCE
    Resource Interdependence
    Task Interdependence
    Role Interdependence
    Communication Interdependence
    Environmental Interdependence

INTERPERSONAL INTERDEPENDENCE
    Identity Interdependence
    Simulation Interdependence

- students' interpersonal interactions are encouraged and structured (interpersonal interdependence).

We will discuss the various types of outcome, means, and interpersonal interdependence listed in Exhibit 6.2, and provide examples of how each is practiced. You can use these different types of interdependence alone, but usually they are more effective when combined, as we will describe later in this chapter.

Outcome Interdependence

Outcome interdependence emphasizes *why* students work together. Outcome interdependence requires group members to work toward the attainment of a group product or group goal. Striving for this outcome motivates students to work together. Using outcome interdependence helps you and your students establish the importance of common learning objectives. There are three types of outcome interdependence: goal interdependence, reward interdependence, and outside force interdependence.

GOAL INTERDEPENDENCE

Goal interdependence exists when all group members must work toward a common goal for the group to succeed. If one group member achieves his or her goal, other group members are helped to achieve their goals. The challenge here is for you to get your students to work together toward a common academic goal (e.g., group presentation) rather than working toward individual goals, or working together for a subversive goal (e.g. distracting the teacher).

One way to increase the likelihood that your students will have a common goal is to have groups participate in setting them. For example, a grade-seven geography class may study different countries of the world in which the goal for each group is to make an oral presentation to the class on a particular country. First, students pick the country that they are interested in studying. Then, you assign them to groups with others who have picked the same country. Group members are likely to be more interested in working together because their com-

mon goal is one they have chosen. Other ways to structure goal interdependence might include having all group members do the following: achieve a certain performance level on a test; create one final group project; prepare and carry out a debate; brainstorm a list of environmental issues; finish a group task before recess; plan a field day for younger grades; and move a heavy mat from the storage room to the gym.

Almost every cooperative activity has positive goal interdependence. It may be the sole source of interdependence, or it may be used in conjunction with one or more of the other types of interdependence that follow.

REWARD INTERDEPENDENCE

The use of rewards is generally not necessary when students' interest in a task or the content is already high. However, in reality, students are not always intrinsically motivated to learn the required material.

Reward interdependence exists when the members of a group all receive the same recognition for the group's accomplishments. Ways of recognizing the group's achievement range widely, from a grade on a single group project to a reward based on the average performance of team members on individual examinations. Rewards can be symbolic (e.g., certificates of excellence or group grades), social (e.g., praise), activity based (e.g., field trips), or tangible (e.g., books).

Not all students are motivated by the same rewards. For example, some students value reward certificates and are excited about showing them to friends and family, while others may show no interest and discard them shortly after receiving them. To be effective, rewards must be powerful incentives for learning. Consequently, you may wish to have each team of students write a learning contract and select their desired rewards from a menu of possibilities.

As noted above, you can base reward interdependence on giving all group members the same grade on an assignment or test. You can determine this common grade by selecting one group member's work at random to evaluate or by averaging the performance achieved by each group member. You must handle using group grades to establish interdependence with caution, however, as peer pressure can become too great if the entire group grade depends on one student's performance. (See Chapter 7: Encouraging Individual Accountability and Chapter 9: Evaluating and Reflecting for a more indepth discussion of this situation.)

One important thing to remember is that all members of a team should share in the group's rewards. Group members should feel responsible not only for their own performance but also for helping others learn. In addition, you need to be clear about where you stand on the issue of rewarding students for working together. (For a discussion of this issue and guidelines about when to use extrinsic rewards, see Chapter 3: Theories of Cooperative Learning).

OUTSIDE FORCE INTERDEPENDENCE

This type of interdependence is also referred to as threat or outside enemy interdependence. When a team is threatened by an outside force, group members usually pull together to overcome the external threat or barrier. In some cooperative learning strategies that use between-group competition, the other groups are the outside force. As long as the competition is fair, remains friendly, and one group does not dominate, students often find this between-group competition motivating. Other people do not need to be the outside force. For example, when a group of outdoor education students on a canoe trip work together to make it through some rough water, the threat of capsizing helps unite the group.

Time can also be a powerful outside force. Challenging a group to finish a task within clear but realistic time limits—meeting book publication deadlines, for example—can draw team members together and encourage them to coordinate their work more effectively.

You need to structure outside force interdependence so that you create or employ a force that challenges your students but can be conquered. If the outside force is too easily overcome, your students will not be challenged. If your students feel that the obstacle is too great, then they will likely become frustrated and give up. Challenging students to beat the class-average score of other schools in a common, board-wide examination is an example of outside force interdependence that may be a realistic challenge for your students.

Means Interdependence

Means interdependence emphasizes *how* students work together to achieve a group goal. In means interdependence, the procedure, process, or manner in which the learning task will be completed is structured so that group members depend on each other. There are five types of means interdependence: resource interdependence, task interdependence, role interdependence, communication interdependence, and environmental interdependence.

RESOURCE INTERDEPENDENCE

Resource interdependence exists when group members must share materials (e.g., markers, worksheets, books, computers) in order to accomplish a learning task. In other words, the resources necessary to complete the task are divided in a way that prevents one individual from accomplishing the task alone. For example, if a group task involves the completion of a worksheet, and you give each individual a copy of the worksheet, it is more likely that group members will work on their own rather than together. In contrast, if a group has only one worksheet, the likelihood that group members will work together to complete the task increases. Nevertheless, you must be careful to provide enough resources to complete the task without having students spend too much time waiting around.

TASK INTERDEPENDENCE

The use of task interdependence divides the learning task so that each group member is responsible for completing part of it. In some cooperative learning methods (see Chapter 12: Jigsaw and Its Variations), group members are responsible for teaching what they have learned to other group members. In other cooperative learning methods, students compile what they have researched independently to create a group presentation (see Chapter 14: Group Project Methods).

For task interdependence, you should use tasks that divide naturally rather than arbitrarily dividing a task that could be completed by one person. Otherwise, your students may resent collaborating on tasks where the need for cooperation is contrived. Task interdependence is particularly appropriate when a wide range of abilities exists within the group and the task has subtasks of varying difficulty or requires varied talents.

You should not use task interdependence to teach hierarchically structured content, that is, content in which students must master one level before they can learn the next. For example, students need to learn how to multiply one-digit numbers before they can learn how to multiply two-digit numbers. Dividing up worksheets so that some students do single-digit multiplication questions and others do double-digit multiplication questions would not help all students learn both of these skills.

ROLE INTERDEPENDENCE

In role interdependence, group members are assigned different responsibilities to perform. The group depends upon all members fulfilling their roles to complete the activity successfully. These roles can be functional (e.g., Recorder, Reader, Time Manager, Materials Manager), cognitive (e.g., Prober, Summarizer, Checker, Elaborator), or interpersonal (e.g., Encourager, Facilitator, Observer, Quiet Monitor). Roles can help facilitate the functioning of the group and should be clearly defined for students. Teachers often distribute role cards such as those in Exhibit 6.3.

Sometimes people confuse task interdependence and role interdependence. Task interdependence

·················· Exhibit 6.3 **Sample Interpersonal, Cognitive, and Functional Roles** ··················

Interpersonal	**Facilitator** You are responsible for inviting everyone to participate and for ensuring that your group is working together harmoniously.	**Encourager** Your job is to encourage your teammates, praise their contributions, and keep up morale in the group.
	Observer You will observe how well your group works together and note any difficulties that arise. Use the observation chart provided.	**Quiet Monitor** You must make sure your group is working quietly together and not disturbing other groups. Remind your teammates to speak softly.
Cognitive	**Summarizer** Your job is to summarize the ideas you and your teammates come up with on a regular basis during your group's discussion.	**Checker** Your job is to check that every member of your group understands the material and can explain how to do the task or the rationale behind your group's answer.
	Prober Your job is to get your teammates to think more deeply about the material and the ideas they come up with.	**Elaborator** Your job is to build on your teammates' ideas and to encourage them to do so by, for example, considering additional alternatives or consequences.
Functional	**Recorder** You are responsible for writing down your group's responses. You must carefully record what the entire group decides.	**Reader** You will read aloud the materials to your teammates. Remember to read slowly and clearly, and to check that your teammates are able to follow.
	Time Manager You are in charge of keeping the group on schedule, ensuring that the work is completed in the allotted time.	**Materials Manager** You are responsible for gathering the materials needed for your group's task and for keeping them organized.

involves the division of content so that each group member completes part of the required work. Role interdependence requires group members to act in different ways to facilitate the accomplishment of the task.

COMMUNICATION INTERDEPENDENCE

Communication interdependence exists when all group members must communicate directly with one another in order to complete the task and achieve the group's learning goal. Effective communication is an important component of cooperative learning. Shaw (1964) suggested that communication lies at the heart of group process. If the group is functioning effectively, its members will be able to communicate productively and easily. In contrast, ineffective groups often have members who either do not communicate often enough or miscommunicate with one another.

Exhibit 6.4 shows the variety of communication patterns that group members can adopt. Not all of these patterns promote effective communication. A five-person team engaged in a wheel pattern of communication forces the team to be dependent on a single student to communicate with others. In contrast, the comcon pattern of communication allows open communication among all team members.

Communication networks in cooperative learning are usually based on group members having equal opportunity to interact with one another. However, as groups increase in size, communication networks become more complex.

There are a number of ways in which you can help your students develop communication patterns consistent with the principle of interdependence. Sometimes using exercises in which the interactions among group members are structured to make students aware of their typical interaction patterns is useful. The teacher, a group member, or a student from another team can observe and record the communication patterns of a group. Team members can then consider which pattern best reflects the way they communicate. Are all patterns equally effective? Which patterns work best with which tasks or students?

You can also structure the interaction for an activity to create different patterns of communica-

tion. This can be useful if you have a meek student you think would benefit from assuming more of a leadership role. The group could be structured in a wheel network, placing that student on the axis. Students would communicate with others only through this student. The central student would have access to and control over the most information. Group dynamics research shows that a person in this position is more likely to emerge as the leader (Shaw, 1981). You could also use this strategy to prevent the few students who habitually take over and control group interactions from doing so by ensuring that they are not in the middle of a communication circuit.

ENVIRONMENTAL INTERDEPENDENCE

Structuring the physical setting so that participants are encouraged to interact with one another promotes student interdependence. Environmental interdependence is almost always used in conjunction with other forms of interdependence, since physical proximity alone is not usually sufficient to ensure interdependence. Exhibit 6.5 presents three examples of environmental interdependence.

Interpersonal Interdependence

Interpersonal interdependence occurs when students are motivated to work together because they have a sense of responsibility, an attraction toward their teammates, or a wish to act on a personal desire to help others. Interpersonal interdependence may include working collaboratively out of a sense of friendship toward teammates, working together because group work is enjoyable, or helping others for personal satisfaction or from indebtedness for past assistance.

Interpersonal interdependence can be enhanced when students engage in activities that promote group cohesiveness and a sense of group identity. Through these activities, students learn to trust each other and feel closer to one another. Once a group identity has been established and rapport exists among group members, teammates will work more effectively together and behave in ways consistent with positive interdependence.

·········· EXHIBIT 6.4 **Communication Networks** ··········

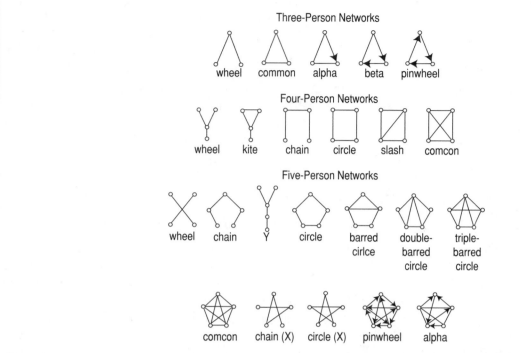

Note: Circles represent positions, lines represent communication channels, and arrows indicate one-way channels.

Source: Adapted from M. Shaw, Communication Networks. In L. Berkowitz (ed.), *Advances in Experimental Social Psychology*, Volume I, New York: Academic Press, 1964, p. 113. Copyright © 1964 by Academic Press, Inc. Used by permission.

·········· EXHIBIT 6.5 **Examples of Environmental Interdependence** ··········

Example 1

A kindergarten teacher gives each of her groups a loop of stretch rope. Students stand inside the rope and use it to form different shapes. The environment within the stretch rope encourages students to practice negotiating with others about where each will stand.

Example 2

A physical education instructor takes her students on a canoe trip. Each group is assigned to a canoe. The limited environment of the canoe encourages students to work together.

Example 3

An elementary language arts teacher takes a first step to establish interdependence by arranging desks into clusters. This environment ensures that group members will be engaged in face-to-face interactions.

Group reflection following a cooperative activity can enhance group cohesiveness (see Chapter 9: Evaluating and Reflecting). Also, most teambuilding and classbuilding exercises use interpersonal interdependence to create in students perceptions that working with others enhances learning and to teach students the value of positive interdependence (see Chapter 4: Classbuilding and Teambuilding). Two types of interpersonal interdependence—identity interdependence and simulation interdependence—are found in activities that bring group members closer together and help them learn to trust one another.

IDENTITY INTERDEPENDENCE

In identity interdependence, group members establish a collective identity through activities that highlight characteristics they have in common. Students come to relate more closely with one another and thus are motivated to work together. These activities include creating a group name, a group sign, a group motto, and so on. You do not need to structure identity interdependence only when the group begins to work together. You can use the structure throughout the group process to ensure that the team continues to function as a cohesive unit. However, you must decide how much time you want to devote to fostering identity interdependence without jeopardizing your coverage of the curriculum. Chapter 4: Classbuilding and Teambuilding contains other activities for building team identity.

SIMULATION INTERDEPENDENCE

Simulation interdependence (also referred to as fantasy interdependence) is created in an activity when students pretend to be in a situation in which they need to depend on one another or need to adopt roles different from the ones they usually play. Simulation interdependence is especially useful for situations where students are stuck in dysfunctional roles. You may have students who think they don't need their peers, or who take over most group tasks and perform them alone. Creating situations in which they realize they *do* need one another can help these students behave more cooperatively in other group tasks. This can lead students to new

ways of relating to one another. Zebulon's Fall (Activity 6.1) is an example of simulation interdependence.

Combining Types of Positive Interdependence

Structures for positive interdependence are rarely used separately. In fact, most cooperative learning activities employ a combination of types of positive interdependence. For instance, if you gave only one worksheet to a group, without using another type of positive interdependence, some group members might take over and complete the worksheet without input from others. You could augment this resource interdependence with role interdependence by having each person in the group do a different job, such as act as Recorder, Reporter, and so on. You could also use reward interdependence by giving group members certificates for obtaining certain group scores calculated from individual tests on the content of an assignment. The more that students realize working together will benefit them, the more they are likely to collaborate with each other. Activity 6.2 demonstrates how different types of interdependence can be structured into one lesson. However, be careful not to overwhelm students with too many directions or with too much structure at one time.

FORMS OF RELATIONSHIPS BETWEEN GROUPS

So far, our discussion of interdependence has focused on the relationship among individuals *within* groups. Similarly, cooperative, competitive, independent, or dependent relationships can exist *between* groups.

Between-Group Cooperation

Positive interdependence exists between groups when the success of one group increases the likelihood that other groups will succeed. You can structure classes in a variety of ways to promote between-group positive interdependence. For example, groups may share tasks when working on the same material; groups may work on different aspects of a project and combine their products at the end; or groups may teach each other what they have learned. Groups may also cooperate by working together to produce a school play or variety show.

Between-group positive interdependence can be a source of peer encouragement. For example, groups may work together to form a cohesive class by first setting a goal that each group must reach. If all groups achieve the goal, the class earns a special reward or acknowledgment. In this way, groups are encouraged to help each other achieve the learning goal. Activity 6.3 demonstrates within-group and between-group positive interdependence.

ACTIVITY 6.1 EXAMPLE OF SIMULATION INTERDEPENDENCE

ZEBULON'S FALL

It is a late fall afternoon. On your way home from school, you and a group of five of your seventh-grade friends stop to play ball in an area several minutes' walk from the street. After a while, Zebulon climbs up to the top of an old wall. He shows off, hopping along the wall on one leg. Suddenly he falls to the ground. You all see Zebulon lying on his back with his left leg tucked under his right one. The bone on his left shin is sticking out through the skin. The wound is bleeding. Zebulon is screaming about the pain. Individually, each group member ranks the order in which you and his other friends should do the following:

_____ Send one friend for help while the others comfort Zebulon.

_____ Wrap a T-shirt or jacket tightly around the wound to stop the bleeding.

_____ Have one friend lift Zeb's right leg, while another puts her hands on Zeb's ankle and pulls gently to straighten out the left leg.

_____ Help Zeb to his feet and support him while he hops up to the street.

_____ Give Zeb a drink of Coke.

_____ Take two strong sticks and use belts to tie sticks onto Zeb's left leg so it won't move.

_____ Tie a belt tightly around the top of Zeb's left thigh to stop the bleeding.

As a group, come to a consensus about the order in which you do the above activities.

Adapted from N. Schneidewind and E. Davidson, *Open Minds to Equality: A Sourcebook of Learning Activities to Promote Race, Sex, Class, and Age Equity,* Englewood Cliffs, New Jersey: Prentice-Hall, 1983, pp. 49–50, 61. Copyright © 1983 by Allyn and Bacon. Adapted by permission.

ACTIVITY 6.2 A LESSON COMBINING DIFFERENT TYPES OF POSITIVE INTERDEPENDENCE

In this lesson on dinosaurs, four different types of interdependence are used. Students are assigned to groups based on the dinosaur they have chosen to learn more about.

Interpersonal interdependence is encouraged by having each group make a sign with the name of its dinosaur written vertically and the name of each group member written horizontally across one of the letters of the dinosaur's name, if possible. This helps each group create an identity. The signs also mark where in the classroom each group will work.

Goal interdependence is created by making each group responsible for completing a group presentation.

Resource interdependence is evident both within groups and between groups because everyone has to share reference books on dinosaurs and art materials. There are not enough books and materials for everyone to use at the same time.

Task interdependence exists because each student is responsible for finding out about a particular aspect of his or her dinosaur (e.g., what they ate, what they looked like, where they lived, etc.). Each student is then responsible for explaining what he or she has learned to their teammates.

Between-Group Competition

Competition, or negative interdependence, exists between groups when the success of one group decreases the likelihood that other groups will succeed. For example, in team sports, such as baseball and hockey, individuals cooperate within their teams but compete against other teams.

In cooperative learning methods where groups compete, teams are rewarded for gaining the most points or producing the best product. In order for students to believe that the competition between groups is fair, assigning them to teams in an equitable manner is important. When team competition is fair, and students learn that doing well depends on working hard as a group, they generally enjoy the between-group competition.

You should also be aware that negative interdependence can occur inadvertently. Sometimes groups that are supposed to be functioning independently may compete. Just as individual students can compete with one another for their teacher's attention and praise, so can groups. For example, groups working on separate projects might compete to see which group finishes first or completes the best project.

Between-Group Independence

Groups function independently when the success of one group has no effect on the outcomes of other groups. The traditional group project, in which groups operate without regard to the functioning of other groups, is an example of between-group independence.

Between-Group Dependence

A dependent relationship between groups may exist when some groups rely solely on others without being able to reciprocate. This may happen when a class is divided into homogeneous groups on the basis of ability. Lower-ability groups may come to depend on higher-ability groups for learning. Between-group dependence is rarely desirable as a structure for classroom learning.

SUMMARY

One major difference between group work and cooperative learning is the presence of positive interdependence, that is, the degree to which group members depend on each other for their learning. In this chapter, we have defined different types of interdependence and have outlined how positive interdependence can develop from a teacher-imposed structure to a student-held value. We have also described different types of interdependence that you can structure into small-group activities to encourage students to cooperate.

ACTIVITY 6.3 EXAMPLE OF WITHIN-GROUP AND BETWEEN-GROUP POSITIVE INTERDEPENDENCE

TEAM CODES

In this game, teams invent letter codes, write messages in their codes, and then decode a message written in another team's code.

Materials: Pencils and paper for each teammate.

Procedure:

1. Divide students into heterogeneous teams of two to four players.

2. Each team secretly prepares a code for the entire alphabet (for example, A = f, B = c, etc.). Each person in the group should contribute an equal number of alphabet substitutions for the code.

3. Each team selects a famous saying. (The passage should be five to twenty words long.) Then each team member translates part of it into code. Teams should verify that the saying is correctly coded.

4. Teams exchange messages and the code for only three letters in their message.

5. Teams try to decode the message. When they finish, they move to another team to help them decode their message. (Teams should move to a team that is not decoding their original message.)

6. Continue playing until the teams have decoded all the sayings.

The major types of interdependence are outcome, means, and interpersonal interdependence. Outcome interdependence encourages students to work toward a group product or goal. Means interdependence concentrates on how students complete a task. Interpersonal interdependence focuses on the attraction or commitment of group members to each other and to their team's success. As you structure positive interdependence within or between groups, and establish a climate of cooperation in your classroom, students will learn how to interact and work together effectively.

REFLECTION ACTIVITIES

1. A teacher can use reward interdependence successfully only when the rewards are consistent with the teacher's philosophy. For example, a secondary language arts teacher decided to reward her entire class if everyone achieved a certain criterion on a test. As the reward, she offered a free period in which students could bring in their own music. The teacher began to think she had suggested an inappropriate reward when her students arrived with portable stereo systems and music she found to be lewd. When the teacher complained, the students revolted, and she threw her arms up in despair and said: "Cooperative learning doesn't work." Her expectations and the students' expectations were not compatible. In this case, what could the teacher have done to avoid this problem?

2. Think about a lesson that you have taught in which you used groups but not cooperative learning. How could you have modified the lesson to incorporate at least two types of interdependence?

3. Along with your colleagues, brainstorm at least three ways you can prevent within-group and between-group dependence.

CHAPTER 7

Brett Lamb

Encouraging Individual Accountability

How will I prevent the problem of free riders and domineering group members?

•

How will I ensure that each student assumes responsibility for his or her learning and completing his or her share of the task?

•

How will I ensure that each student assumes responsibility for helping other members learn and accomplish their share of the task?

Individual accountability is one of the critical components of cooperative learning. It permits identification of each group member's contribution to the group's work. The concepts of positive interdependence and individual accountability are closely linked. While positive interdependence focuses on the complementary relationship among group members, individual accountability focuses on the responsibilities of each member in that relationship. Through individual accountability, each student's contributions to his or her own learning and to the learning of others is maximized. When individual accountability is high, the performance of each group member is apparent to the other group members. Each individual feels responsible for the group's success and contributes to it.

Not all cooperative learning methods emphasize individual accountability. For example, methods that recognize only a group product without identifying the contribution of individual group members have low individual accountability. In this chapter, we will outline the components of individual accountability and discuss ways you can structure it.

DEFINITION: WHAT IS INDIVIDUAL ACCOUNTABILITY?

Individual accountability involves two components: (1) each group member is individually responsible for his or her own learning and (2) each member is responsible for helping the other members of the group learn. Individual accountability enhances group work in a number of ways. First, it ensures that each student has important responsibilities that are apparent to all team members. Second, it can signal if a student needs support and help. Third, it decreases the possibility of unnecessary duplication of group members' efforts.

THE UNDERMINING EFFECTS OF NONACCOUNTABILITY

When you assign students to groups, and individual accountability is absent, individual productivity during group work may diminish. Some students may realize that their efforts are not required, since other teammates will do virtually all the work. These students are called *free riders*, and what they do is called *social loafing*. (See Chapter 2: Group Processes and Productivity.) The workers in the group eventually come to resent being "workhorses" and doing the jobs of others. To avoid being "suckers," they too may reduce the amount of effort they exert during group work. These two effects, social loafing and sucker avoidance, are common difficulties experienced in group work. Together, they reduce the overall productivity of the group.

Is it just laziness that makes some individuals exert less effort on group tasks than on individual tasks? Why does social loafing occur and how can individual accountability lessen its effects? In Chapter 2, we reviewed several factors that contribute to social loafing: group members who share unequally in the work; individual contributions that cannot be clearly identified; members who are uncertain about whether their efforts will contribute, are redundant, or duplicate other members' efforts; and

tasks that are boring, easy, or uninvolving. Based on these factors, Shepperd (1993) proposed that group members will reduce their individual efforts if they feel contributing is (a) not worth it, (b) not necessary, or (c) too costly.

Some approaches you might take to counteract social loafing include:

- increase students' intrinsic motivation (e.g., allow students some choice in topics or tasks)
- use extrinsic incentives (e.g., provide individual and group rewards)
- make individual contributions unique, necessary, and indispensable (e.g., assign a task that is too complex or too large for one student to complete alone)
- reduce the costs, or the perceived costs, of contributing (e.g., make individual group tasks manageable and realistic; ensure group members assess the contributions of individuals)

Unless your students are learning a skill or a concept they all need to master, you should design group tasks so that the work done by different students is not duplicated. If students feel that their work is being duplicated by another group member, or, worse, done better by another member, they may perceive that their contribution is not necessary, and they will lose motivation. Failure to specify how each individual will accomplish the group task may also lead to a lack of responsibility. When there is ambiguity about the way to successfully complete a task, students may assume that someone else will do the work, and the task may never get done.

THE DEVELOPMENT OF INDIVIDUAL ACCOUNTABILITY

Individual accountability develops in the same way that positive interdependence does—beginning with teacher-imposed structures. The structures set the stage so that student perceptions, behaviors, and values of individual accountability can develop.

Individual Accountability As a Teacher-Imposed Structure

Cooperative learning groups are often composed of students with varied abilities, interests, and motivations. Sometimes their commitment to helping each other learn and contributing to the group task is high and arises naturally, with each student feeling responsible for the group's success. Often, however, you may need to employ specific strategies designed to increase individual effort and accountability.

When individual commitment and responsibility have become internalized, and are values held by all group members, teacher-imposed structures may not be necessary. In fact, students who have already assumed such responsibility may resent your attempt to control their behavior and may perceive it as a lack of trust. Shepperd's model (1993) suggests that teacher-imposed structures may not be required when individual members perceive that contributing is worth their while, is necessary and unique, and is fair. Exhibit 7.1 presents some classroom situations in which structuring individual accountability may be particularly important.

Individual Accountability As a Student Perception

If you merely impose a structure of individual accountability, your students may not perceive that accountability has a meaningful influence on their learning. Students' perceptions of accountability are associated primarily with students' beliefs that the accomplishment of the learning task depends on them. This belief—that each student is responsible to the group—should motivate students to work toward a group goal.

Students are usually motivated to work on tasks if there is a reasonable likelihood that they will suc-

··················· EXHIBIT 7.1 **When to Structure Individual Accountability** ························

Structuring individual accountability is particularly important when any of the following conditions apply:	Rationale/ Dimension
1. Students find the task uninteresting.	Contributing is not worth the effort.
2. The learning goal or reward is not attractive to group members.	Contributing is not worth the effort.
3. The task can be completed by one individual alone.	Contributing is unnecessary.
4. The size of the group is large.	Contributing may be unnecessary and may not be noticed.
5. There is little teacher supervision.	Effort is unmonitored, so the cost of contributing is perceived as unfair.
6. The composition of the group is highly heterogeneous.	The cost of contributing is perceived as unfair (perceived risk of being called a sucker).
7. Cooperation is not the norm of the class or school.	Individual accountability has not been internalized as a student value.

ceed, if they value the task, and if they believe that success is within their control. You must communicate clear expectations that each group member is capable and is responsible to the group. You may wish to consult Cohen (1994a), who has developed specific strategies for publicly recognizing the value of group members' abilities and contributions. In addition, we have listed below several things you can say and do to communicate that each student is capable and responsible.

Words

- "You can do it!"
- "Your group is counting on you."
- "You guys make a great team!"
- "Here's a job your group can do."
- "Everybody should pull their weight."

Actions

- Have frequent eye contact with all students.
- Assign tasks or roles.
- Post and reward improvement points.
- Point out individuals' strengths.
- Select students at random to answer questions.

When you structure individual accountability appropriately, your students will perceive that their contribution to the group is vital to the group's success. This perception should motivate students to participate actively in the group task. Making each student's contribution to the group outcome visible to all helps students see that they are accountable.

Individual Accountability As a Student Behavior

If students perceive that their contribution is important to the group, they are likely to behave in ways that support the group in attaining its goal. These behaviors include being on task, expressing positive attitudes toward others, seeking help and giving help, asking for and providing explanations, and so on.

Individual Accountability As a Student Value

Ultimately, students should develop a feeling of personal responsibility to the groups in which they work. Nonetheless, there are many factors in addition to accepting individual accountability as a value that affect the degree of commitment and responsibility each student feels toward the group. These include the perceived likelihood of success, the degree of intrinsic interest in the task, the perceived commitment of and effort exerted by the other members, the perceived importance of members' individual contributions, and the interpersonal relations among group members.

WAYS OF STRUCTURING INDIVIDUAL ACCOUNTABILITY

Generally, you can structure individual accountability by ensuring that (a) the learning outcomes of individual students are identifiable and students are responsible for them (outcome accountability); (b) the means for achieving those outcomes require the involvement of individual students (means accountability); and (c) the social relations between students are structured to create personal responsibility (interpersonal accountability). These approaches can be used alone or in combination to strengthen the degree of accountability required. Exhibit 7.2 provides examples of outcome, means, and interpersonal accountability structures.

Outcome Accountability

Having each student responsible both for his or her individual performance and for making a substantial contribution to the group outcome makes it very difficult for some students to sit back and let other group members do all the work. Some teachers use a combination of individual and group assessment to encourage responsibility, noting the importance for students to have individual feedback. You may also want to assess students on their contributions toward the learning and performance of their group members. Instead of or in addition to your assessment, ask your students to evaluate their own performance and that of their teammates in contributing to the final group product. For more detail and specific suggestions, see Chapter 9: Evaluating and Reflecting for ways to evaluate individual contributions to group products.

One way to ensure accountability is to assign a group grade or evaluation based on the average of members' individual test scores. You could also select a group member at random whose individual test results, worksheet, and/or oral performance are used to represent the team's performance. This holds all group members responsible for ensuring that every member has learned the material and can perform at the required level.

Another way to increase individual accountability based on test scores is to develop an incentive system in which each group member contributes points toward a common group goal. The group receives the agreed-upon reward (e.g., the selection of a special activity), when they have achieved their goal (see Exhibit 7.3). Such incentives encourage individual accountability both for students' own learning and for helping others learn, without putting individual grades in jeopardy.

To maintain outcome accountability while recognizing ability differences, you can use individual improvement scores on tests or quizzes, rather than raw scores, as contributions toward a group score. For example, a student whose test results improved by seven percentage points from the previous test would bring seven bonus points to his or her team, regardless of the absolute score on the test. Using individual improvement points means that all students, regardless of their ability or prior achievement, have an equal opportunity to contribute to the team score. Thus, all students are motivated to improve their performance and to help their team-

·················· EXHIBIT 7.2 **Examples of Individual Accountability Structures** ·····················

OUTCOME ACCOUNTABILITY
  Individual testing and evaluation
  Group rewards based on individual improvement scores
  *Grades based on the average of team members' scores
  *Grades based on a random selection of team members' answers
  Giving the group one point for each person who reaches his or her criterion
  Peer and self-assessment of individual academic contribution (e.g., evaluation of individual contribution to the
    group product)

MEANS ACCOUNTABILITY
  Role assignment (with each role necessary for task completion)
  Task division (e.g., mini-topic presentations)
  Member signature denotes agreement and participation
  Participation regulation (e.g., Talking Chips)

INTERPERSONAL ACCOUNTABILITY
  Observation and feedback about individual participation and social skills
  Teambuilding activities that require individual input (e.g., Uncommon Commonalities)
  Group identification that requires individual contribution (e.g., a group name composed of letters of teammates'
    names)

* We recommend that you use these options with caution.

mates improve. You will find an example of one method of using improvement points in Chapter 11: Student Team Learning Methods.

Means Accountability

Means accountability specifies the way in which the group activity should be completed, with each member having a specific role or task to perform. Giving each member a clear task or role encourages students to perceive their contributions as unique and indispensable to the group. Means accountability also includes the responsibility of supporting teammates in their task or role assignments.

Assigning members specific responsibilities makes it much easier for you or other group members to intervene during the activity to encourage individuals and keep them on task. Such intervention should not be accusatory (e.g., "Jean Marc, why aren't you doing your job?"). Rather, you should assist members in fulfilling their roles or completing their portions of the assignment (e.g., "Jean Marc, I notice you're getting stuck. May I offer a suggestion?"). You may need to teach students how to encourage group members to respect their tasks or roles. Exhibit 7.4 shows how the selective use of role or task assignments can also be used to help keep domineering students in check and to assign authority to more shy students. Finally, the participation of group members in group discussion activities can be regulated by using procedures that require members to take turns. See Exhibit 7.5 for one way to regulate individual participation.

Interpersonal Accountability

In addition to the structures related strictly to the academic task are structures that help students develop personal responsibility toward their group. This accountability is often encouraged through nonacademic activities that highlight the importance of each individual's contribution to group identity. Teambuilding activities that emphasize the importance of each member in the group and build trust among teammates are ways of structuring interpersonal accountability (see Chapter 4: Classbuilding and Teambuilding). An enhanced sense of commitment to and trust in fellow group members

··················· EXHIBIT 7.3 **Using Incentives to Increase Outcome Accountability** ···················

A grade-four teacher uses a combination of group and whole-class incentives to promote individual accountability for learning and helping others learn. At the front of the class is a drawing of a large bubble gum machine containing numerous white (outlined) bubble gums. The class goal is to color in all the bubble gums (earned according to a performance schedule described below), and thus attain their reward. The teacher determines the number of bubble gums to make attaining the reward challenging but feasible within a reasonable time frame. The reward one class agreed upon was watching a video in class.

To earn the right to color in bubble gums, the following procedure is used. After a team learning unit, students are evaluated on individual quizzes. The points earned by each team member on the quiz are used to generate an average team score. Each of the team scores then contributes toward the coloring in of bubble gums as specified below:

Team average of 9/10 or 10/10 earns 4 colored gums
Team average of 7/10 or 8/10 earns 3 colored gums
Team average of 5/10 or 6/10 earns 2 colored gums
Team average of 4/10 or less earns 1 colored gum

Variations
For older students, use a thermometer, with the goal of reaching a predetermined temperature. Or use a mountain climber for whom students would earn altitude increments toward the final goal of reaching the summit.

will reduce the likelihood of individuals withholding effort for fear of being taken advantage of.

Interpersonal accountability is further enhanced by having group members clearly communicate their individual responsibilities for completing the group task and their commitment to each other for meeting those responsibilities. Observations of and reflections on students' participation during an activity and noting the degree to which effective social skills were used can also provide group members with feedback on whether they are acting in ways consistent with interpersonal accountability (see Chapter 8: Developing Interpersonal and Cognitive Skills for examples).

SUMMARY

In this chapter, you have seen that group activities in which some members "free ride" and others do all the work are devoid of individual accountability.

EXHIBIT 7.4 **Intervening to Support Means Accountability**

Fazia takes over the lettering on a poster from Ida because she feels she can do the job better. Mr. Levesque notices this and without accusing anyone of wrongdoing drops by the group to verify who was assigned the role of "writer."

Ida: "It's my role."

Fazia: "Ida doesn't print very well."

Ida: "It's just that my letters don't stay the same size and I run out of room."

Mr. Levesque: "That doesn't sound like too big a problem. Fazia, do you have any suggestions for Ida that would make it easier?"

Fazia (to Ida): "Maybe you could draw lines in pencil as a guide."

Ida: "Okay, I'll try that."

Mr. Levesque: "Good. Now, Fazia, what role did you choose?"

(Mr. Levesque returns a few minutes later to check on progress and to praise Ida for her lettering job.)

EXHIBIT 7.5 **Structuring Means Accountability by Regulating Participation**

TALKING CHIPS
Equal participation can be created by imposing a structure over a regular small-group discussion. Everyone in the group is given a poker chip. After they have a turn talking they place their chip in the centre of the table. They must wait until all of the chips are on the table before they can speak again. Once everyone has spoken, all the chips are retrieved and the turns begin again. (Participants' pens can be used instead of poker chips.)

After a few rounds, take time to discuss how people felt during this activity. Typically, quiet people feel pressured to speak and those who usually talk the most feel constrained. This activity makes students more aware of their degree of participation and highlights unequal rates of participation. After using the approach a few times, students should begin to participate more equally.

Source: Adapted from S. Kagan, *Cooperative Learning Resources for Teachers*, San Juan Capistrano, California: Resources for Teachers, 1990. Copyright © 1990 by Spencer Kagan. Used by permission.

To encourage individual accountability, students must believe that their individual contributions to the group task are necessary, worthwhile, and achievable. We have discussed how teachers can structure individual accountability to create the perception in students that they are responsible for their learning and for the success of their teammates. Perceptions of accountability promote appropriate behaviors, which cause students to eventually internalize accountability as a value. In this chapter, we have also presented structures for outcome accountability, means accountability, and interpersonal accountability that you can use to encourage your students to work effectively with their teammates.

REFLECTION ACTIVITIES

1. Refer to Exhibit 7.1 and give specific examples of teaching situations in which you would need to structure individual accountability.

2. Think about the definition of individual accountability presented in this chapter and the definition of individualistic classroom structures presented in Chapter 6. How are they similar and how are they different?

3. Think of a group activity that you have experienced. How did the presence or absence of individual accountability contribute to group dynamics and outcomes?

Paul Till

CHAPTER

8

Developing Interpersonal and Cognitive Skills

How will I select the interpersonal and cognitive skills to be developed?

•

How will I develop students' awareness of their use of these skills?

•

What techniques will I use to help students develop the selected skills?

•

What behaviors do I expect to see students engaged in during group work?

Today's rapidly changing society is increasing the need for schools to help students develop interpersonal and cognitive skills. Divorces and smaller families in which both parents work reduce the number of interactions between parents and children and between siblings. Families are more transient. Extended families are less common and neighborhood support systems are less evident. In the past, children who would have learned communication, negotiation, leadership, and cooperation skills from their parents, grandparents, siblings, and other family members no longer have as much opportunity to do so.

In business today, work teams are increasingly common. Employees need to communicate and negotiate with one another effectively, think flexibly and creatively, and transfer their learning skills to new contexts. The rapid pace of change in modern society also means that people must continually acquire new information and skills throughout their lives, and are likely to change careers several times. Students need to go beyond the acquisition of a set-content curriculum; they need to acquire the cognitive skills that will allow them to continue to learn, to set their own learning goals, and to select appropriate strategies for achieving them.

Thus, students need to learn effective interpersonal and cognitive skills to make life in the classroom more pleasant and productive, and to improve their interactions with their families, friends, and future colleagues outside of school.

Two key assumptions underlie this chapter. First, we believe that interpersonal and cognitive skills need to be developed *for* effective and productive cooperation. Second, we contend that the development of these skills is facilitated *through* cooperation with others in carefully designed group work.

In this chapter, we will (1) outline the interpersonal and cognitive skills that students need to learn, (2) discuss why these skills are necessary for effective group work and how cooperative interaction can enhance their development, (3) provide guidelines for teaching interpersonal and cognitive skills, and (4) describe concrete techniques. Throughout the chapter, you will find examples of activities you can use to develop your students' interpersonal and cognitive skills.

Definitions

Interpersonal skills, such as listening, sharing, and encouraging, are used to engage in verbal and nonverbal interactions with others. They are sometimes referred to as social skills, communication skills, prosocial skills, collaborative skills, cooperative skills, or group maintenance skills.

EXHIBIT 8.1 **Interpersonal and Cognitive Skills**

facilitating interaction	resolving conflicts	evaluating ideas
respecting others		analyzing
accepting differences	negotiating	justifying opinions
using humor appropriately		summarizing
participating enthusiastically		comparing and contrasting
disagreeing politely	criticizing ideas, not people	probing for deeper meaning
keeping self-control		generating alternatives
describing feelings		elaborating
caring for others	recognizing others'	applying
showing appreciation	perspectives	integrating ideas
including everyone		checking for understanding
taking turns	paraphrasing	expanding others' ideas
sharing space and materials		clarifying ideas
encouraging others		verifying answers
avoiding put downs	listening actively	asking for clarification
praising		estimating
using quiet voices		sequencing
saying please and thank you		categorizing
using names	asking for help	describing concepts
		asking questions
		contributing ideas
		brainstorming
		recalling information
		identifying
		staying on task

COMPLEXITY (↑)

Interpersonal Skills ← → Cognitive Skills

Cognitive skills are thought processes involved in learning, including the abilities to process information, determine relationships, and make reasoned conclusions and decisions. They are sometimes referred to as thinking skills, learning skills, or task skills.

Increasing attention is being given to training in meta-cognitive awareness. *Meta-cognitive awareness* refers to learners' knowledge about the learning skills or strategies they are using, their ability to select appropriate strategies for a particular situation or purpose, and their ability to monitor the usefulness of the strategies and modify them as necessary.

INTERPERSONAL AND COGNITIVE SKILLS: A CONTINUUM

Since many skills, such as paraphrasing and considering another's perspective, clearly involve both interpersonal and cognitive aspects, it is useful to view interpersonal and cognitive skills on a continuum, rather than as two mutually exclusive categories. Exhibit 8.1 categorizes a sample of skills into three broad categories along this continuum: interpersonal skills, cognitive skills, and skills that require aspects of both.

Exhibit 8.1 also lists the skills vertically in approximate order of complexity. Generally, we recommend that teachers of younger children and students new to cooperative group work start with skills toward the bottom of the list. For example, if your students are young or often interrupt one another, you can use Talking Stick (Activity 8.1) to develop their skill at taking turns. Older students may need to develop more complex skills. Activity 8.2 describes an activity that helps students learn to resolve conflicts—an advanced skill involving both interpersonal and cognitive components.

The actual level of skill complexity will depend on various factors, including your students' maturity and experience and the difficulty of the content. For instance, if your students are very familiar with their group members and the content to be worked on, they will find it easier to apply more complex skills.

A productive group is one in which attention is given to both interpersonal and cognitive skills. Cognitive skills help group members learn the course content, complete their task, and reach their goal. Interpersonal skills are needed to maintain a united, cooperative climate in the group, where each member feels supported and appreciated. If consideration is given only to task completion, productivity may drop as conflicts arise among group members. Conversely, if students focus only on enjoying each other's company, little learning will take place and the task will not be accomplished. Remember to consider both ends of the continuum when selecting the skills your students will need for productive and enjoyable learning in groups.

SKILL DEVELOPMENT WITHIN COOPERATIVE LEARNING

Interpersonal Skills

In addition to the interpersonal challenges in traditional classrooms, many classrooms today contain students with a diversity of ethnic and racial backgrounds. This requires that students have better interpersonal skills to interact effectively with people who may have different customs and values. While this puts additional stress on teachers and schools, it also provides greater opportunities to build intercultural and interracial understanding.

The assumption underlying some cooperative learning methods, such as Student Teams-Achievement Divisions (STAD) and Teams-Games-Tournaments (TGT), is that students have already developed sufficient interpersonal skills to engage in effective collaboration with others. For other methods, such as Learning Together, the assumption is that interpersonal skills have to be directly taught.

Even without direct instruction, the interpersonal skills of students in cooperative groups are improved when compared to students learning in competitive or individualistic classrooms. However, because many students have had limited experience interacting and learning with others in the classroom, they often need more explicit guidance in developing these skills. Perspective-taking activities such as "I" Statements (Activity 8.3) help students develop interpersonal skills.

Cognitive Skills

Education typically engages lower-level thinking—what Costa (in Bellanca and Fogarty, 1991) classifies as information "gathering" skills. These are characteristic of many school tasks in which students count, describe, match, name, recite, select, recall, and tell. Match and Master Marathon (Activity 8.4) is a cooperative learning activity that involves students in matching and rehearsing information.

Advanced cognitive skills training attempts to engage students in higher-level thinking about the content. Students are required to "process" the material actively, through tasks requiring comparing and contrasting, explaining, classifying, and inferring. Students are further trained to "apply" what they have learned in tasks that require evaluating, judging, predicting, speculating, and exploring implications. You can use an activity such as Venn Diagram (Activity 8.5) to give students practice in comparing and contrasting. Send-A-Problem (Activity 8.6) engages students in knowledge application.

As we discussed in Chapter 3: Theories of Cooperative Learning, cooperative learning can provide an ideal context for developing students' cognitive skills. Errors or omissions in students' thinking are revealed much more readily through feedback in interaction with others. Group members ask each other to justify responses and opinions, clarify ideas, and elaborate responses. Through this interaction, students' thought processes are verbalized and made available for evaluation by themselves and others. Furthermore, group members contribute multiple perspectives to a problem, offering a much wider range of arguments and evidence than a single individual is likely to develop alone. Word-Webbing (Activity 8.7) is an activity designed for concept development and exchange.

By creating a supportive, interdependent environment, cooperative learning encourages students to be more open-minded and to value varied perspectives. Students will be less likely to persist in doggedly defending their personal viewpoints and will be more open to considering evidence and arguments from others. Finally, group members can provide each other with immediate assistance and feedback when they apply and practice these skills during group work.

GUIDELINES FOR SKILL DEVELOPMENT

You are confronted by several questions when considering interpersonal and cognitive skill development. What skills should I teach? Should these skills be explicitly taught? Should they be integrated with subject matter instruction or taught separately? Which approach will best help my students transfer a given skill to new contexts? Although there are

---

ACTIVITY 8.1 TALKING STICK

1. Give one student a stick or a small object and ask him or her to start the discussion.

2. When that student has finished talking, the stick should be handed to the person who wishes to continue. Only the person holding the stick may talk. You can give instructions about handing over the stick (such as boy, girl, boy, girl, etc.).

3. Be very firm if students interrupt the speaker, and repeat the instructions if necessary. Soon students will notice the interruptions themselves and learn they must wait their turn to speak.

4. When the discussion is over, students should talk about the problems they experienced waiting for their turn, and how they felt about being interrupted.

ACTIVITY 8.2 RESOLVING DIFFERENCES

This structure was developed to help students learn how to resolve differences of opinion stemming from multiple perspectives. In this process, students are led to develop a better appreciation of the perspectives of others. Students learn that such understanding makes it easier to respect others and resolve differences graciously. Stories or scenarios appropriate to the age of the students can be chosen, making this structure applicable for all levels (e.g., Cinderella for use with young children, a courtroom drama for use with older students).

1. The teacher chooses a story with several characters, each representing different perspectives, and assigns students to groups so that the number of group members equals the number of characters.

2. Each group member is assigned a different character.

3. Students regroup with others who have been assigned the same character, and explore the story from the perspective of their character, sharing their thoughts about what their character would think and feel.

4. These groups then write an adapted version of the story from their character's perspective.

5. The class is given a new problem that relates to the story.

6. The groups develop a case for solving the problem.

7. The students return to their original mixed-character groups.

8. Each member presents the case for his or her character.

9. Group members rotate positions and present the case of the member to their right.

10. The groups then reach consensus, resolving the problem.

11. The groups reflect on the process, and discuss how what they have learned could be applied to resolving their own conflicts amicably.

ACTIVITY 8.3 "I" STATEMENTS

When people describe their own behavior, they are usually less critical than when others exhibit the same behavior. This structure helps students develop awareness of this tendency and promotes respect for others.

1. Assign "I" statements to groups. Some examples are:

   - I am an optimist.
   - I usually agree with my classmates.
   - I believe it is important to be fashionable.
   - I occasionally get angry.
   - I have high moral principles.
   - I treat my parents' ideas with respect.
   - I believe that a penny saved is a penny earned.
   - I am flexible.
   - I choose my friends carefully.
   - I believe in getting my fair share.

2. Students create, and record in writing, different perceptions by transforming "I" statements into "You" and "She or He" statements. For example, "I am firm. You are obstinate. He is pigheaded."

3. In groups, students share the "You" and "She or He" statements they've created.

4. In their groups, students discuss whether they have ever found themselves taking these different perspectives. Why do they think people do this? In what circumstances do people do this more frequently? How does this inhibit communication?

no definitive answers to these questions, we make the following recommendations for you to consider below.

Select the Skills to Be Improved

Careful analysis of the task assigned for group work can reveal which interpersonal and cognitive skills your students will need to complete the assignment successfully in a group. For example, if the task demands that students reach consensus on a controversial subject, they may need training in skills such as as respecting others, negotiating, and integrating ideas.

Learning the strengths and weaknesses of your students can also help you narrow down which skills would benefit most from explicit attention. Observe your students informally as they interact with their classmates. Do they demonstrate the skills needed to work together effectively?

ACTIVITY 8.4 MATCH AND MASTER MARATHON

The Match and Master Marathon activity can be very successful in encouraging students to work together to master academic content. It should be used for high-consensus material, for which there are clear right and wrong answers. It is effective either for practice of recently presented content, or as a review in preparation for a test.

Preparation:

- Create a deck of cue and response cards. The cue cards contain information that needs to be matched with information on the corresponding response cards.
- Make multiple-color copies of the deck of cue and response cards, so that each group is working with a different-color deck.
- Each team receives a deck of response cards.
- Decks of the corresponding cue cards are laid on a table in the front of the room.

Directions to groups:

1. Deal out the response cards until they are all gone. All members should hold the response cards in their hands and not combine them with the other members' cards (i.e., one member should not do all the matchings while the others watch).

2. The group decides which member will begin the activity (e.g., the member with the next birthday begins).

3. The member who begins the activity comes to the front table and selects *one* cue card from the deck in his or her group's color and returns to the team.

4. Members consult and try to match the correct response card with the cue card.

5. Each member is responsible for matching the response card(s) in his or her hands, but the entire group should verify the matching.

6. The member holding the matching response returns to the front for the teacher to verify:

   - if match is correct, the member selects a new cue card and returns to the team
   - if match is incorrect, the member repeats Step 4.

When a group successfully completes all the matchings, return both cue and response cards to that group. Group members can then review the material further by playing a matching card game, such as Fish or Memory. (Alternatively, give a master sheet with cues and responses to the group from which to study for a quiz.)

Examples

1. Match dates with historical events. (history)

2. Match geometric pictures with descriptions. (geometry)

3. Match answers with mathematical problems. (mathematics)

4. Match baby animals with their parents. (kindergarten)

5. Match paintings with their painter. (fine arts)

You may also involve your students in deciding which skills are important or need to be taught. Small groups could do this by brainstorming skills needed for cooperative group work, or by consulting a list, such as the one in Exhibit 8.1, and ranking the skills from most important to least important. One advantage of having students select at least some of the skills is the added commitment they will feel toward the development of these skills.

Provide Direct Instruction

Once you have identified the skills, you must decide how to develop them. We recommend at least some form of direct instruction or focus on the skill to be learned. If the skill is taught separately, you should make applicability to course content and academic tasks explicit. In other words, learning how to cooperate on nonacademic tasks may not be sufficient; students also need to develop the ability to apply these skills while learning course content in groups. If the skill is integrated with content instruction, you should promote its transfer by highlighting the critical elements of the skill itself, and by discussing other contexts in which the skill could be usefully applied. Reintroducing specific skills across varied content and tasks will also promote their transfer.

Develop Meta-Cognitive Awareness

Developing students' strategic use of a variety of interpersonal and cognitive skills through meta-cognitive awareness is critical to encouraging transfer and maintenance of these skills. Students must learn how to assess the task assigned, design a plan for completing the task, decide which skills or strategies to apply, monitor the success of their approach, and modify it if necessary. Without this meta-cognitive awareness, students risk learning both the course content and the procedures by rote, and consequently may be unable to apply either the acquired knowledge or the skills in new situations. You can promote meta-cognitive awareness by having students share their strategies with each other, reflect on the process they went through in completing a task, and evaluate the relative success of their approach.

Take a Cyclical Approach

Acquisition and refinement of an interpersonal or cognitive skill is a cyclical process that takes time. The model in Exhibit 8.2 illustrates this process. As we have suggested above, training should begin with some direct teaching of the skill, including developing students' motivation through awareness

---

ACTIVITY 8.5 VENN DIAGRAM

A Venn diagram is a structure to help students visualize the similarities and differences of ideas, concepts, or simple objects. Cognitive skills of comparing and contrasting, categorizing, analyzing, synthesizing, and judging are all used for this structure. To create a Venn diagram:

1. Draw two circles so that one overlaps the other by about one-third.

2. Ask students to brainstorm what makes one concept unique, the other concept unique, and what attributes they have in common.

3. Students can use this information to generate reports, essays, or presentations.

Below is an example generated by students in a high-school biology class.

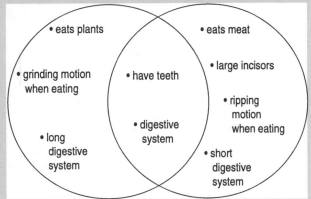

- eats plants
- grinding motion when eating
- long digestive system
- have teeth
- digestive system
- eats meat
- large incisors
- ripping motion when eating
- short digestive system

of the need for the skill. Following this, students must have the opportunity to practice the skill, perhaps with a peer or the teacher as observer. In order to promote strategic use of the skill, providing specific, descriptive feedback to your students and having them reflect on their interaction and learning behaviors during the activity is important. Reflection alone, however, may not ensure goal-directed growth. Following reflection, students should set goals for improving their use of the skills. This may then lead back to more direct teaching, or to additional practice of the skill, thus beginning the cycle again. Techniques you can use at each stage of this cycle are discussed below.

TECHNIQUES FOR SKILL DEVELOPMENT

Techniques are procedures that teachers can apply within an activity or lesson for a specific purpose.

ACTIVITY 8.6 SEND-A-PROBLEM

Send-a-problem is an ideal structure for having students generate their own learning materials for review or further exploration of a topic. Students must think carefully about the material both to develop appropriate questions for another group and to respond to questions sent to them by another group. The three steps are:

1. *Students author review questions.*
   Each group member creates a review problem and writes it down on a flash card. (Encourage high-consensus problems that have right or wrong answers, verifiable by the text.) Authors pose their questions to their teammates. If there is consensus, each author writes the answer on the back of the card. If not, the question is revised so that it produces consensus. The side of the card with the question is marked with a "Q." The side of the card with the answer is marked with an "A."

2. *Teams send-a-problem.*
   Teams pass their stack of review questions to another team.

3. *Teams respond.*
   Student 1 reads the first question. Each team member individually writes down his or her answer. The team members then compare and discuss their answers. When they reach consensus, they turn the card over to see if they agreed with the sending group. If not, they write their answer as an alternative answer. Student 2 reads the next question, and the procedure is repeated. The stacks of cards can be sent to a third and fourth group, and so on.

Upon return of the cards to the senders, there is opportunity to discuss and clarify any questions indicated on the back of the cards.

Variation: *Open-ended Send-a-Problem*
Send-a-problem could also be used for more open-ended questions, without clear-cut right or wrong answers. The authoring team would simply formulate the question, without determining the answer. The responding team would then consider the problem they were sent and come to a consensus. The two groups would then meet to discuss their responses to each other's questions. If the size of the combined group would be too large, half of each group could meet. It should be made clear to the students that all members of each original group would be responsible for understanding their group's conclusion and rationale, and thus be able to represent their teams.

Mixed subject area examples

1. Write a question about the motivation behind a character's actions in a book your class has read. (language arts)

2. Write a question about a particular period or event. (history)

3. Write a word problem. Ask for its solution. (mathematics)

4. Write a question about the environment in a particular region. Ask about its influence on the economy of that region. (geography)

Source: Adapted from S. Kagan, *Cooperative Learning: Resources for Teachers*. San Juan Capistrano, California: Resources for Teachers, 1992. Copyright © 1992 by Spencer Kagan. Used by permission.

They can be adapted for use in most any lesson, since they do not interfere with the overall design of the lesson itself. Several techniques for developing students' interpersonal and cognitive skills are described below and include (a) defining skills via T-charts, (b) modeling skills, (c) assigning roles for skill practice, (d) observing and reflecting on skill use, (e) reinforcing desired behaviors, and (f) setting goals for skill refinement.

Defining Skills via T-Charts

When introducing a new interpersonal or cognitive skill, it is often easier for students to understand and apply the skill if it is operationalized through clear, concrete examples of expected behaviors. For example, if you remind students to check that everyone in their group understands, you might hear them verifying answers without actually explaining or asking others to explain how the answer was

---

ACTIVITY 8.7 WORD-WEBBING

Word-webbing is a powerful tool for concept development and exchange. A simpler version of more complex concept mapping strategies, it is well suited for quick visual representation of a group's prior knowledge of a topic before a more in-depth exploration. It can be particularly effective for externalizing beliefs or attitudes held implicitly by students and acts as a catalyst for exchanging views.

Individual Webs—Groups Discuss:

1. Each student writes the "core concept" in the center of a sheet of paper and draws a rectangle around it. Next, major related concepts are added, circled, and connected with a line to the core concept. Finally, more detailed concepts are added and connected to the related core or major concepts.

2. Within their groups, students compare their word-webs, discussing similarities and differences. They may also be encouraged to probe for underlying differences in perspectives or attitudes.

Group Word-Webbing:

1. Give each group a large sheet of paper, and each group member a different colored pen. Have them write the core concept in the center of the sheet (in a rectangle). Then, in a Round Robin, members each add one major related concept and circle it. Following this, in a Free-for-All, members add additional related concepts and connections as they feel the urge. This method allows easy cognitive assessment because the colors indicate individual contributions.

2. Upon completion, group members examine their word-web and each student shares his or her thoughts about the concepts she or he contributed.

3. Word-webs from different groups are compared. This can be done in a variety of ways (e.g., teams tour the room and examine the word-webs of other groups; teams pair up and explain their word-webs to each other; each group presents its word-web to the class, etc.).

Diamond Word-Webbing:
Diamond word-webbing is a less elaborate and more structured version of word-webbing. It is very useful when introducing a new concept for discussion. It works best in groups of four.

1. Give each group a sheet of paper and each member a different colored pen. Have each group draw a diamond-shaped structure. Assign the core concept, and ask each group to write it in the top box.

2. Groups split into pairs. Each pair enters a related concept in one of the next two boxes.

3. Each member individually enters one related concept in the following four boxes.

4. Members again pair up and decide on a word for one of the next two boxes that is related to both of the words connected to it.

5. The whole group comes to a consensus on the last word uniting the two concepts leading to it.

6. The group examines and discusses its word-web.

7. Word-webs are compared across groups (see Group Word-Webbing).

reached. T-charts define the skill through teacher- and student-generated examples of verbal and nonverbal behaviors. You should construct the T-charts with your students in order to incorporate their own expressions and cultivate their commitment to practicing the skill.

The steps for creating a T-chart and suggestions for its use are given below (Johnson, Johnson, and Johnson Holubec, 1993). Exhibit 8.3 illustrates an example of a cognitive skill defined using a T-chart.

1. Select the cooperative skill to be taught.

2. Make a T-chart with your students:

   (a) Write the name of the skill and draw a large T underneath it.

   (b) Label the left side of the T with either "Looks like" or "Actions" and the right side with "Sounds like" or "Words." For young children, draw a picture of eyes and an ear; for older students you may use the terms "nonverbal" and "verbal."

   (c) Ask students, "If I were observing your groups, but couldn't hear what you were saying, what would you be doing that would show me you are using this skill?" Write these nonverbal behaviors on the left side.

   (d) Ask students, "What phrases or words would you be saying to each other that would tell me you are using this skill?" Write these verbal behaviors on the right side.

3. Tell students you will be observing their use of these verbal and nonverbal behaviors while they are working in groups.

4. Have students practice the skill during group work.

6. Observe and reinforce their use of the skill.

7. Have students reflect on their use of the skill and set goals for improvement.

8. Repeat this procedure until the skill is well integrated.

······················· EXHIBIT 8.2 **A Cyclical Model of Skill Development** ·······················

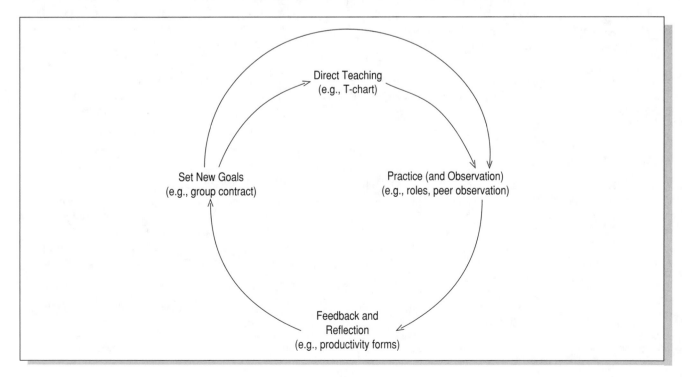

Modeling Skills

Students learn a lot about how to employ interpersonal and cognitive skills by observing them being used effectively. You should model the skills that you expect your students to display. You will be more likely to earn your students' respect if you "practice what you preach."

In presenting new content and procedures, you can explicitly incorporate many of the cognitive skills and strategies you wish your students to use during group work. For example, if you want your students to engage in critical questioning, justifying responses, and exploring multiple perspectives during group work, you must open your teaching to such practices as well. Ask questions that encourage your students to challenge textbook and lecture material and to probe underlying rationales.

You can also act out particular interpersonal and cognitive skills. One grade-three teacher, for example, constructed a T-chart with her students on the skill of disagreeing politely. She then decided to role-play it with a colleague. In the role play, the two teachers discussed where to eat supper. They exaggerated the gestures and phrases listed on the T-chart to illustrate "disagreeing politely" in action. The T-chart and modeling gave students a concrete picture of the skill and helped them to apply it during subsequent group work. As students observe a skill used frequently and in varied contexts, they will develop greater

awareness of its potential, and will be more likely to apply it in their own work.

Assigning Roles for Skill Practice

To encourage students to practice particular skills, roles can be designed and assigned to members of the group. These roles can be used to practice interpersonal skills (e.g., Encourager) or to engage students in more cognitively complex interactions (e.g., Prober). In addition to interpersonal and cognitive roles, you can assign functional roles that are closely related to the completion of the task (see Chapter 6: Fostering Positive Interdependence for sample role cards that you can distribute to your students).

Your selection of appropriate roles will depend on the type of task assigned. As your students gain more experience with roles, you may share responsibility for selection with them, eliciting from them the roles they think would best enhance the quality of their group work. You should stress to students that, in addition to the specific role they have been given, all group members are expected to participate in completing the work assigned, and all are responsible for how well they work together. It is a good idea to rotate the roles among group members so that each student has an opportunity to develop and practice the skills required for all the roles.

At the end of the session, you can have the group reflect on how well their members assumed their roles and how this helped them to work together

EXHIBIT 8.3 **Sample T-Chart of Cognitive Skills**

INTEGRATING IDEAS	
Looks like . . .	Sounds like . . .
eye contact gesturing to contributors of ideas eyebrows furrowed in thought	"How might we combine both of these ideas?" "That's related to what Julia said earlier..." "To add to what you were saying..." "What consensus can we reach that would include our ideas?"

effectively. As students learn the important aspects of each role, and what it contributes to the group's functioning, the lines separating the various roles may become blurred and role rigidity may be relaxed.

Observing and Giving Feedback

While students are involved in group work, practicing interpersonal and cognitive skills, it may be useful for you or a group member in the role of observer to record the behaviors of group members. After observation, students should receive concrete feedback on how they are progressing in their attainment of interpersonal and cognitive skills. Both the observations and feedback should be descriptive, not evaluative. For example, the observer should report how frequently group members exhibited the behaviors or actual examples of phrases or nonverbal behaviors, rather than make statements such as, "Marco is good at encouraging." Groups can then

use the results to reflect on their functioning and set their own personal and group goals for improvement. See Chapter 9: Evaluating and Reflecting for additional information and forms for observation of and feedback on interpersonal and cognitive skills.

FISHBOWLING

Fishbowling (Aronson, Blaney, Stephan, Sikes, and Snapp, 1978) is a fairly elaborate technique for observing and reflecting upon group interaction. For a fishbowling activity, a small group sits in a circle and discusses a topic or completes an activity, while the rest of the class sits in a larger circle surrounding the small group. The group on the outside observes the interactions of the group members inside the "fishbowl," using the observation criteria in Exhibit 8.4. Afterward, the outside group moves inside the fishbowl and reacts to the first group's process. Through focused observation and discussion, this technique helps sensitize students to the impor-

····· Exhibit 8.4 **Fishbowling Observation Form** ·····

1. **The energy level of the group.**
   Are participants sitting up or slouching?
   Do they appear interested, or do they seem withdrawn from the discussion?
   What might be the reasons for lack of interest *or* active participation?

2. **Group leadership.**
   Who starts the group moving on a particular topic? Can one person in the group easily be called the leader? Does the leader facilitate the group's discussion by summarizing what has been said so discussion may proceed?
   Does one member help the group stick to the topic and not wander off?

3. **The climate of listening in the group.**
   Are people making eye contact with one another and nodding?
   Are they rephrasing and summarizing what other people have said, indicating active listening?

4. **Participation in the group.**
   Are all members invited to share their ideas, or do they have to interrupt to say something?
   Does every member participate, or do some members sit silently?

5. **Other.**
   Who is talking to whom?
   What kind of nonverbal communication is used?
   Are there other important occurrences?

Source: Adapted from E. Aronson, N. Blaney, C. Stephan, J. Sikes, and M. Snapp, *The Jigsaw Classroom,* Beverly Hills, California: SAGE Publications, 1978, pp. 171-173. Used by permission.

tance of interaction and its impact on group climate and productivity.

MICROTEACHING ASSIGNMENTS AND VIDEO ANALYSIS

Microteaching assignments isolate particular skills and allow students to practice them in a safe, structured setting. Videotaping group interactions allows students to see themselves as they actually interact within their groups. When used in a nonthreatening atmosphere, this technique can provide constructive feedback to students on their interpersonal and cognitive skills, which may be superior to using only a student or a teacher's observations.

Reinforcing Desired Behaviors

You may elect to modify student behaviors by rewarding students tangibly or symbolically for engaging in positive behaviors. Using reinforcement principles generally means that students receive acknowledgment for acting properly, rather than criticism and punishment for acting improperly. You may first wish to establish a baseline—a record of the initial frequency of use of the skill among individuals or groups. You may then contract with students concerning the behaviors to be modified and the reward to be given for demonstrating the desired behaviors. You may give rewards frequently when the skills are first being acquired, then offer them intermittently, and eventually withdraw them.

Reflecting on Skill Use

Reserving some time during or at the end of a group activity for students to reflect on the cognitive and interpersonal skills they employed is well worth the effort. Reflection increases meta-cognitive awareness and helps students become more independent, self-directed learners. Johnson, Johnson, Stanne, and Garibaldi (1990) showed that as little as five minutes of group reflection per day can improve students' interpersonal skills.

At first, students may find reflection awkward. However, through regular practice in a climate of trust and openness, they will develop more confidence and comfort in talking about group functioning and skill development. In Chapter 9: Evaluating and Reflecting, we present various approaches to conducting reflection.

Setting Goals for Skill Refinement

Student reflection on interpersonal and cognitive skills should conclude with setting concrete goals. After discussing the quality of their interactions and learning, groups or individual group members can be asked to write down what skills they think they should improve, how they will work on them, and how they will assess whether they reach their objective. Goal setting completes the cycle of skill development and prepares the students for additional teaching or practice of the skill.

SUMMARY

Cooperative learning provides an ideal context for interpersonal and cognitive skill development. It provides a supportive environment for positive interactions and for generating new ideas. Students explore multiple perspectives and solutions to resolve both interpersonal and academic conflicts. It encourages students to reason aloud and critically examine their own opinions and beliefs. Rather than listening to the teacher most of the time, students are given increased opportunity to practice skills and, through feedback, to build upon each other's strengths and experiences.

Proponents of interpersonal and cognitive skill development employ the techniques and activities described in this chapter in various combinations. For example, Spencer Kagan's most recent approach to teaching interpersonal skills, "Skill of the Week" (Kagan, 1992), calls for the teacher to identify the skill that needs most work, use T-charts to teach specific phrases and behaviors that reflect the skill, use activities to highlight and practice the skill, reinforce students who use the skill, and have groups reflect on their use of the skill.

In this chapter, we have outlined some of the interpersonal and cognitive skills that students need to learn, and we have suggested different techniques and activities for developing them. Many of the activities in Chapter 4: Classbuilding and Teambuilding can also improve students' skills for cooperation, as can the reflection activities and forms described in Chapter 9: Evaluating and Reflecting.

REFLECTION ACTIVITIES

1. Referring to Exhibit 8.1, determine which interpersonal and cognitive skills you currently stress in your teaching. How much emphasis do you place on interpersonal and cognitive skills? Compare your results with those of a colleague. Reflect on the reasons why you emphasize the ones you do.

2. Choose one skill you think your students need to develop and design strategies for training that skill. Remember to include each of the stages in the cyclical model of skill development depicted in Exhibit 8.2.

3. Which cognitive skill do your students need to work on most? Design a cooperative learning activity that would help them practice that skill.

Cathie Archbould

9

Evaluating and Reflecting

WHAT WILL BE EVALUATED—INTERPERSONAL AND
ACADEMIC LEARNING?

•

WHO WILL EVALUATE PERFORMANCE—SELF, PEER,
OR TEACHER?

•

WHAT PROPORTION, IF ANY, OF INDIVIDUAL
GRADES WILL BE BASED ON GROUP PERFORMANCE?

•

HOW WILL I MONITOR AND ASSIST GROUPS IN
ACHIEVING THE LEARNING OBJECTIVES?

•

HOW WILL I GET STUDENTS TO REFLECT ON THEIR
INTERPERSONAL AND ACADEMIC DEVELOPMENT?

I n cooperative learning, as in most types of instruction, evaluation can be a problematic and complex issue. You must make decisions concerning why you evaluate, what you want to evaluate, who will evaluate, how to evaluate, and who will be evaluated. Having students reflect upon their learning is an important aspect of cooperative learning. In this chapter, we outline reasons for evaluating students, define terms related to evaluation and reflection, and explore techniques and issues regarding evaluation and reflection within cooperative learning.

WHY EVALUATE?

You can evaluate your students for a variety of purposes—to inform, select, direct, or motivate (Natriello, 1989). For information purposes, students are evaluated to determine if they have reached a certain level of mastery. For selection purposes, students are identified for entry into or promotion in a program of study. For direction purposes, evaluation provides feedback to you about whether your students are learning. With this information, you can realign your objectives or restructure your teaching, if necessary. Finally, evaluation can be conducted to motivate students to work toward academic goals.

Evaluation in cooperative learning is conducted most often to gain information about group members' understanding of the material, to motivate group members to work toward the group goal, or to provide direction for both your students and you. Evaluation in cooperative learning is less often used for selection purposes.

DEFINITIONS

There are several terms that are used in educational evaluation, such as evaluation, summative evaluation, formative evaluation, and reflection, and their meanings are often unclear. We will define these terms so you will understand what we mean when we use them in this chapter.

Evaluation refers to the appraisal of students' knowledge and skills. In cooperative learning, both content acquisition and interpersonal and cognitive skills should be considered for evaluation.

Summative evaluation determines students' grades. The word "summative" indicates that this type of evaluation sums up information about what a student has learned. When summative evaluation is based on a group product, as sometimes happens in cooperative learning, you should structure some form of individual accountability to ensure that all group members have completed their share of the task.

Keep in mind that not every cooperative activity needs to be graded. Students may engage in group work purely for discussion, for practice and rehearsal, or to enhance the classroom climate. Finally, if your students have had an opportunity to assess their learning through formative evaluation (see below) before summative evaluation takes place, and if the summative evaluation takes a varied, portfolio format (described under Evaluation by Teachers below), it will be perceived as a more accurate, fair, and less threatening judgment of their progress.

Formative evaluation gives feedback to teachers and students about their current progress, and provides information about where they need to improve their respective teaching and learning. For-mative evaluations can help you align your expectations with your students' outcomes, and help you adjust your pacing and/or teaching strategy. The feedback that students receive from formative evaluation can help them decide where they need to improve and, thus, where to focus their efforts.

Reflection refers to students' or groups' self-analysis of their learning for formative evaluation purposes. Sometimes referred to as processing, reflection involves students thinking about and discussing how effectively they performed as individuals and/or as a group. Students can reflect upon their learning of academic content and on their use of interpersonal and cognitive skills. Reflection plays a critical role in cooperative learning by helping group members learn to work together effectively.

WHAT WILL BE EVALUATED?

At the outset of an instructional unit, you should clearly establish the objectives—how learning will be assessed—and the criteria for meeting those objectives. Sometimes instructional objectives are set solely by you. However, if you want your students to learn to take greater responsibility for their learning, then you should consider involving them in the setting of instructional objectives. However they are determined, the objectives, criteria, and procedures must be communicated to all students in order to avoid misunderstandings about the evaluation process.

Frequently, educational objectives and evaluation are defined solely in terms of academic skills or content to be acquired. Be sure to include interpersonal and cognitive skill objectives as well, if you intend to include them in your teaching and evaluation. Teachers are sometimes required to report on their students' interpersonal skills, especially at the elementary level.

WHO WILL EVALUATE AND HOW?

You, and sometimes your students, will need to decide whether evaluation will be conducted by the teacher, by team members or classmates, or by self-assessment. Decisions must also be taken on how evaluation will be carried out, such as by portfolio assessment, observation and feedback, reflection activities, and so on.

Evaluation by Teachers

You can assess your students' learning by building a portfolio of their test scores, assignments, homework, projects, and writing samples. You can also assess your students' learning process by observing them as they work in groups. Using both these approaches will give you a more accurate picture of your students' progress.

PORTFOLIO ASSESSMENT

One alternative to frequent testing is to use individual portfolios comprised of varied samples of students' work. These portfolios can also include copies of work completed in a group and feedback from observations. Portfolios allow for a more balanced and thorough evaluation of your students' learning. They may also include results from self- and peer evaluations—techniques that we will describe below.

OBSERVATION AND FEEDBACK

To supplement traditional evaluation procedures, such as testing and collecting samples of students' work, you may wish to assess learning through direct observation during group work and provide formative feedback to the group. Observing also provides you with feedback about the appropriateness of the task or the assignment.

The behaviors or skills you want to observe should be clearly defined. For example, looking to see if "students are getting along" is much too vague to help you give specific feedback to groups. A checklist with the behavior "criticizes ideas not people" is more specific and easier to observe. Exhibit 9.1 shows a structured observation form that can be used to record the frequency with which individual students use specific interpersonal and cognitive skills, such as encouraging. In addition, Clarke, Wideman, and Eadie (1990) offer the following suggestions for conducting systematic observations.

1. Tell students what task and social skills will be observed.

2. Decide how many groups to observe and for how long.

3. Be unobtrusive; avoid hovering over student groups while they are working.

4. Prepare observation sheets, such as checklists, in advance.

5. Use one observation sheet for each group.

6. Make notes or jot down questions that come to mind which may not fit into the categories on the observation sheet.

You need to set aside time to consider the observations you have made and share them with your students. This enables you and your students to clarify problems, consider solutions, and set new goals to improve how their groups function.

You need to decide whether your feedback will merely describe what occurred or whether you wish to incorporate praise, encouragement, rewards, and criticism. For example, you may smile, or recognize a group by stating, "Your group should be proud of how well it negotiated your group's tasks," or provide rewards, such as bonus points.

You can give feedback to the whole class or to particular groups about the effective and ineffective behaviors you observed. However, avoid singling out specific groups or individuals for criticism. General feedback, such as, "You were a good group today" is usually less effective than specific feedback, such as, "I noticed that you took the time to make sure everyone understood the material." Whenever possible, you should emphasize effective behaviors rather than focus on negative ones.

If a group is experiencing difficulty, you may decide to intervene to give immediate feedback. However, frequent intervention by you may lead to reduced cooperation within the group and may prevent your students from learning from one another by giving them the message that you are the only one who can solve their problems (Cohen, 1994a). One way of handling task-related questions without intervening is to redirect them to the groups. Try not to solve a group's problem yourself; give the group real responsibility for finding its own solution.

················· EXHIBIT 9.1 **Sample Teacher and Student Observation Form** ····················

Encouraging		
Group members	Frequency	Examples
Raphael	///	High-five signal; "Uh huh"
Mahmoud	/	"Good idea!"
Alain		
Zito	////	"Yeah"; nods

Source: Adapted from D. W. Johnson, R. T. Johnson, and E. Johnson Holubec, *Cooperation in the Classroom*, Revised Edition, Edina, Minnesota: Interaction Book Company, 1988. Copyright © 1988 by David W. Johnson. Used by permission.

··················· EXHIBIT 9.2 **Group Productivity Reflection Form** ·····················

Your name: _____

Group name: _____

ASSESSMENT OF GROUP PRODUCTIVITY

Directions: Please evaluate the functioning of your group on the task just completed. Circle the number that best represents how you would rate the performance of your group.

1. Effective use of time:

1	2	3	4	5
much time spent without purpose		did well, once ideas clear		no wasted effort— stayed on target

2. Development of ideas:

1	2	3	4	5
little done to generate ideas		ideas imposed by one or two members		ideas encouraged and well explored

3. Ability to decide issues:

1	2	3	4	5
poor resolution— couldn't agree		made compromises to get job done		genuine support and agreement

4. Group involvement:

1	2	3	4	5
little group interaction— everyone worked alone		one or two members took over—others left out		everyone participated in group product

5. Overall productivity:

1	2	3	4	5
did not accomplish our goal or task		barely accomplished our goal or task		held a highly productive session

You might establish a policy of answering questions only if all students in the group agree that they have tried to solve the problem but do not have the answer.

If groups encounter problems with interpersonal skills, your first intervention would include giving feedback on group functioning or teaching the skills directly (see Chapter 8: Developing Interpersonal and Cognitive Skills). If your students are still unable to solve the problem, then consider assigning roles to students that will keep them on task, breaking the group into two smaller groups, or changing the composition of the group.

Individual and Group Reflection

Traditionally, evaluation has been conducted solely by the teacher. Inviting students to participate in the evaluation process gives them a sense of control (Moorman and Dishon, 1983). Students get the message that their opinions are valued and develop ownership of their learning. In addition, students' independence in learning is cultivated by involving them in formative evaluation through individual or group reflection.

In cooperative learning, group members are often asked to reflect on their skills at working together. How well did our group function? How did each member contribute to the effectiveness of the group's interactions? How can we improve our skill at working together next time? Three to Glow and One to Grow is a procedure that allows students to reflect upon how their groups function. Following a group activity, students are asked to respond to the following prompts: (a) list three things that your group did that helped the learning process, and (b) name one area in which your group can improve.

If you have explicitly taught or defined particular skills in advance, more specific questions can be asked. For example, if you have taught "encouraging equal participation," you could ask your students to reflect on whether all their group's members participated equally during group work, or whether one member dominated, while another was left out. Sometimes, you may wish to have students complete structured reflection forms. Older students can reflect on their group productivity by using the form in Exhibit 9.2. Exhibit 9.3 shows a form elementary students can use to rate themselves on the interpersonal skills they displayed during a group activity.

However the reflection is structured, you should also encourage groups to think about how they used the skills and to set goals for how they can improve in the future (see Exhibit 9.4).

It can be difficult for students of any age to discuss the effectiveness of their group behaviors frankly. If a trusting relationship has been established, an honest and open evaluation is more likely (see Chapter 4: Classbuilding and Teambuilding).

Another way to promote reflection is through the use of dialogue journals. In dialogue journals, students write about their experiences in group work, assess their contributions and those of their teammates, and describe their feelings about the process. You read and respond to the students' comments. Depending on the level of your students and the degree of trust that exists, you might have base-group members read and respond to each others' journals.

Students can also be involved in conducting structured observations of their peers engaging in group work. When students are the observers of group work, you should provide clear guidelines and teach the specific skills that they will need to be effective observers. We suggest the following steps in structuring peer observations.

1. Select one student from the group to be the observer, either randomly or by having students take turns.

2. Explain the role of the observer. The observer does not participate in group interactions but only records particular behaviors specified beforehand. Stress the importance of nonevaluative feedback statements.

3. Select a predetermined skill or skills or have the groups decide what skill(s) they want to focus on. Keep the number of behaviors small, especially for novice observers.

4. The observer indicates on a form, such as the one in Exhibit 9.1, each time a group member engages in the particular behavior(s) being

observed. The observer, however, does not intervene.

5. Individually, students reflect on how they used the skills that were focused on.

6. The observer then gives feedback. Statements such as, "I saw Zito encouraging four times," are better than, "Zito, you encouraged the most." It is very important to be nonjudgmental when giving feedback.

7. Together, group members decide what skills they need to work on to improve their group interactions and what specific goals to set.

8. The role of observer is rotated so that all group members can learn how to give and receive feedback.

Self- and Peer Evaluation

Some teachers view student participation in grading as part of the process of making schools more dem-ocratic. You can have individual students evaluate their own performance, group members rate each other's participation in group activities, and/or have all students evaluate group projects or presentations.

At first, teachers and students are often uncomfortable with the redistribution of responsibility for evaluating students' work. Sometimes teachers are not sure whether students are capable and responsible enough to evaluate their peers. Students may lack experience in peer evaluation and may worry about offending their classmates. Your students may experience difficulty evaluating one another, especially when the evaluation is negative. To make the evaluation a more instructive exercise for your students, and to relieve the pressure they feel when evaluating each other for marks at the conclusion of a project, have your students conduct self- and peer assessments several times throughout the project. This will provide in-progress feedback on each member's contributions, help students realign expectations and effort, and allow students to set

· Exhibit 9.3 **Individual Reflection of Interpersonal Skills** ·

Color in the boxes to show how much you did the following things.				
a great deal				
somewhat				
not at all				
	I listened to my teammates.	I shared with my teammates.	I helped my teammates.	I enjoyed today's work.

new goals. You can then collect these self- and peer assessments to use for final evaluation purposes.

Often when students complete group projects, it is impossible to determine if everyone carried his or her weight or if one or two students seemed to do most of the work. To assess individual contributions to a group product, have your students assess how much each teammate contributed to the group product (see Exhibit 9.5).

You can also have classmates evaluate group presentations or projects (see Exhibit 9.6). These evaluations can be returned to the group to reflect upon or be used by you in determining the group's grade.

INDIVIDUAL VERSUS GROUP GRADES

A critical issue when evaluating student outcomes in cooperative learning is individual versus group grades. To what extent, if at all, should evaluation of group performance be a component of individual students' grades?

Some educators believe that successful team work is important and use group grades to motivate students to work together. Therefore, they argue, group grades should be an integral component of student summative evaluation. Exhibit 9.7 contains suggestions for incorporating group grades into students' individual evaluations.

You should be cautious when using group grades. Some educators believe that while group members should be responsible for the learning within the group, summative evaluation should remain individual. Peer encouragement can turn to overwhelming peer pressure and resentment toward the weaker student if everyone's grade depends on one student. This can lead to the refusal of students to work with certain classmates.

SUMMARY

Evaluation is a difficult issue. Making evaluation as clear and objective as possible helps ease the difficulty. In this chapter, we have presented the why,

EXHIBIT 9.4 **Group Reflection Form**

Group Reflection Form					
What happened in my group?	never 1	2	3	4	always 5
1. Did everyone have the chance to speak?	1	2	3	4	5
2. Did we listen to each other?	1	2	3	4	5
3. Did any member(s) dominate?	1	2	3	4	5
4. Did we encourage each other?	1	2	3	4	5
5. Did we help each other?	1	2	3	4	5

MY GOALS for improving cooperative skills
During the next group activity, I will:

1. _____

2. _____

my name _____

my group's name _____

who, what, and how of evaluation in cooperative learning. Although we have provided some examples of evaluation forms and procedures (such as portfolio assessment, observation and feedback, individual and group assessment, and self- and peer evaluation), you are encouraged to adapt these to create your own instruments according to your teaching objectives. You should consider what academic material and interpersonal and cognitive skills will be evaluated. You should also consider

···················· EXHIBIT 9.5 **Teammate and Self-Evaluation Form** ····················

TEAMMATE AND SELF-EVALUATION SHEET

Project title _____

Teammate names: Your name:
1. _____   _____
2. _____
3. _____
4. _____

Please assign the ratings you feel appropriate for each of your teammates and yourself in the categories below. Use the following grade scale in making your judgments:

- A+/A   exceptional
- A−/B+   good
- B   acceptable
- B−/C+   marginal
- C   poor
- F   no contribution

	Self Rating	Teammate Ratings			
		# 1	# 2	# 3	# 4
Attended planned meetings.					
Prepared for his or her contribution to project.					
Gave supportive and helpful suggestions and feedback.					
Allowed and encouraged others to present their ideas; did not dominate or intimidate.					
Overall Rating of Participation and Contribution					
Additional comments:					

Source: Adapted from S. Kagan, *Cooperative Learning: Resources for Teachers*, San Juan Capistrano, California: Resources for Teachers, 1990. Copyright © 1990 by Spencer Kagan. Used by permission.

EXHIBIT 9.6 **Presentation Evaluation Form**

PRESENTATION EVALUATION FORM

Presenting Group: _____   Topic: _____

Your name: _____

What was one particularly interesting thing you learned during the presentation?

_____

_____

_____

What question would you like to ask the presenters about their topic?

_____

_____

_____

What did you like best about the format of the presentation?

_____

_____

_____

What do you think would have improved the presentation?

_____

_____

_____

EXHIBIT 9.7 **Ways to Incorporate Group Grades**

Some suggestions for incorporating grades in the spirit of enhancing positive interdependence include each student receiving:

1. an individual score plus bonus points based on a pre-set criterion met by all members of the group
2. an individual score plus the average score for the group
3. the average improvement score of all group members
4. an individual score plus bonus points based on the group's average improvement score
5. the group score from a single group product, with peer assessment of the contribution of each member
6. one member's randomly selected score

Source: Adapted from D. W. Johnson, R. T. Johnson, and E. Johnson Holubec, *Cooperation in the Classroom*, Revised Edition, Edina, Minnesota: Interaction Book Company, 1988, pp. 4:28–4:30. Copyright © 1988 by David W. Johnson. Used by permission.

how your students will reflect upon their learning and group processes, how they will be involved in the evaluation process, and what types of evaluation you will use.

REFLECTION ACTIVITIES

1. What skills do you think your students need to learn? Focusing on one skill, design three different evaluation forms for that skill: an evaluation for you, a self-evaluation for each student, and a peer evaluation for the students' classmates.

2. What percentage, if any, of your students' grades do you think should be obtained from a group product? Discuss this with your colleagues and with your students. Do they agree with your percentage?

3. Students often have difficulty assessing their teammates. They may assign overly positive assessments and may not be willing to negatively evaluate students who are not contributing to the learning of the group. With a colleague, brainstorm some steps you can take to avoid these difficulties.

Brett Lamb

10

Using Cooperative Learning in Your Classroom

How will I select appropriate content and tasks for cooperative group work?

•

How will I adapt my materials for cooperative group work?

•

How will I match my learning objectives to appropriate cooperative learning structures?

•

How can I find support for my implementation of cooperative learning?

•

What are some possible solutions to difficulties I might encounter?

Having read about what cooperative learning is, how it works, and what your choices are in implementing it, you may still be thinking to yourself, This sounds great, but what about *my* classroom? How should I start? How can I implement my curricula cooperatively? Where will I find support for my efforts as I struggle through the initial stages? How will I continue to develop my knowledge and skills in cooperative learning? And last, but not least, how will I handle all those potential problems I may be faced with?

This chapter begins with suggestions for how to take the first step in implementing cooperative learning. Next, we provide guidelines and a format for creating your own cooperative learning lessons based on your curriculum. This format will help you apply and integrate the essential elements of cooperative learning covered in the previous chapters. Then we will present issues and problems experienced by other teachers implementing cooperative learning and discuss some of the solutions they employed to overcome these challenges. Finally, we will discuss how collegial support can help you persist and refine your skills in cooperative learning.

THE FIRST STEPS

If you are new to cooperative learning, you may find the following suggestions useful (see Exhibit 10.1). Start where you feel comfortable. If there is a particular subject or class you feel most at ease with, then try your first activity with that subject or class. This way, you can focus on the cooperative activity design, rather than struggle with the content or a difficult group of students. As you gain confidence and experience, you will be ready to try an activity in more challenging circumstances.

Start small. Limit the size of the group, the duration of the activity, and the complexity of the task. Try one simple, short activity before committing yourself to anything more ambitious. Johnson, Johnson, and Johnson Holubec (1992) suggest starting with pairs. Kagan's Think-Pair-Share (1990) (see Chapter 4: Classbuilding and Teambuilding), in which students think about an item, tell a partner about it, and then tell the whole class anything they feel is particularly interesting, is an easy-to-use structure suitable for all age and ability levels. Remember, cooperative learning may also be new to your students and you won't want to overwhelm them either.

Don't feel as though you need to include a cooperative activity in every class. After your first experience with a cooperative activity, take ample time to reflect on what was successful and what you'd like to improve the next time. Repeating what you did well is as important as overcoming some difficulties you experienced. Giving yourself sufficient time for reflection before implementing another activity will provide you with valuable insights that will increase your chances of success.

Persevere. It takes time to feel comfortable using new techniques and to adapt them to your teaching situation. Be patient; don't give up if everything doesn't go smoothly from the start.

INTEGRATING COOPERATIVE LEARNING WITH YOUR CURRICULUM

You want to begin using cooperative learning, but don't know how to implement it with the existing workbooks, texts, or learning packets that you have on hand. What do you do? Examine the materials and resources available to see if they have been

·············· EXHIBIT 10.1 **Hints for Getting Started with Cooperative Learning** ····················

- Increase your chances of success! Start with a class or subject that you are most comfortable with.
- Start small! Try pairs first and move to groups of three or four later.
- Keep it short! Begin with a ten-minute activity to see how your students respond.
- Keep it simple! If your first attempts are too complicated, your students will get frustrated.
- Use cooperatively structured tasks! For successful cooperative learning, you need tasks designed for use in groups, not for individual use.
- Vary your approach! Experimenting with different methods will enable you to discover which methods will help your students reach particular learning objectives.
- Reflect on your implementation! After a cooperative learning activity, take time to celebrate your successes or find solutions for overcoming difficulties.
- Set realistic goals! Plan ahead and set attainable goals for your next cooperative learning activity.
- Persevere! It takes time to feel comfortable using new techniques and to adapt them to your teaching situation.

designed for use by groups of students. If not, you will need to adapt them for cooperative group work. This section will help you select and design activities suitable for effective group work.

Many instructional programs incorporate the ability to work in groups as an objective, and cooperative learning methods have either been integrated with the curriculum or can be added easily; others have been planned along individualistic lines and need to be adapted. Some cooperative learning methods have developed materials in specific curriculum areas. You will find references to materials and lesson plans at the conclusion of this book in Appendix B: Selected Resources.

Keep in mind that cooperative learning can be integrated in many different ways, and need not be a lengthy group project lasting several periods. For example, if you do decide that some whole-class lecturing is required, you will involve your students more actively by intermittently using brief student interaction techniques, such as Think-Pair-Share, that require students to respond to what you've said or to generate questions or predictions about upcoming information.

Selecting Appropriate Tasks for Group Work

As you consider your course objectives and the material you plan to cover in the next class, one of the decisions you will need to make is what tasks or materials will be appropriate for group work. Cooperative learning is now one of many teaching strategies available to you and will not be appropriate for all learning tasks. With experience, you may discover that more learning objectives than you had imagined can be effectively achieved through student interaction, but there will still be content that is best communicated through teacher lectures, individual seat work, computer-assisted instruction, or other pedagogical methods.

How do you decide what to teach using cooperative learning strategies? First, do your students have sufficient prior knowledge among themselves to complete the task? If not, are appropriate resources available to them? If they do not have the

required information and have nowhere to seek it, they will continue to depend upon you for this knowledge. You may find yourself running from group to group answering the same questions or explaining the same concept. This is clearly frustrating for both you and your students.

Next, consider the task. Can the task you have in mind be better completed by an individual than by a group? If so, chances are when asked to work together, students may find very creative ways of completing the work alone. Teacher-imposed structures can help students work together on a group task, but nothing is as powerful as a task that truly profits from a group endeavour. Is the task too large or too complex for one individual to complete? Does the task require a variety of talents, abilities, or perspectives, all of which are not likely possessed by one individual? Is the exchange between students mutually beneficial? If the answers to one or more of these questions is yes, you have hit on ideal material for group work.

In Chapter 2: Group Processes and Productivity, we presented an overview of some theory and research on the nature of tasks and the potential productivity of groups that can help you decide on the suitability of your tasks for group work. Can the task be broken down into subcomponents? Which is more important—the quantity produced or the quality of performance? Is there a group product? Can team members decide how to contribute? How are individual inputs related to the group's product? In addition, Chapter 2 summarized the effects of group productivity for six types of tasks. Additive tasks, which require individual inputs to yield a group product, result in a product superior to that produced by the strongest member working alone. In contrast, unitary conjunctive tasks, which require that each individual complete them, typically result in a group product equal to that produced by the weakest group member working alone.

INTERACTIVE GROUP PROJECTS
Sharan (1990) outlined eight principles that justify the use of interactive group projects. This checklist can be useful when considering whether your assignment is appropriate for group exploration.

1. Each individual's knowledge or experience is required.

2. The final product is collective and dependent upon each individual doing his or her part.

3. The task involves choices and decisions to be made.

4. There are no right or wrong answers; questions are either open-ended or there are multiple ways of getting to the right answers.

5. The task involves multiple modes of expression, learning styles, or abilities.

6. Individual group members are given time to generate and prepare their ideas.

7. There is closure to the activity involving a linking of tasks that provides a reason for listening to others and completing one's own part of the task.

8. The teacher shares responsibility with the students for the lesson and the direction it takes.

REVIEW AND REHEARSAL

Cooperative learning strategies may also be used for review and rehearsal of course material. Indeed, students often spontaneously form study groups or meet with a friend to prepare for a test. This type of interactive group work involves different requirements from exploratory group work. Guidelines for peer rehearsal or review activities are outlined below.

1. Clear right or wrong answers to verify members' responses are available within the group or are provided.

2. All group members are challenged and can benefit from the review.

3. Students have developed skills in justifying their responses and explaining their rationale to others.

4. Students are committed to and held responsible for helping other group members learn.

At first, it may be difficult to judge what material will work best for cooperative group work. Consider the guidelines offered above, make your decision, and go with it. Then take time to reflect on what was most successful and what you would want to modify next time. Teachers have often told us that at first it was difficult for them to conceive of alternative ways of teaching material they had traditionally taught via lectures. Yet, as they acquired experience in using group work, ideas for group activities began to spring to mind as they prepared their lessons.

Adapting Materials and Designing Cooperative Activities

Teachers sometimes feel cooperative learning is a completely new method that requires them to start from scratch in designing their classes and creating materials. In fact, most current texts and other learning material can be easily used or adapted for group work. Some strategies you might consider include:

- dividing the material into sections and assigning each section to a different group member to read and prepare to teach to others

- assigning each group member a different exploration topic or mathematics problem from the end of a textbook chapter, which all members would review and discuss in their small group

- having groups read the course material and develop their own discussion questions that they could exchange with other groups

As you can see, *how* you use the material and structure the group task is particularly important.

Each chapter of Part Two: Implementation highlighted one component of cooperative learning and presented questions that you should consider when using cooperative group activities with your students. Now it's time to put it all together. We developed the questions in Exhibit 10.2 to help you do so.

Following these guidelines, fill in Exhibit 10.3 as you consider and specify how each cooperative learning component is structured into your activity. It does not provide space for a description of the activity (that is, its procedures, steps, and time for each step), so you may wish to do this on a separate sheet.

When first starting out with cooperative learning, we suggest you adapt one of the sample activity structures presented throughout this book. Because the basic structure of the activity is already provided, you have only to incorporate your own course content to prepare it. Alternatively, you may have already used some group work with your students, but you may now wish to structure it more clearly following cooperative learning principles. In this case, work directly with the planning guidelines to ensure that each component has been included. For example, could a teambuilding activity be added as a first step to help the group members establish good working relations? Can you enhance the degree of positive interdependence in the activity by assigning roles or dividing up the task? Have you considered how you will ensure individual accountability? If you're unsure about your options for a given component, go back and review the corresponding chapter and the examples provided in it.

·············· EXHIBIT 10.2 **Planning Guidelines** ··············

Grade and Subject:	
Content:	
Group task: *What must the group accomplish?*	
Estimated time for entire activity: *How much time will I need to allot for the activity, including grouping, giving instructions, carrying out the task, and reflecting and evaluating?*	
Resources/materials: *What resources and materials are needed for this activity?*	
Grouping *How many students per group will I assign?* *What students' characteristics will I consider when assigning them to groups?* *Will I use heterogeneous or homogeneous groups?* *What technique will I use to group the students?* *How long will the students work in the same group?*	**Positive Interdependence** *How will I structure the activity to ensure active participation of all students?* *Will I use group rewards to motivate students to work together?* *Will I divide the task or assign roles?* *Will I have students share materials?* *How will I encourage students to recognize the benefits of cooperating?*
Individual Accountability *How will I prevent the problem of free riders and domineering group members?* *How will I ensure that each student assumes responsibility for:* 1. *his or her learning and completing his or her share of the task?* 2. *helping other members learn and accomplish their share of the task?*	**Interpersonal and Cognitive Skills** *How will I select the interpersonal and cognitive skills to be developed?* *How will I develop students' awareness of their use of these skills?* *What techniques will I use to help students develop the selected skills?* *What behaviors do I expect to see the students engaged in during group work?*
Evaluation and Reflection *What will be evaluated—interpersonal and academic learning?* *Who will evaluate performance—self, peer, or the teacher?* *What proportion, if any, of individual grades will be based on group performance?* *How will I monitor and assist groups in achieving the learning objectives?* *How will I have students reflect on their interpersonal and academic development?*	**Extension Activity** *What additional task will I assign to the groups who finish early?*

When designing your activity don't forget to consider carefully the prerequisite knowledge and skills. No matter how well designed the cooperative activity, if your students are not sufficiently prepared to complete the task, it will be a frustrating and unrewarding experience for both you and them. Remember, if you notice that many groups are experiencing similar difficulties during group work, stop the activity and provide clarification of the task or content. Maintaining flexibility is important in teaching, so don't hesitate even to postpone a planned activity until the following class if you feel your students are not yet ready for it.

Finally, keep in mind that some groups will finish the activity before others. For these students, it's best to have an extension task available that will challenge them and further develop their understanding of the material. For example, if the groups had been working on strategies for solving word problems in mathematics, each member could be

···· EXHIBIT 10.3 **Planning Form** ····

Grade and subject:	
Content:	
Group task:	
Estimated time for entire activity:	
Resources/materials:	
Grouping	Positive Interdependence
Individual Accountability	Interpersonal and Cognitive Skills
Evaluation and Reflection	Extension Activity

asked to create an additional problem, exchange it with another member, and solve the problem they received. Or, in language arts, if a group finishes discussing a decision made by a literary character from a novel, members could be asked to discuss any similar situations they have been in and how they reacted. An extension task, therefore, performs two functions. First, it discourages students from racing through an activity in order to obtain free time. Second, it encourages more able students who have worked well and efficiently together to expand their learning, thus making more productive use of class time.

Reflecting on the Cooperative Activity Experience

After implementing an activity, you should take some time to reflect on the experience and consider the outcomes of each decision you made regarding the components of cooperative learning. For example, was group size appropriate? Did the positive interdependence structures result in everyone participating actively? What aspects were particularly successful? What changes might improve this activity? These and other questions are included in the Reflection Guidelines in Exhibit 10.4. Use the Reflections Form in Exhibit 10.5 to organize and record your thoughts.

When cooperative learning activities are well planned, consistent with your approach to teaching, and appropriate to the learning situation, students are usually willing to work together. Once you have mastered one or two strategies, plan to add more to your teaching repertoire. Be patient with yourself! It may take several years to become proficient in cooperative learning. Follow the same steps that you took in choosing your first cooperative learning activity, carefully considering your options in cooperative activity design, and taking time to reflect upon your experiences.

TROUBLE-SHOOTING

Teachers who are incorporating cooperative learning into their teaching strategies are faced with many questions. Teachers must evaluate their learning objectives, assess the effectiveness of the strategies chosen, and reflect on their appropriateness to the curriculum. In this section, we address commonly asked questions by teachers implementing cooperative learning in their classes.

Organizational Issues

How you organize your classroom affects the success of your cooperative learning implementation. Dealing with space and time constraints are challenges that you might encounter.

SPACE CONSTRAINTS

How do I physically arrange my classroom? Although it is much easier if the desks can be rearranged into small clusters so that students face one another, you can implement cooperative learning in a classroom where the desks are bolted to the floor. Not all grouping techniques require rearranging the classroom. Informal groups, in which students briefly consult with a neighbor, require the least amount of change in the classroom configuration.

For brief activities, students do not need to move desks and chairs but can simply move themselves around one desk for consultation. For longer activities, have students move only their chairs to meet around one desk or have them meet in groups seated on the floor. This cuts down on both time and noise. If your students are capable of working with minimal supervision, you can let them work in the hall or library. Finally, if you are making any permanent changes to the configuration of your classroom, caretaking staff should be consulted.

TIME CONSTRAINTS

How do I fit cooperative learning into my already overloaded curriculum? Cooperative learning is not a separate subject. Lessons structured cooperatively should be a part of your daily plan. Depending on the grade level, the curriculum to be covered, and the individual teacher, the timeline for cooperative learning is different. Some activities, when structured cooperatively, take longer to complete than if they are done individually, while others take less time. If one of your goals is to teach higher-order cognitive or interpersonal skills, and you have time for students to discuss and grapple with complex issues, cooperative learning can provide practice in these skills. However, if there is a great deal of pressure to cover the course content, then it would be best to use cooperative learning only for short, structured activities. Considerable time can be saved if you have students do individual preparation or follow-up work as homework assignments. Individual preparation improves the quality of the group interaction, enhances individual accountability, and helps make the most of the class time available for group work. Finally, as students

···················· EXHIBIT 10.4 **Reflection Guidelines** ····················

Grade and subject:	Time allotted: *Was the time sufficient?*
Textbook reference:	
Objective(s): *Were the objectives achieved?*	
Group task: *Was the task appropriate for group work?*	
Prerequisite knowledge/skills: *Were the students sufficiently prepared?*	
Resources: *Were the resources provided sufficient?*	

IMPORTANT COMPONENTS TO CONSIDER IN YOUR LESSON PLAN

Grouping *Was the grouping effective?* *What were the successes? the difficulties?*	Positive Interdependence *Did all group members actively participate and contribute to completion of the task?* *Did group members help each other accomplish the learning objectives?*
Individual Accountability *Were students' individual responsibilities clear to them?* *Did each student successfully complete his or her task and learn the material?* *Were there any free riders? Did anyone dominate?*	Interpersonal and Cognitive Skills *Did I determine and review the required target skill(s)?* *Did students engage in the behaviors I anticipated?* *What other interpersonal and cognitive skills did I observe?* *What skills need further work?*
Teacher's Role *Did I model the task?* *Did students immediately move on task?* *How did I monitor for skill development?* *Did I intervene—why, with whom, how?*	Evaluation and Reflection *Were the groups productive?* *Did I have students reflect on their learning and interaction?* *What sort of feedback did I give the students on their performance?*

Extension Activity
Did I provide the groups with an extension activity? Was it engaging and challenging?

Successes *What aspects of this activity were particularly successful?*	Recommended Changes *What difficulties did I experience?* *What changes might improve this activity?* *What considerations should I keep in mind for future activities?*

develop group interaction skills, they will become faster and more efficient during group work.

Classroom Management

Classroom management is an issue of considerable concern to many teachers. In your new role as a facilitator in the cooperative classroom, you may need to alter how you deal with noise, discipline, and pacing.

TOO MUCH NOISE

What do I do about increased noise level during group work? There is definitely more noise in a

·············· EXHIBIT 10.5 **Reflections Form** ··············

Grade and subject:	Time allotted:	
Textbook reference:		
Objective(s):		
Group task:		
Prerequisite knowledge/skills:		
Resources:		
IMPORTANT COMPONENTS TO CONSIDER IN YOUR LESSON PLAN		
Grouping	Positive Interdependence	
Individual Accountability	Interpersonal and Cognitive Skills	
Teacher's Role	Evaluation and Reflection	
Extension Activity		
Successes	Recommended Changes	

cooperatively structured classroom than in one where students work individually. When there are thirty-two students working in small groups of four, it means that about eight students are speaking at any given time. You may recognize this new noise as constructive, but nonetheless it is noise. You must communicate to the principal, fellow teachers, and parents that the increased noise is not evidence of lack of control, but of students actively engaged in learning.

In order to reduce the amount of noise, some teachers use a large noise meter posted in the room. Anyone who feels that it is getting too noisy can raise the red line on the meter to indicate to classmates that they should speak more quietly. Other teachers use a large, red circle, or some other cue, which is given to a group that is making too much noise. The circle is removed when the noise level goes down. This technique clearly indicates the noise problem, but doesn't interrupt the group's interaction. Some teachers challenge students to speak quietly enough so that only their group can hear their interactions. You can encourage your students to use "arm's length," "twelve inch," or "twenty centimeter" voices. Another solution is to assign the task of noise control to one member of each group. A Captain Quiet or a Sound Manager is responsible for keeping the noise level at an acceptable level by reminding group members to keep their voices down, to whisper, or to lean forward when interacting. However, there may be times when you simply must stop the activity and discuss the noise problem with students before resuming.

MAINTAINING DISCIPLINE

How do I maintain discipline in a cooperative learning classroom? Students have a natural need to interact with each other. Cooperative learning gives them a constructive outlet for this need and usually decreases disruptive, off-task behavior. In cooperative learning, teachers and students must learn to share responsibility for learning and discipline. Because many discipline problems stem from a power struggle with the teacher, giving students more autonomy and responsibility actually reduces some discipline problems.

You can begin this shift in responsibility by having your students create their own group and class behavior guidelines (see Chapter 4: Classbuilding and Teambuilding). It is also helpful to engage in other classbuilding and teambuilding activities to build a sense of cohesion and mutual commitment to learning. It may take some time before you feel comfortable with this shift in power structure within your classroom, but don't give up.

PACING GROUPS

How do I deal with different groups finishing at different times? In any classroom activity, teachers are faced with some students finishing the task before others. Sometimes groups rush through an activity superficially, without taking care to involve every group member and to ensure that everyone understands. When a group claims to have finished the task, first verify that everyone in the group has in fact completed and understood the work.

For those groups that have finished early, it's always a good idea to have on hand an extension activity related to the content. This doesn't require the preparation of a completely new activity; it may simply mean offering the group a new challenge based on the materials they have just used. Sometimes, you may want to involve these students as helpers for the other groups that have not finished. Be careful, however, to monitor whether this involvement is useful, rather than disruptive.

Dealing with Diverse Students

You will undoubtedly encounter students with varied charactistics. You will need to deal with various uncooperative behaviors, such as rejecting group members and refusing to participate. Some students may be shy or may lack the skills to participate effectively. Others may attempt to dominate their team mates. Evaluating these diverse students in a group context can be a challenge.

CLIQUES

How do I keep cliques from interfering with effective group interactions? When students are allowed to group themselves, they often choose to work only with their friends, thereby promoting the development of cliques and rejecting some students. It also restricts their opportunities to benefit from the diverse viewpoints that a mix of students brings to a group.

To give students practice working with diverse others, you will usually want to assign students to groups yourself (see Chapter 5: Grouping Students). Students will be more accepting of their assigned teammates if, when introducing cooperative group work to your students, you make it clear to them that in your class each student will work with every other student at one time or another. You should indicate that this will enable them to develop skills in working with others, something they will need in every aspect of their lives.

RELUCTANT PARTICIPANTS

How do I develop teams with students who do not want to be part of a cooperative group? When introducing cooperative learning, be sure to highlight for students the advantages of working in groups. For example, you can explain to students the importance of teamwork for many business and professional careers. If there are still some students who do not want to participate in group work, you may want to discuss their reservations with them privately to determine the source of their hesitation. Keep these reasons in mind when considering the following options.

Students who are reluctant participants sometimes need to experience success with cooperative learning. You can build an activity that highlights the talents or strengths of unwilling participants. You can also create situations in which students develop trust in each other before they work together on academic content. If you feel a student may be willing to work with one other student, then consider beginning with pair work. You cannot force a student who adamantly refuses to participate. Therefore, if all else fails, give this student the option of sitting out an activity. However, we suggest that you do not modify the requirements of a group task to accommodate individual completion, so the student will come to appreciate the benefits of working with others. You can also leave the door open for the student to join a group at any time he or she feels ready. You may find that some bright

students are occasionally reluctant participants. You may have to allay their concerns about decreased learning or lowered grades by explaining the benefits of discussion and elaboration.

SHY STUDENTS

How do I involve the shy student in cooperative small group learning? Start with groups of two or three, since groups of this size will be less threatening for all students, especially the shy ones. Use classbuilding and teambuilding activities (see Chapter 4: Classbuilding and Teambuilding), such as icebreakers and appreciation activities, to involve all group members. With young children, you can try asking shy students to use props or puppets if they are reluctant to talk directly to their group members.

When you group a shy student with a compassionate student, be sure to brief the compassionate student on how to help the shy student get involved before the group activity begins. Such advance briefing will help the more outgoing student see that working with a shy classmate is not a punishment but an important role in a small group. As you monitor group work, remember to encourage all students and highlight their unique abilities, being sure to mention a special ability or talent that a shy student has. At the same time, however, don't draw too much attention to shy students, making them feel uncomfortable.

DOMINEERING STUDENTS

What do I do with a student who takes over the group and does not allow everyone to participate? If the activity has been structured cooperatively, positive interdependence and individual accountability are built in. Students who feel that they can do all the work have not begun to adopt interdependence as a behavior or value. You should stress this interdependence when planning activities (see Chapter 6: Fostering Positive Interdependence).

Establishing classroom norms and small-group norms that include the importance of equal participation in small-group interactions is important. For a student who actively dominates the group, the role of observer could be assigned. His or her job would be to use a checklist to observe the interpersonal skills used during a group activity and then to give feedback. This will help show a domineering student how others engage in more effective interpersonal behaviors.

STUDENTS WITH LIMITED ENGLISH PROFICIENCY

What do I do with students who have English as a second language? In recent years, the classroom has seen increasing numbers of ESL students. This poses a challenge to group work, since these students need to interact with their peers more than they do in a traditional classroom. At the same time, group work provides opportunities for these students to practice their language skills through interaction with native speakers.

You can help ESL students participate more effectively in group work by assigning them roles that capitalize on their strengths and do not make unrealistic demands on their limited English skills. You could also assign a buddy to an ESL student whom you have prepared to help out. This buddy would provide assistance to the student and would model language skills. Gradually, the ESL student would assume increasing responsibility within the group. You may wish to vary the buddies you assign if you feel they would perceive the task as a burden.

If you have several students who speak the same language, you may want to group them together to allow them to explore more complex concepts in their first language. Then have them report their conclusions in English, thus encouraging transfer of knowledge to their new language.

EVALUATING INDIVIDUALS IN GROUPS

How do I evaluate individual students within groups? Even though your students may be working in groups and helping each other learn, it is not the group that learns, but each individual within the group. All students need individual feedback on their progress, both on the acquisition of group interaction skills and on academic learning. Thus, there is no contradiction between group work and individual assessment.

One way to provide individual feedback is to give individual quizzes or assignments following a cooperative learning activity. Students can then use the results of the quiz or assignment to reflect on whether they've assumed their responsibilities for learning and for helping their fellow group members learn.

When assessing group products, be sure to have each member responsible for an identifiable component that you can assess individually. Or, have students complete self- and peer assessments of contributions to group work (see Chapter 9: Evaluating and Reflecting). Students should be able to explain the final product and the process of completing the task.

WORKING TOGETHER IN PROFESSIONAL DEVELOPMENT

Often in professional development, teachers attend workshops by themselves, become inspired, and return to their classrooms. When they experience difficulties in attempting to apply the new strategies with their students, they have no one around to provide ongoing support. The isolation teachers often experience makes innovation particularly difficult. As we toil away in our corner without anyone to encourage us, provide confirmation of new ideas, or brainstorm solutions to problems we encounter, our enthusiasm for the new strategies wears off. Collaboration and mutual support among teachers, administrators, and parents can encourage persistence in the use of new teaching strategies.

Collegial Support Groups

What are collegial support groups and how do they function? Collegial support groups take many different forms. They can be informal chats over the telephone, discussions over a drink after work, or formal staff meetings with set agendas. Regardless of their form, collegial support groups should be gatherings where teachers choose to be; where they feel heard, understood, and supported. They are not gripe sessions but opportunities for teachers to discuss their teaching, to share positive experiences, and to seek solutions to difficulties they've encountered. Teams of teachers may spend the time collaborating on lesson planning; others may reflect together on previously implemented activities. Many teachers also find it useful to observe each other implementing cooperative learning in their classrooms, or to team teach cooperative lessons. Principals are instrumental in helping this happen by arranging for release time (either filling in themselves or hiring substitute teachers) or by coordinating spares so that teachers are free to co-plan or visit each other's classes.

Working collaboratively with colleagues not only models the cooperation that you ask your students to engage in, but it also makes your attempts at cooperative learning more manageable and enjoyable. Often, collaboration is easier if you have a structure to follow, so we suggest that you use the planning forms provided earlier in this chapter.

Networking with Other Teachers

There are many regional, national, and international associations that help educators with similar interests make contacts and share ideas. The International Association for the Study of Cooperation in Education (IASCE) brings together educators involved in cooperative learning through frequent conferences and a quarterly magazine called *Cooperative Learning*. It's also the umbrella organization for many regional cooperative learning associations that hold local conferences and circulate newsletters. Find out if such an association exists in your area and get involved. If an association doesn't exist, think about getting together with some of your colleagues and starting one yourself.

Involving Parents and Other People in Your Community

To inform parents about cooperative learning, explain the rationale behind this approach in notes students take home and on occasions such as Meet the Teacher Night. Few parents will have experienced cooperative learning in their educa-tion, except for the traditional group project, which they may have found ineffective. Outline how cooperative learning is different from group projects, and what they can expect their children to learn from the process. Assure parents that their children will be exposed to a balance of goal structures to prepare them for the real world. Invite parents into your classroom, make them feel welcome as participants, and give them meaningful educational tasks. Many parents are happy to make cooperative materials, work with small groups, and perform some administrative jobs.

There may be individuals in your community who would like to speak to your students about the importance of teamwork, interpersonal skills, and cooperation in the workplace. This will help your students, particularly older ones, relate what they're doing in cooperative group work to the real world.

SUMMARY

In this chapter, we have recommended that you start small, gradually increasing the frequency and complexity of the strategies you implement as you and your students become more confident with cooperative group work. We asked you to consider carefully whether the task you're assigning is appropriate for group work. You may find that you need to adapt your existing materials or create new activities for cooperative learning. We have provided you with both guidelines and forms for doing so. Don't forget to take the time to reflect on your experiences and modify future activities in light of your reflections.

Following the strategies and suggestions outlined in this book will maximize your chances of a successful cooperative experience, but difficulties and challenges still await you. We have outlined some common problems experienced by teachers using cooperative learning and suggested possible options for resolving those problems.

Finally, we have encouraged you to work collaboratively with others to enhance your professional development. Collegial support groups, in which teachers co-plan their lessons, reflect, and solve problems together, are important sources of motivation and ideas. Administrators, parents, and other community members can also provide you with assistance and support in your efforts to create successful cooperative learning experiences in your classroom.

REFLECTION ACTIVITIES

1. With a colleague, design an activity for your classes. Use the cooperative activity planning forms in this chapter (Exhibits 10.2 and 10.3), considering each of the cooperative learning elements.

2. After implementing a cooperative activity with your students, use the forms provided in this chapter (Exhibits 10.4 and 10.5) to reflect upon your experiences. Discuss your reflections with a colleague. Celebrate your successes, brainstorm improvements, and set goals for your next activity.

3. Meet with other teachers interested in cooperative learning. Set concrete goals and state how you will help each other achieve your goals.

PART

THREE

SELECTED

METHODS

Cathie Archbould

CHAPTER

11

Student Team Learning Methods

WHAT ARE TGT, STAD, TAI, AND CIRC?

•

ARE STUDENT TEAM LEARNING METHODS
APPROPRIATE FOR THE OBJECTIVES I WANT TO
ACHIEVE?

•

HOW DO I ASSIGN MY STUDENTS TO GROUPS?

•

WHAT METHOD CAN I USE TO TEACH MATH TO A
VERY HETEROGENEOUS CLASS?

•

WHAT MOTIVATES STUDENTS TO WORK TOGETHER
IN STUDENT TEAM LEARNING METHODS?

•

HOW DO I KEEP THE TOURNAMENT COMPETITION IN
TGT FAIR?

Robert Slavin (1986, 1990a, 1991c) and his colleagues at Johns Hopkins University have developed a number of Student Team Learning methods based on the beliefs that students are not always intrinsically motivated to learn the subject matter and that, in traditional educational settings, students do not have equal opportunities to succeed. Given these two assumptions, two general methods, Student Teams-Achievement Divisions (STAD) and Teams-Games-Tournaments (TGT) were designed both to provide equal opportunity for all students to succeed and to extrinsically motivate students so that they encourage and help each other learn. STAD and TGT are very similar except that STAD uses improvement points gained on individual quizzes as the basis of team scores, while TGT uses tournament points won in face-to-face competition.

In addition, Slavin and his colleagues have also designed two curriculum-specific methods—Team-Assisted Individualization (TAI) and Cooperative Integrated Reading and Composition (CIRC). TAI addresses some of the problems in using cooperative methods in mathematics classes, primarily for grades two through eight. CIRC extends cooperative learning methods to the teaching of reading and writing and is for grades one through eight. All four methods—STAD, TGT, TAI, and CIRC—incorporate team rewards, individual accountability, and equal opportunities for success, but each incorporates them in different ways.

In this chapter, we will provide a detailed description of STAD followed by an illustrative example. Then we will discuss the differences between STAD and TGT. Because TAI and CIRC are curriculum-specific methods, they are not described here. Slavin and his colleagues also modified the Jigsaw learning method to employ group rewards for individual achievement. Jigsaw II is described in Chapter 12: Jigsaw and Its Variations.

Finally, Student Team Learning methods focus on the enhancement of student achievement as a primary objective of instruction. No provision is made for systematic instruction in interpersonal skills development. Instead, interpersonal skills improve as students work purposefully together to promote each other's learning.

STUDENT TEAMS-ACHIEVEMENT DIVISIONS

STAD and TGT can be used when learning objectives are divisible into small and manageable units. Both methods employ frequent cycles of direct instruction, team study, and evaluation. Teachers may elect to adapt their own materials or to use curricular material already prepared for STAD and TGT by the Johns Hopkins staff. Student Team Learning curriculum units, forms, number cards, and single copies of worksheets and quizzes, which can be reproduced for classroom use, are available for mathematics (grades two to eight), consumer mathematics (grades nine and ten), metric education (grades five and six), algebra 1, high-school geometry, language arts (grades three to eight), life science (grades seven to nine), physical science (grades seven to nine), and U.S. history (grades seven to ten).

Implementation of STAD

The major elements of STAD are (1) assignment of students to teams, (2) whole-class instruction, (3) team study, (4) individual quizzes, (5) improve-

ment scores, and (6) team recognition. The steps for implementing these elements are described below.

Step 1. Assigning students to teams: STAD groups consist of four- or five-member student teams of mixed ability, gender, and ethnicity. Each team should be a microcosm of the whole class. Assign students to teams based on these variables and on your knowledge of which individuals are likely to work well together. For example, if two students are dire enemies, don't put them on the same team. In assigning students to teams, strive to create a mix of students within teams but make sure each team is about equal to the others in terms of prior achievement.

(a) Rank students from the highest to the lowest on their previous achievement in the subject of the STAD unit. You can use test scores, earlier grades, or your personal judgment of the students' abilities to rank them. However, your ranking should be as accurate as possible.

(b) Decide on the number of teams you will divide the class into. For example, if there are 22 students in your class, you will have five teams of four and two extra students that you will assign to two of the teams. Thus, you will end up with three four-member teams and two five-member teams.

(c) Assign students to their teams in the following manner. Divide the class of ranked students into three sections—the top 25 percent, the bottom 25 percent, and the remainder. If you do not have a number divisible by four, take the extra students (from one to three students) from the midpoint of the class. Use these students to make up the fifth members of the five-student teams. Assign students to each team beginning at the top of the high-performing students and moving down, beginning at the bottom of the low-performing students and moving up, and beginning at the centre of the average-performing students and moving away from the center in both directions. Each team will now have one high-ability student, two middle-ability students, and one low-ability student, resulting in teams that are about equal in the average prior achievement of their team members. (To double-check this composition, calculate the average of the ranks for each team. The averages should be approximately equal.)

(d) Check the teams for ethnic, racial, and gender balance. You may exchange students of similar prior achievement on different teams to achieve a better team mix or to avoid combining students who just cannot work together.

(e) Finally, assign the extra students to five-member teams. Since the extra students are about average in achievement and are ranked in the middle, adding them to a team should not affect the team's average prior achievement. Students stay in the same teams for the duration of the unit, usually about five or six weeks. After this time, you should begin STAD again and assign students to new teams so that they have the opportunity to work with other classmates.

Step 2. Whole-class instruction: Teach a specific lesson on the topic being covered in the unit. You should make the learning objectives clear so that students know exactly what they are expected to learn. Likewise, ensure that all students have grasped the fundamental concepts of the lesson before they engage in team practice.

Step 3. Team study: Team study replaces all independent seat work and some of the direct instruction that is common in traditional classrooms. Arrange the desks or tables so that team members can easily communicate with each other. Give each team two worksheets and two answer sheets. The worksheets consist of items that provide students with practice to help them prepare for the quiz.

Circulate among groups and provide help if no one on the team knows the answer. To encourage team learning, avoid answering questions from individual students unless it is clear the student has checked with the group first.

Promote positive interdependence by reminding students to do their best "for the team" and teams to do their best for their members. Also remind students that the learning goal is more than individual mastery; it also includes team mastery. Although students will be tested individually, the whole team cannot succeed unless everyone understands the material. Finally, you can assign individual homework, but it should not be the team worksheets.

Step 4. Individual quizzes: Give students individual quizzes, preferably weekly, on the specific content of the worksheets. These quizzes may include a variety of evaluation procedures, but you should ensure that the format of the quiz allows for fairly fine distinctions in achievement.

Students do not work together on these quizzes. The quizzes are assessments of the individual student's mastery of the material, which ensures individual accountability. Quizzes are best marked on the basis of "percent correct" rather than on "the curve." You can either collect and then correct the quizzes, or have students exchange quizzes to score them. In addition, the overall difficulty of the quizzes should remain fairly uniform throughout STAD.

Step 5. Improvement scores: The purpose of improvement points is to make it possible for each team member to contribute equally to the team score regardless of individual student ability. Using improvement scores presents an equal challenge to all students; the learning task becomes more difficult for more able students and more manageable for less able students. Consequently, low-ability students can bring as much glory to their team as high-ability students.

Students earn points for their teams based on the degree to which their weekly quiz scores differ from their base scores. The base score may be a function of a student's prior grade or the average of smaller tests previously taken. Thus, base scores are predictions of how well each student is expected to perform.

The awarding of improvement points may be exact (the absolute difference between the base score and the test score), or it may be approximate as in the illustrative example that follows. Large gains in performance are recognized by assigning students maximum improvement points. Note that students are never "punished" for poor performance. No points are deducted when students perform below expectations.

Periodically, you should calculate each student's base score by averaging the quiz scores. This ensures that improvement scores are an accurate assessment of the student's progress. The new base scores are especially useful when students change teams and begin a new round of STAD.

Step 6. Team recognition: You can calculate the team scores by recording each student's improvement points on a team summary sheet. The team score is the average score of all team members taking the quiz. As soon as possible after the quiz, teams are recognized and congratulated for their performance via newsletters distributed to each student or by bulletins posted in the classroom.

Teams that make small gains are GOOD TEAMS, those that make moderate gains are GREAT TEAMS, and those that make large gains are SUPER TEAMS. Weekly results of STAD are cumulative. At the end, distribute appropriate rewards, such as certificates and buttons, to the deserving teams during a recognition ceremony.

In general, Slavin (1991c) recommends that individual quiz scores should be used to compute students' report-card grades, not their improvement scores or team scores. However, if participation or effort are included on the report card, then you can use team scores or improvement points.

Variation: Using team improvement points
STAD encourages students to try their best by recognizing the extent to which students improve their

·············· EXHIBIT 11.1 **Method of Assigning Students to Heterogeneous Teams** ···············

Rank			
Section	Student	Order	Team
Top Performers	Lisa	1	A
	Tracy	2	B
	Leeann	3	C
	Kapil	4	D
	Yair	5	E
Middle Performers	Janik	6	E
	Joelle	7	D
	Heather	8	C
	Brian	9	B
	Rachel	10	A
	Adam	11	*
	Avi	12	*
	Candice	13	A
	Harmon	14	B
	Derek	15	C
	Peter	16	D
	Natalie	17	E
Bottom Performers	Carol	18	E
	Ravi	19	D
	Shawn	20	C
	Michael	21	B
	Larry	22	A

*These students will be assigned to teams as fifth members after the teams have been checked for heterogeneity for other variables (gender, ethnicity, etc.).

In this example, the average rank of team members on each team equals approximately 11.5. There is heterogeneity *among* team members, but the teams are similar, on average, in the ability of their members.

Source: Adapted from R. E. Slavin, *Using Student Team Learning*, Third Edition, Baltimore, Maryland: The Johns Hopkins Team Learning Project, September, 1986, p. 16. Copyright © by The Johns Hopkins University. Used by permission of Robert Slavin.

performance over time (e.g., on unit tests given once a week). These individual improvement points (IIPs) form the basis of a team score. After one or more weeks of cooperative learning, you may find that teams differ in the average amount of improvement. In such cases, you can use team improvement points (TIPs) to recognize and encourage teams to improve their performance.

Illustrative Example of STAD

Level and subject: Grade seven mathematics

Content: Fractions

Objectives: To compare fractions and to identify equivalent, smaller, and larger fractions, to reduce fractions to their simplest form, and to solve problems involving fractions.

Materials: Worksheets and answer keys for each objective, individual quiz on each week's work, a newsletter at the end of each week, and stickers, certificates, or buttons for rewards at the end of the unit.

Procedure:

Step 1. Assigning students to teams: Create five teams from the 22 students in your class. Use the results of the summative test of the last mathematics unit as the basis for ranking and assigning students to teams (see Exhibit 11.1).

At this point, you can make further adjustments to the teams based on gender, ethnicity, and compatibility, but be careful not to disturb the balance of abilities. For example, it might make sense to switch the team assignments of Lisa and Tracy, but switching the assignments of Lisa and Michael would create two teams that are unequal in average ability.

Step 2. Whole-class instruction: Begin the first class on fractions by teaching the first objective. Use manipulatives and other teaching aids to make sure that your students understand the concept of comparing the size of fractions.

Step 3. Team study: During the next mathematics period, tell your students that they will work in their teams and practice comparing the size of fractions. Distribute two worksheets to each team (see Exhibit 11.2). Encourage students to work together and to make sure that everyone gets a turn to answer. Also remind them that the team score will be based on each team member's improvement.

Circulate among the teams while they are working and make sure that everyone is contributing to the worksheets. Encourage team members to ask each other for help before they send a spokesperson to you for assistance. When team members have completed their worksheet, and have agreed that the answers are correct, give each team an answer key to check the answers. If teams complete the worksheet with time remaining, they can create some questions and answers that you could use on a subsequent class quiz.

Step 4. Individual quizzes: During the final class period on this objective, give students an individual quiz containing questions similar to those on the worksheets. Have students exchange quizzes and correct them. Or collect the quizzes and score them yourself.

Step 5. Improvement scores: Calculate each student's improvement points over his or her base score using the method shown in Exhibit 11.3. For example, Peter has a base score of 72 and earns 75 on the first quiz. He brings 20 improvement points to his team. Since Lisa had a very high base score (98) and a perfect quiz result (100), you would give her full improvement marks (30). Calculate the team scores by recording each student's individual improvement points on a summary sheet (see Exhibit 11.4). Note that the team score is the average score of all team members taking the quiz. (After one or more weeks of STAD, you may wish to recognize teams and encourage them to *improve* their performance by calculating team improvement points.)

Step 6. Team recognition: Prepare a newsletter publicizing and congratulating teams and students who have done well (see Exhibit 11.5). At the end of the entire unit on fractions, calculate the cumulative team scores and give teams that have done well an appropriate reward, such as stickers, certificates, or buttons. As we discussed in Chapter 6: Fostering Positive Interdependence, you should use rewards that students value, otherwise they will not motivate your students.

An analysis of the important features of this illustrative example of STAD is presented in Exhibit 11.6.

Teams-Games-Tournaments

TGT is very similar to STAD. However, instead of individual quizzes, it uses academic tournaments—competitions between students from different teams. Although some criticize TGT for using face-to-face competition, the tournaments introduce a "game" element to learning, further engaging the interest of students who might otherwise be bored by the material. In the original TGT (DeVries, Slavin, Fennessey, Edwards, and Lombardo, 1980), student teams competed against one another for rewards and recognition (between-team competition). However, TGT was revised (Slavin, 1986) to allow student teams to compete against preset criteria for rewards and recognition (between-team independence).

Implementation of TGT

The major elements of TGT are very similar to those of STAD. Students (1) are assigned to teams, (2) are taught by the teacher, (3) study in their teams, (4) engage in academic tournaments, (5) bring points to their teams, and (6) have their teams recognized for doing well through newsletters and awards. *Steps 1, 2, and 3: Assignment of student teams, whole-class instruction, and team practice* are implemented in the same way as STAD. *Steps 4 to 6* are described below.

Step 4. Tournaments: Tournaments are academic games in which students from different teams are assigned to ability-homogeneous tournament tables.

·············· Exhibit 11.2 **Sample Worksheet on Evaluating the Size of Fractions** ················

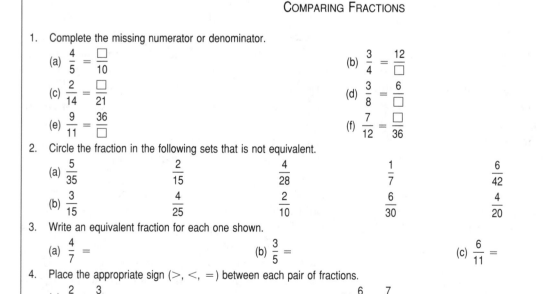

WORKSHEET 1
COMPARING FRACTIONS

1. Complete the missing numerator or denominator.

   (a) $\frac{4}{5} = \frac{\Box}{10}$ (b) $\frac{3}{4} = \frac{12}{\Box}$

   (c) $\frac{2}{14} = \frac{\Box}{21}$ (d) $\frac{3}{8} = \frac{6}{\Box}$

   (e) $\frac{9}{11} = \frac{36}{\Box}$ (f) $\frac{7}{12} = \frac{\Box}{36}$

2. Circle the fraction in the following sets that is not equivalent.

   (a) $\frac{5}{35}$ $\frac{2}{15}$ $\frac{4}{28}$ $\frac{1}{7}$ $\frac{6}{42}$

   (b) $\frac{3}{15}$ $\frac{4}{25}$ $\frac{2}{10}$ $\frac{6}{30}$ $\frac{4}{20}$

3. Write an equivalent fraction for each one shown.

   (a) $\frac{4}{7} =$ (b) $\frac{3}{5} =$ (c) $\frac{6}{11} =$

4. Place the appropriate sign ($>$, $<$, $=$) between each pair of fractions.

   (a) $\frac{2}{7}$ $\frac{3}{5}$ (b) $\frac{6}{7}$ $\frac{7}{11}$

   (c) $\frac{1}{3}$ $\frac{3}{9}$ (d) $\frac{2}{3}$ $\frac{3}{4}$

Students then compete to correctly answer questions on the material they have studied, thereby winning points for their teams. This type of competition allows students at all levels to contribute equally to their team's score.

(a) *Assigning students to tournament tables:* Calculate the required number of tournament tables by dividing the number of students by three. If the number is not equally divisible by three, make the top one or two tournament tables consist of four students. List students from top to bottom according to the criteria first used to assign students to teams. Assign the top three students to one table, the next three to a second table, and so on. Try not to make the ability level of each table known in order to avoid having students make negative comparisons. Whenever possible, make sure that students who are in the same team are *not* assigned to the same tournament table, so they will not compete against one another.

(b) *Tournament participation:* At the beginning of the tournament, announce the composition and location of each tournament table. Ask the students to go to their assigned tables. Distribute special tournament rules to each table and make sure that students know about taking turns and challenging incorrect answers.

Students participate by attempting to answer objective questions that they pick from a deck

·············· EXHIBIT 11.3 **Approximate Method of Calculating Improvement Points** ··············

A. Individual Improvement Points (IIPs)

Quiz Score Minus Base Score	Improvement Points
More than 10 points below	0
1 to 10 points below	10
0 to 10 points above	20
More than 10 points above	30
A perfect quiz score	30

Source: Adapted from Robert E. Slavin, *Using Student Team Learning,* Third Edition, Baltimore, Maryland: The Johns Hopkins Team Learning Project, September, 1986, p. 19. Copyright © by The Johns Hopkins University. Used by permission of Robert Slavin.

B. Variation: Team Improvement Points (TIPs)

Weekly Team Score Minus Team Base Score	Team Improvement Points
More than 10 points below	0
1 to 10 points below	10
0 to 10 points above	20
More than 10 points above	30
All perfect quiz scores	30

Team base score is the average team score for one or more weeks of cooperative learning. *Total team score* is the average of teammates' IIPs for the week, plus team TIPs for the week. For differential weighting, multiply IIP and TIP by fractions that add to 1.0. For example, to weight TIP less: 0.75IIP + 0.25 TIP.

Source: Philip C. Abrami, Bette Chambers, Sylvia d'Apollonia, Mona Farrell, and Christina De Simone, *Failing Groups: The Relationship between Team Learning Outcome, Attributional Style, and Student Achievement,* July, 1990, Paper presented at the biannual meeting of the International Association for the Study of Cooperation in Education, Baltimore, Maryland.

of numbered 3″ × 5″ cards. All the tournament tables are given the same set of questions. At the end of the tournament, ask each tournament table to submit a game score sheet with the number of correct answers for each player and the name of each player's team.

(c) *Bumping:* Students change tables for the next tournament depending on their performance in the most recent one. The winner at each table is "bumped up" to the next higher-ability table and the lowest scorer is "bumped down." The student who scores in the middle remains at the same tournament table. Bumping allows students to reach their true level of performance if initially they have not been correctly assigned. In addition, bumping serves to vary the composition of the tournament tables and to continually motivate students to work hard. Remember, whenever possible, to avoid having two members from the same team at the same tournament table.

·················· EXHIBIT 11.4 **Teacher's Summary Sheet for STAD** ··················

Team	Student	Base Score	Individual Quiz	Individual Improvement	Week 1 Team Average	Base Score	Individual Quiz	Individual Improvement	Week 2 Team Average	Overall Team Average
A. No One Likes Peas	Lisa	98	100	30	17.50	100	95	10	15.00	16.25
	Rachel	76	65	0		76	78	20		
	Candice	74	70	10		74	72	10		
	Larry	53	65	30		53	60	20		
B. X-Rated	Tracy	95	98	20	20.00	95	96	20	20.00	20.00
	Brian	79	83	20		79	81	20		
	Harmon	74	73	10		74	76	20		
	Michael	55	66	30		55	60	20		
C. The Math Cats	Leeann	93	95	20	15.00	93	82	0	5.00	10.00
	Heather	81	70	0		81	79	10		
	Derek	70	74	20		70	65	10		
	Shawn	68	69	20		68	64	0		
D. Rolling Beans	Kapil	92	81	0	14.00	92	99	20	20.00	17.00
	Joelle	81	86	20		81	*			
	Avi	75	73	10		75	80	20		
	Peter	72	75	20		72	79	20		
	Ravi	66	67	20		66	66	20		
E. Math Busters	Yair	91	97	20	24.00	91	100	30	30.00	27.00
	Janik	82	93	30		82	93	30		
	Adam	75	74	10		75	87	30		
	Natalie	72	84	30		72	84	30		
	Carol	62	75	30		62	75	30		

* Absent
Team score of 15 = GOOD TEAM, 20 = GREAT TEAM, 25 = SUPER TEAM.

·············· EXHIBIT 11.5 **Sample STAD Newsletter** ··············

THE RAP SHEET

Week Two

The Math Busters are "busting" records with their performance this week. Yair, Janik, Adam, Natalie, and Carol each earned 30 improvement points for their team. Janik says the secret to their success is "practicing together until everyone gets it." So far, the Math Busters are on schedule for a SUPER TEAM award with a cumulative team points average of 27.00 after two weeks of working together. Bravo!

Also doing well this week were the X-Rated and Rolling Beans. Each scored twenty points. Congratulations on a job well done.

This Week's Scores

No One Likes Peas		X-Rated		The Math Cats	
Lisa	10	Tracy	20	Leeann	0
Rachel	20	Brian	20	Heather	10
Candice	10	Harmon	20	Derek	10
Larry	20	Michael	20	Shawn	0
Team Average	15.00	Team Average	20.00	Team Average	5.00

Rolling Beans		Math Busters			
Kapil	20	Yair	30		
Joelle	*	Janik	30		
Avi	20	Adam	30		
Peter	20	Natalie	30		
Ravi	20	Carol	30		
Team Average	20.00	Team Average	30.00		

Season's Standings Second Week

Team	Season Score
No One Likes Peas	16.25
X-Rated	20.00
The Math Cats	10.00
Rolling Beans	17.00
Math Busters	27.00

Step 5. Distribution of points: After each game, points are distributed to each tournament player and brought to his or her team to calculate team scores. A student can contribute a maximum of six points or a minimum of two points to the team score.

Step 6. Team recognition: Recognizing teams that have done well is the same as in STAD.

Illustrative Example of TGT

We will use the same situation we used to illustrate STAD—teaching a unit on fractions—to show you how to use TGT to teach a grade-seven class with the same objectives.

Materials: Worksheets and answer keys for each objective, tournament rules, tournament cards with an answer key, a newsletter at the end of each week, and stickers, certificates, or buttons for rewards at the end of the unit.

Procedure:

Steps 1, 2, and 3: Assignment of students to teams, whole-class instruction, and team practice are the same as the illustrative example for STAD.

Step 4. Tournaments:

(a) *Assigning students to tournament tables:* Assign your 22 students to seven tournament tables as illustrated on the left side of Exhibit 11.7. Note that the top table will have four players.

(b) *Tournament participation:* At the beginning of the tournament, announce the composition and color of each tournament table. Tell students to go to the table that is draped in the appropriate color. Distribute the tournament rules to each table and ask students if they have any questions about the rules. Announce how long the tournament will last (e.g., twenty minutes). Have each tournament table select a player to start the round. The rules for TGT are provided in Exhibit 11.8.

•••••••••••••••••••• Exhibit 11.6 **Analysis of STAD Illustrative Example** ••••••••••••••••••••

Grade and subject: Grade-seven mathematics
Content: Fractions
Group task: Practice fractions with team members to prepare for individual quizzes.

Grouping	Positive Interdependence
• Four to five students are assigned to each team. • Teams are grouped heterogeneously for ability. • Teams stay together for the duration of STAD.	• Reward: Team performance is recognized in newsletters and by certificates. • Goal: To learn fractions in order to earn improvement points for the team. • Resource: Students share worksheets.
Individual Accountability	Interpersonal and Cognitive Skills
• Team members write individual quizzes. • Each member contributes improvement points to the team's score.	• STAD does not include systematic instruction in interpersonal skills; the focus is on mastering academic content.
Evaluation and Reflection	Extension Activity
• Evaluation includes weekly quizzes, individual improvement scores, and team scores. • There is no systematic reflection during or after STAD.	• During team study, groups that finish early create sample questions and answers, some of which the teacher may use on the quiz.

At the end of the tournament, ask each tournament table to submit its scores, which have been entered onto a game score sheet. Collate the score sheets as shown on the right side of Exhibit 11.7. Note that the higher-ability tables will likely have completed more questions than the lower-ability tables.

(c) *Bumping:* After the first tournament, bump students to the appropriate tournament table for the next game (see Exhibit 11.9). In the event of ties, you may find it necessary to bump students anyway, although you would not change their tournament points. Inform students of their placements for the next tournament in the

··············· EXHIBIT 11.7 **Initial Assignment of Students to TGT Tournament Tables,** ···············
Week-One Game Score Sheets, and "Bumping"

Initial Assignment to TGT Tournament Tables				Sample Game Score Sheets and "Bumping"			
Players	Team	Tournament Table	Items Correct	Level* (from high to low)	TGT Score	Next Week's Table	Level*
Lisa	A	Red	13	1	6	Red	1
Tracy	B	Red	10	1	4	Red	1
Leeann	C	Red	9	1	3	Red	1
Kapil	D	Red	8	1	2	Green	2
Yair	E	Green	16	2	5	Red	1
Janik	E	Green	16	2	5	Green	2
Joelle	D	Green	8	2	2	Blue	3
Heather	C	Blue	14	3	4	Blue	3
Brian	B	Blue	16	3	6	Green	2
Rachel	A	Blue	10	3	2	Yellow	4
Adam	E	Yellow	15	4	6	Blue	3
Avi	D	Yellow	13	4	4	Yellow	4
Candice	A	Yellow	11	4	2	Orange	5
Harmon	B	Orange	13	5	3	Orange	5
Derek	C	Orange	14	5	6	Yellow	4
Peter	D	Orange	13	5	3	White	6
Natalie	E	White	13	6	6	Orange	5
Carol	E	White	12	6	4	White	6
Ravi	D	White	10	6	2	Gray	7
Shawn	C	Gray	13	7	6	White	6
Michael	B	Gray	10	7	4	Gray	7
Larry	A	Gray	7	7	2	Gray	7

* Do not disclose to students.

················· EXHIBIT 11.8 **Rules for TGT** ·················

1. To start the game, shuffle the deck of numbered cards and place it face down on the table. Also place the answer sheet face down on the table. Decide who will be player number 1. Play proceeds in a clockwise direction from player number 1.

2. Each player, in turn, takes the top card from the deck, reads the item corresponding to that number aloud, and does either (a) or (b) below:

   (a) states that he or she does not know the answer and asks if another player wants to give an answer. If no one answers, the card is placed on the bottom of the deck. If another player gives an answer, he or she follows the procedure described under (b).

   (b) answers the question immediately and asks if anyone wants to challenge the answer. The player to the left of the person giving the answer has the right to challenge first and give a different answer. If he or she passes, the next player to the left can challenge.

3. When there is no challenge, the player to the right checks the answer:

   (a) if the answer is correct, the player keeps the card.

   (b) if the answer is wrong, the player puts the card on the bottom of the deck.

4. When there is a challenge and the challenger gives an answer:

   (a) if the answer is correct, the challenger receives the card.

   (b) if the challenger is incorrect and the original answer is correct, the challenger must give up one of his or her other cards, if any, and place it on the bottom of the deck.

   (c) if both the challenger's answer and the original answer are wrong, only the card in play is placed on the bottom of the deck.

5. The game ends when there are no more cards in the deck. Each player counts up the number of cards he or she has and records this number as the score on the game score sheet. The player with the most cards is the winner. If there is time, students reshuffle the deck and play until the end of the tournament period.

Source: Adapted from R. E. Slavin, *Using Student Team Learning*, Third Edition, Baltimore, Maryland: The Johns Hopkins Team Learning Project, September, 1986, pp. 24–25. Copyright © by The Johns Hopkins University. Used by permission of Robert Slavin.

················· EXHIBIT 11.9 **Illustration of the Bumping Mechanism in TGT** ·················

The winner (top, T) at each table is "bumped up" to the next highest table (e.g., from Table 3 to Table 2) and the low scorer (L) is "bumped down" as shown below. M stands for the middle scorer who remains in place for the following tournament.

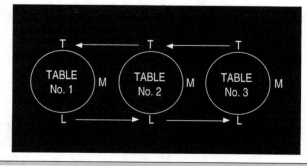

Source: Adapted from R. E. Slavin, *Using Student Team Learning*, Third Edition, Baltimore, Maryland: The Johns Hopkins Team Learning Project, September, 1986, p. 43. Copyright © by The Johns Hopkins University. Used by permission of Robert Slavin.

newsletter or by a note on the bulletin board. Exhibit 11.7 also shows how students are bumped to higher or lower tables for their next tournament.

For example, Adam wins at the Yellow table by answering the most questions correctly (15). He will be bumped up to the Blue table for the next tournament. Candice gets the fewest answers correct (11) at the Yellow table. She will be bumped down to the Orange table for the next tournament. Avi's score of 13 correct answers is between Adam's and Candice's scores. Avi will continue to participate at the Yellow table in the next tournament.

Step 5. Distribution of points: Calculate the points that each player will bring to his or her team. Rules for the distribution of tournament points for two-, three-, and four-player games are given in Exhibit 11.10. The points distribution for the illustrative example are given in Exhibit 11.7.

Step 6. Team recognition: The TGT newsletter is similar to the STAD newsletter. It should be distributed shortly after each tournament and contain both the results of the latest tournament and the cumulative standings for each team. At the conclusion of TGT, use rewards to recognize teams that have done well using the following criteria: average team score of 4.00 = GOOD TEAM, 4.50 = GREAT TEAM, 5.00 = SUPER TEAM.

An analysis of the important features of this illustrative example of TGT is presented in Exhibit 11.11.

· · · · · · · · · · · · · · · · · · · EXHIBIT 11.10 **Distribution of TGT Tournament Points** · · · · · · · · · · · · · · · · · · ·

POINT DISTRIBUTION FOR TWO-PLAYER GAME		
Player	No Tie	Tie
Top Scorer Low Scorer	6 2	4 4

POINT DISTRIBUTION FOR THREE-PLAYER GAME				
Player	No Tie	Tie Top	Tie Low	Three-Way Tie
Top Scorer Middle Scorer Low Scorer	6 4 2	5 5 2	6 3 3	4 4 4

POINT DISTRIBUTION FOR FOUR-PLAYER GAME								
Player	No Tie	Tie Top	Tie Mid	Tie Low	Three-Way Tie Top	Three-Way Tie Low	Four-Way Tie	Two-Way Tie Top and Low
Top Scorer High-Middle Scorer Low-Middle Scorer Low Scorer	6 4 3 2	5 5 3 2	6 4 4 2	6 4 3 3	5 5 5 2	6 3 3 3	4 4 4 4	5 5 3 3

Source: Adapted from R. E. Slavin, *Using Student Team Learning,* Third Edition, Baltimore, Maryland: The Johns Hopkins Team Learning Project, September, 1986, p. 42. Copyright © by The Johns Hopkins University. Used by permission of Robert Slavin.

SUMMARY

Student Team Learning methods recognize that students are not always intrinsically motivated to learn course content, and so use group rewards as extrinsic incentives. Two of the Student Team Learning methods—STAD and TGT—are general methods and two—CIRC and TAI—are specific to reading and mathematics, respectively. All of these methods encourage every student to achieve by providing peer support and equal opportunities for success.

The major elements of STAD are assignment of students to teams, whole-class instruction, team study, individual quizzes, improvement scores, and team recognition. The major elements of TGT are very similar to those of STAD. Students are assigned to teams, taught by the teacher, study in their teams, engage in academic tournaments, bring points to their teams, and have their teams recognized for doing well through newsletters and awards.

REFLECTION ACTIVITIES

1. Describe the conditions that would influence you in choosing either STAD or TGT for a high-school algebra class.
2. Considering what you have read in Part Two: Implementation, what are some of the possible shortcomings of Student Team Learning methods and what could you do to mitigate these effects?
3. Experiment with a colleague who teaches the same content. Decide that one of you will teach the content using STAD and the other will use TGT. Compare your experiences.

ᴇxʜɪʙɪᴛ 11.11 **Analysis of TGT Illustrative Example**

Grade and subject: Grade-seven mathematics	
Content: Fractions	
Group task: Practice fractions with team members to prepare for weekly tournaments.	
Grouping • Four to five students are assigned to each team. • Teams are grouped heterogeneously for ability. • Teams stay together for the duration of TGT.	**Positive Interdependence** • Reward: Team performance is recognized in newsletters and by certificates. • Goal: To learn fractions in order to earn tournament points for the team. • Resource: Students share worksheets.
Individual Accountability • Each team member competes in a weekly tournament. • Each member contributes tournament points to the team's score.	**Interpersonal and Cognitive Skills** • TGT does not include systematic instruction in interpersonal skills; the focus is on mastering academic content.
Evaluation and Reflection • Evaluation includes weekly tournaments, individual tournament points, and team scores. • There is no systematic reflection during or after TGT.	**Extension Activity** • During team study, groups that finish early create sample questions and answers, some of which the teacher may use in the tournaments. • During tournaments, tables that finish early go through the tournament questions again.

Cathie Archbould

Jigsaw and Its Variations

Is Jigsaw an appropriate strategy for the content I want students to learn?

•

What type of interdependence does Jigsaw employ?

•

How will I divide the task so that each student will be responsible for about the same amount of work?

•

How do I adapt Jigsaw to make it less complex?

Jigsaw was one of the first structured cooperative learning strategies. It was originally developed by Elliot Aronson and his colleagues (Aronson, Blaney, Stephan, Sikes, and Snapp, 1978; Aronson and Goode, 1980) at the University of Texas. Aronson developed Jigsaw to solve some of the problems of school desegregation. Even though by the mid-1970s schools in the United States had been desegregated for several years, there was still little positive interaction between black and white students. Aronson solved this problem by placing students in small heterogeneous groups, and by subdividing the group task and resources so that each student had unique information required by all group members. Thus, the degree of interdependence among the students was very high, and the teacher's role as information giver was correspondingly reduced. In this chapter, we will describe original Jigsaw and a few of its variations.

ORIGINAL JIGSAW

The name "Jigsaw" captures the essence of this cooperative learning strategy. The material to be learned is divided, or "jigsawed," into pieces with each piece given to only one team member. The puzzle—learning about all the content—cannot be solved until all the pieces are reassembled. Consequently, the responsibility of each team member is to master his or her piece of the content and then teach it to other team members. In other words, Jigsaw relies heavily on task and resource interdependence to motivate students to learn cooperatively. Furthermore, to assist team members in mastering their pieces of the content, they work with students from other teams who have been assigned the same material to learn.

Jigsaw was originally designed for grade-five and grade-six classes; however, it has been widely used in primary through college classes. As most Jigsaw tasks require at least minimal reading proficiency, it is best implemented with students above the second or third grade.

Implementation of Original Jigsaw

In original Jigsaw, students work in two groups: the counterpart group (also known as the expert or exploration group), where they work together to learn common material, and the Jigsaw group (also known as the home group), where they teach the material they have just learned to their peers. Original Jigsaw requires that each member of the Jigsaw group be given a unique subsection of the curricular material, which is comprehensible on its own but forms only part of the content. Students from different Jigsaw groups who have the same material meet together in counterpart groups to study the information. They also discuss methods of teaching the material to their respective Jigsaw group members. When the Jigsaw groups re-form, each student teaches the others his or her section of the material.

There are seven major aspects of original Jigsaw: selection and division of curricular materials, assignment to Jigsaw groups, teambuilding, Jigsaw group meetings, counterpart groups, Jigsaw group reports, and evaluation.

STEP 1: SELECTION AND DIVISION OF CURRICULAR MATERIALS

Since Jigsaw relies heavily on task and resource interdependence, it is most appropriate for content that is *not* hierarchical in nature. Also, the material should not require mastery to the same level of proficiency by all students; students usually learn best the material that they teach to their Jigsaw groups. The content must be divisible into roughly equal parts for each student to have about the same amount of work to cover. This means you will sometimes have to rewrite existing materials. For younger students, or for small Jigsaw exercises, you may find it useful to transfer the material to be learned onto cards that are sequentially numbered. Jigsaw is especially appropriate for subjects such as social studies, history, or geography, and for learning situations that emphasize in-depth exploration of a topic and improvement of expository skills. In these cases, use books and other materials that already exist on the topic, ensuring that each group has about the same amount of material to learn. You can also use Jigsaw to review material that has already been taught.

Finally, you can experiment with how you assign curricular material to Jigsaw group members. You can assign the material randomly or selectively to ensure that counterpart groups have the composition of students you desire. If your students are relatively homogeneous in ability and the material is at roughly the same reading level, allow Jigsaw group members to decide which topic they want to explore.

However, if your students have a wide range of reading levels, you may want to divide the material up so that the material for some topics is easier to master than for others. In this case, assign lower-ability group members to the topics for which you have the easier material. Coelho and Winer (1991) have published some innovative Jigsaw units, with varying reading difficulty, for ESL learners.

STEP 2: ASSIGNMENT OF STUDENTS TO JIGSAW GROUPS

Assign students to heterogeneous Jigsaw groups of three to seven members. Aronson and others (1978) recommend that you may need to reduce the number of students per Jigsaw group depending on how much experience they have with cooperative learning and the number of topics to be covered. Jigsaw groups should be heterogeneous for ability, race, gender, popularity, and so on. Aronson, however, recommends assigning students to teams *randomly*, adjusting for reading ability, if necessary. Initially, you should select a team member to function as a facilitator and organizer from each Jigsaw group. It is important that team facilitators work effectively with you and model the role of team leader for the other students. After two to three meetings, the role of team leader should rotate, and each Jigsaw group should choose a different leader.

STEP 3: TEAMBUILDING

In original Jigsaw, teambuilding occurs before students begin work on the academic task and continues occasionally after work has begun. Teambuilding serves to accomplish two broad objectives: (1) developing trust and communication among Jigsaw group members and (2) cultivating the interpersonal skills required for cooperative learning.

STEP 4: JIGSAW GROUP MEETINGS

Students meet in their Jigsaw groups to get their text and any last-minute instructions from their group leaders before meeting with their counterpart groups to learn the academic content. Subsequently, students will continue to meet briefly in their Jigsaw groups to improve their interpersonal and leadership skills and to check on group members' progress.

STEP 5: COUNTERPART GROUPS

To become expert in their units of academic material, students re-form into counterpart groups composed of individuals from different Jigsaw groups working on the same content. Counterpart group members work together to understand the material and discuss how they will teach it to their Jigsaw group members. Approximately 30 percent of the time spent in a Jigsaw lesson should be spent in counterpart groups. Aronson and others (1978) recommend selecting counterpart group leaders before each Jigsaw class.

You may want to control the assignment of students to the subtopics and their respective counterpart groups. If all the material you have jigsawed is of equal complexity and length, you may want to ensure that counterpart groups contain students with the requisite skills and abilities to help others both to learn the material and to develop ways to instruct it. If each counterpart group does not contain a mix of students, some counterpart groups will falter, while others may get too far ahead. Under these circumstances, each counterpart group should be as heterogeneous as each Jigsaw group.

Sometimes, you may want to have counterpart groups that are homogeneous in skills and abilities. For example, you may want to assign ESL students to the same counterpart group so that they have an opportunity to learn and explore easier material at their own pace. When these students return to their Jigsaw groups, they may be better able to instruct their teammates than they would have been otherwise. Under these circumstances, you will probably want to jigsaw the material into subunits that are unequal in complexity and length.

STEP 6: JIGSAW GROUP REPORTS

Students return to their Jigsaw groups to teach each other the curricular material in a specified order, if necessary. Jigsaw group members then review the material to ensure that everyone understands the content. When the group is finished learning the material, they spend time discussing and reflecting on the process they went through. Approximately 60 percent of the time spent in a Jigsaw lesson should be spent in Jigsaw groups.

STEP 7: EVALUATION

After the Jigsaw groups' review, students take individual tests on all the material. The task interdependence used in Jigsaw means that students can do well on the individual tests only if they cooperate effectively. Consequently, Aronson and others (1978) did not incorporate any form of team recognition or reward in the design of original Jigsaw.

Illustrative Example of Original Jigsaw

To help you gain a better understanding of original Jigsaw, we have provided an example of how you can implement this learning method in your classroom.

Level and subject: Grade-four science and language arts

Content: Dinosaurs

Objectives: To generate questions about dinosaurs, to synthesize information, to present material orally, to paraphrase ideas of others, and to listen actively.

Materials: Research books and magazines (at various reading levels), presentation package, individual quizzes, dictionaries, and art supplies.

Procedure:

Step 1. Selection and division of curricular materials: Assemble books on dinosaurs. Divide the books on specific dinosaurs into separate piles equal to the number of counterpart groups that you want to have. Equally divide the rest of the books among these piles, making sure that each pile has books of different reading difficulty.

Step 2. Assigning students to Jigsaw groups: Using an adapted version of Category Cards (see Chapter 5: Grouping Students), prepare sets of cards with dinosaur names divided into four segments. Randomly distribute the cards and have students form groups by matching their cards to complete a dinosaur name. Make sure that students who do not get along are not in the same Jigsaw group and that you have students of different abilities and ethnic backgrounds in each group. Assign the role of group facilitator for the day to one student in each group.

Step 3. Teambuilding: Jigsaw groups brainstorm and make note of all the information that group members know about dinosaurs. As a teambuilder, groups prepare a group sign based on their knowledge of dinosaurs.

Step 4. Jigsaw group meetings: Each group member lists the top three dinosaurs that he or she would like to research from the list provided by the teacher. Based on these choices, the group reaches consensus about which dinosaur each group member will study. Jigsaw groups may also meet briefly at midweek to check on each member's progress in their counterpart groups, to clarify objectives, and so on.

Step 5. Counterpart groups: Students regroup into counterpart groups with others who are studying the same dinosaur. Each group takes the books about its dinosaur and begins to study the material. For approximately 30 minutes each day for a week, counterpart group members help each other learn everything they can about their dinosaur, and help each other prepare to teach their Jigsaw groups. Counterpart groups share the general books about dinosaurs and the books they have brought from home with other groups. Each group also prepares four questions about dinosaurs to be used in the individual test.

Step 6. Jigsaw group reports: After returning to their Jigsaw groups, students spend part of each day taking turns teaching what they have learned about their dinosaurs to their teammates. After all students have shared their information, group members complete a Group Productivity Reflection Form (see Chapter 9: Evaluating and Reflecting) and discuss the functioning of their group.

Step 7. Evaluation: Students take individual tests, which are composed of the questions prepared by the counterpart groups.

Exhibit 12.1 presents an analysis of this Jigsaw illustrative example.

JIGSAW VARIATIONS

For the remainder of this chapter, we will discuss some variations of original Jigsaw: Jigsaw II, Partner Jigsaw, Within-Team Jigsaw, and Team Jigsaw.

Jigsaw II

Slavin (1986) has modified original Jigsaw. His variation, Jigsaw II, incorporates some of the features of the Student Team Learning methods (see Chapter 11). First, the content to be learned is highly structured; specific materials are always prepared and divided evenly into small chunks that groups can master in a short period of time. Second, no group facilitator is assigned. Third, no teambuilding is used. Finally, Slavin has introduced a group reward based on individual improvement. Thus, Jigsaw II includes task interdependence, reward interdependence, and individual accountability. The six steps of Jigsaw II are outlined below.

Step 1. Curricular materials: Select text from your existing curricular material. The material should be brief if students are to read the text in class. The material can be longer if it is to be assigned for homework. For each unit, prepare an expert sheet consisting of several topics central to the text. The expert sheet gives guidance to students about what to concentrate on in the text. You should also prepare some form of test that has at least two questions per topic or design a project to provide students an opportunity to demonstrate their learning. You can also prepare an optional discussion guide to help students discuss the topics in their counterpart groups.

Step 2. Assigning students to Jigsaw groups: Assign students to heterogeneous Jigsaw groups of four to five members as you would in STAD. A leader is not selected in Jigsaw II. Students function equally to help each other learn the material. There is also no teambuilding in Jigsaw II. The group reward is supposed to motivate students to work collaboratively and to learn the material.

Step 3. Jigsaw group meetings: Students initially meet in their Jigsaw groups to obtain their text and expert sheets for the topics you will assign. Students either read the text in class or as homework.

Step 4. Expert groups: Students with the same topic meet to discuss it using the expert sheet. Appoint a discussion leader who is responsible for leading the discussion.

Step 5. Jigsaw group reports: Students return to their Jigsaw groups to teach each other their topics. They then review the material to ensure that everyone understands the content and is prepared to take an individual quiz on the material.

Step 6. Group recognition: Students take an individual quiz that is scored as it would be in STAD, including improvement points and team-scoring procedures. Successful groups are rewarded in the same manner as in STAD and TGT.

·················· EXHIBIT 12.1 **Analysis of Jigsaw Illustrative Example** ····················

Level and subject: Grade-four science and language arts	
Content: Dinosaurs	
Group task: Learn in counterpart groups and then teach Jigsaw groups about dinosaurs.	
Grouping • Four students are randomly assigned to Jigsaw groups. • Counterpart groups of students who study the same dinosaur are created.	Positive Interdependence • Task: The material to be learned is divided among Jigsaw group members, each of whom must teach other members about one dinosaur. • Goal: Each counterpart group will produce four questions. • Resource: Counterpart group members will share resource books.
Individual Accountability • Each Jigsaw group member must teach material in order for group members to pass the test.	Interpersonal and Cognitive Skills • Students will practice active listening. • Students will practice their explanation and summarization skills.
Evaluation and Reflection • Each student takes an individual test. • Each student completes a group productivity form and discusses it with his or her Jigsaw group members.	Extension Activity • Counterpart or Jigsaw groups can work on making a class book about dinosaurs.

Partner Jigsaw

Partner Jigsaw is one variation of original Jigsaw that simplifies the strategy by eliminating the reorganization involved in having large exploration groups. Partner Jigsaw is like original Jigsaw except that students meet to learn their material with only one other student. It is often used for brief Jigsaw lessons or when the material to be mastered is not too complex. Partner Jigsaw takes less coordination than original Jigsaw, since each student pairs up with a student from a nearby group who has the same material.

Within-Team Jigsaw

Kagan (1992) has devised many variations of Jigsaw. Within-Team Jigsaw is even simpler than Partner Jigsaw and also requires less reorganization of groups. Students simply work on separate material individually and then teach that material to their Jigsaw groups. There is no counterpart or expert group. Within-Team Jigsaw should be used only for very basic content that you are sure all students will have no difficulty mastering and teaching to their group members.

Team Jigsaw

Another variation of Kagan's is Team Jigsaw (1992). This strategy eliminates the first Jigsaw group meeting. In Team Jigsaw, students begin in exploration teams of four students, and then pairs or individuals from each exploration team teach their material to students from other exploration teams.

SUMMARY

In this chapter, we have outlined the original Jigsaw strategy and some of its common variations, all of which rely on task and resource interdependence to encourage students to learn cooperatively. Keep in mind that not all material is appropriate for use with Jigsaw. You must be able to divide the material into approximately even sections and be sure that each section is understandable on its own. Because students need to have fairly sophisticated group skills to work closely with two different groups, teambuilding and interpersonal skills training are important for original Jigsaw and some of its variations. In place of teambuilding, Jigsaw II uses individual improvement points and team scores to encourage individual accountability and outcome interdependence.

REFLECTION ACTIVITIES

1. If you wanted to introduce your grade-four class to fractions, would you use any of the Jigsaw strategies. If you wouldn't, explain why. If you would, which one would you use?

2. Get together with a colleague who teaches the same subject and grade as you do. Select material that you think would be appropriate to use as a Jigsaw activity. Try out the activity with your respective classes, then get together to discuss the results.

3. Looking back at the section on interracial and interethnic relations in Chapter 2: Group Processes and Productivity, how could the Jigsaw strategies promote interracial and interethnic friendships? What concerns would you have?

Cathie Archbould

CHAPTER

13

Learning Together

WHAT ARE THE SOCIAL AND ACADEMIC OBJECTIVES
I WANT TO TEACH?

•

HOW WILL I STRUCTURE THE GROUPS?

•

HOW WILL I STRUCTURE POSITIVE
INTERDEPENDENCE?

•

HOW WILL I DEVELOP STUDENTS' COOPERATIVE
SKILLS?

•

WHAT IS MY ROLE DURING TEAM LEARNING
ACTIVITIES?

•

WHO AND WHAT SHOULD I OBSERVE?

•

HOW WILL I EVALUATE STUDENTS' ACADEMIC AND
SOCIAL ACCOMPLISHMENTS?

The cooperative learning method called Learning Together (Johnson, Johnson, and Johnson Holubec, 1992; 1993) emphasizes the psychosocial development of the learner. The Johnsons refer to Learning Together as a conceptual, rather than a mechanistic, approach to cooperative learning because it comprises essential elements that teachers can combine and apply to most areas of the curriculum and to all grade levels. The emphasis of Learning Together is on fostering positive group interaction skills, rather than on the mastery of academic material, as in STAD and TGT (see Chapter 11: Student Team Learning Methods), or on the development of cognitive learning skills, as in Co-op Co-op (see Chapter 14: Group Project Methods).

WHAT IS LEARNING TOGETHER?

In Learning Together, students are expected to learn academic content, but the primary focus is on understanding and promoting positive group interactions and interpersonal skills. This is achieved both by direct teaching, monitoring, and intervening to improve interpersonal skills and by students reflecting on their group interactions.

In Learning Together, positive interdependence is fostered in several ways. One of the primary means is through the assignment of specific roles to each group member, such as Encourager, Recorder, and Facilitator. Students are encouraged to look to each other for support, assistance, and feedback while engaging in their respective roles. Learning Together also employs other types of positive interdependence, such as goal interdependence, in which each group produces one product, and task interdependence, in which the group's success is dependent on each group member doing a separate part of the work and contributing in a distinct way to the group outcome.

During each cooperative learning session, time is spent discussing group functioning, a critical aspect of Learning Together. Through this process, students reflect on their use of both cognitive and interpersonal skills and focus on how to build and maintain good working relationships with their teammates. Teachers play a more directive role in Learning Together than in more student-centered methods, such as Co-op Co-op or Group Investigation. It is your responsibility to structure the groups, assign the learning goals and procedures, structure positive interdependence and individual accountability, monitor group functioning, intervene when necessary, and evaluate students' learning. Your students can also take responsibility for some of these aspects, depending on their developmental level and your instructional goals.

Learning Together can be described as a set of classroom elements that promote the development of effective cooperative groups. You are responsible for structuring group learning to include positive interdependence, individual accountability, face-to-face promotive interaction, interpersonal and small-group skills, and group processing.

Positive Interdependence

Like most proponents of cooperative learning, the Johnsons (1992) believe that positive interdependence is the heart of cooperative learning. From the Johnsons's perspective, positive interdependence exists when all group members believe that they need each other in order to attain the group goal.

The Johnsons outline three steps in incorporating positive interdependence into your instruction:

assign a clear, measurable task, create and communicate a meaningful group goal, and include other types of positive interdependence in addition to goal interdependence (see Chapter 6: Fostering Positive Interdependence).

Face-to-Face Promotive Interaction

In addition to positive interdependence, having students actively interacting with one another motivates them to achieve, creates caring, committed relationships, and promotes positive feelings about self and others. Face-to-face promotive interaction means that students encourage one another and work together to achieve group goals. It maximizes student participation, interaction, and communication. Students need to work together in a positive setting rather than simply sit next to each other. Some behaviors that are characteristic of promotive interactions include:

- providing each other with assistance
- sharing resources
- giving each other feedback
- challenging each other's ideas
- encouraging each other to work hard
- demonstrating enthusiasm

Advocates of Learning Together suggest that the process of encouraging promotive interaction involves scheduling regular times for groups to meet, emphasizing how interdependent group members are, and promoting interaction by monitoring groups and recognizing effective interactions.

Individual Accountability

Individual accountability includes assessing the performance of each individual and communicating the results to everyone in the group. Each individual should understand that his or her contribution is essential to both individual success and group success. At the end of a cooperative learning lesson, each individual should be able to demonstrate knowledge of the concept studied in the group (see Chapter 7: Encouraging Individual Accountability).

Interpersonal and Small-Group Skills

Improving interpersonal and small-group skills is one of the primary goals of Learning Together. The Johnsons believe that these skills need to be taught directly because many children no longer learn these skills at home or in traditionally structured classes. Consequently, the appropriate use of cooperative skills cannot be taken for granted when structuring cooperative learning activities. Improving these skills follows a developmental progression from very basic group-forming skills to more sophisticated formulating skills. For example, "using quiet voices" and "staying with the group" are very basic skills, while "justifying opinions" and "criticizing the idea but not the person" are higher-level ones.

The Johnsons suggest five steps for teaching cooperative skills (see Exhibit 13.1).

The Johnsons recommend the use of T-charts for teaching these skills. (See Chapter 8: Developing Interpersonal and Cognitive Skills to learn about T-charts, lists of skills that students need to learn, and for additional ways to enhance these skills in your students.)

Group Processing

Teaching cooperative skills is only the first step in helping your students become effective group members. Students also need to reflect upon, or process, their use of these skills to ensure that they become deeply engrained. Processing can occur at different times during a group activity and at its conclusion. Processing enables students to recognize the effective behaviors they have employed, make suggestions for eliminating ineffective behaviors, and set goals for their next cooperative activity. You need to set aside regular times for group processing; otherwise it is an aspect of cooperative learning that can be easily omitted. Try to provide your students with a variety of ways to reflect upon both their academic and their social skills; doing so will help maintain your students' interest. You should also encourage students to give positive feedback to one another, emphasizing the use of the skills they are developing.

Implementation of Learning Together

The Johnsons (Johnson, Johnson, and Johnson Holubec, 1993) do not provide a "recipe" for cooperative learning sessions; however, they do suggest the five steps listed in Exhibit 13.2. These steps should help you incorporate the Learning Together elements—positive interdependence, face-to-face promotive interactions, individual accountability, interpersonal and small-group skills, and group processing—into your teaching.

Step 1. Select a lesson: You need to choose a lesson that will be appropriate for group work. You should have clear objectives for both the academic content and the collaborative skills to be learned.

······· Exhibit 13.1 **Teaching Cooperative Skills** ·······

1. Have students recognize the need for the skill.	4. After practice sessions, have students process—receive feedback on—the degree to which group members used the skill.
2. Ensure students understand what the skill is and when to use it. A good way to do this is to have students give examples of what the skill—for instance, encouraging—sounds like (e.g., what people say when they are encouraging someone to participate) and what the skill looks like (e.g., the facial expressions and posture people assume if they are encouraging someone to participate).	5. Ensure students practice the skill until it becomes natural. Even if the behaviors are exaggerated and somewhat artificial initially, the Johnsons recommend persisting in the development of the skill and reinforcing the occurrence of suitable behaviors through rewards, until the students employ the behaviors automatically.
3. Arrange practice situations and foster mastery of the skill.	

Source: Adapted from D. W. Johnson, R. T. Johnson, and E. Johnson Holubec, *Cooperation in the Classroom,* Revised Edition, Edina, Minnesota: Interaction Book Company, 1988, p. 4:4. Copyright © 1988 by David W. Johnson. Used by permission.

Step 2. Make decisions: Make decisions about (a) group size, (b) the assignment of students to groups, (c) time spent in groups, (d) room arrangement, and (e) the materials you will need.

(a) *Group size:* The Johnsons recommend starting with small groups (two or three members) and working up to larger groups if, and when, appropriate.

(b) *Assigning students to groups:* Groups should be as heterogeneous as possible, taking ability, motivation, and working style into account. Students who need specific skill development can be placed in groups where they are likely to see this skill modeled. Skill deficits can be balanced within a group, so that among its members, the group has all the requisite skills needed for a task.

(c) *Room arrangement:* The physical arrangement of the room sends important messages to students about how they are to act and interact with their teammates; therefore, you must arrange the room accordingly. Desks should be grouped together to make communication easy and group work comfortable and unencumbered.

(d) *Materials:* Be sure that the materials required for the task are cooperatively structured. They should be designed so that a group would have less difficulty using them than would an individual working alone.

(e) *Assigning roles:* Each student should be clear about his or her responsibilities. Having a clear role can help achieve this goal. Roles assigned on the basis of the learning task can vary greatly. If, for example, your students are involved in learning geography and navigational skills by planning a ship route from England to the New World, you could assign such roles as captain, quartermaster, navigator, and meteorologist.

The roles do not have to be assigned for a long period of time. It is a good idea to rotate the roles among group members so that each student learns the skills involved in executing them. Role rotation also allows each student to view the cooperative learning process from a different perspective. As students learn the important aspects of each role and what it contributes to the functioning of the group, the lines among the various roles may become blurred and rigid role playing may not have to be maintained.

Step 3. Set the lesson:

(a) *Explain the academic task:* You must structure group tasks and activities so that collaboration is required to complete them. Even if you instruct students to work together, if a task can

---

···················· EXHIBIT 13.2 **Teacher's Steps in Learning Together** ····························

1. Select a lesson
   Specify objectives for:
   (a) academic content
   (b) social skills

2. Make decisions
   (a) group size
   (b) assignment to groups
   (c) room arrangement
   (d) materials
   (e) assigning roles

3. Set the lesson
   (a) explain the academic task

   (b) structure positive interdependence
   (c) create individual accountability
   (d) set criteria for success
   (e) explain expected behaviors

4. Monitor and process
   (a) find evidence of expected behaviors
   (b) observe
   (c) make plans for processing

5. Evaluate outcomes
   (a) task achievement
   (b) group functioning

Source: Adapted from D. W. Johnson, R. T. Johnson, and E. Johnson Holubec, *Cooperation in the Classroom*, Edina, Minnesota: Interaction Book Company, 1993, Copyright © 1993 by Johnson and Johnson. Used by permission.

easily be done by a single student, collaboration may not occur. You must also clearly communicate to your students what the academic objectives of the lesson are and how the task is to be completed (e.g., how students will interact).

(b) *Structure positive interdependence:* One of the most common ways to structure positive interdependence in Learning Together is through the use of role interdependence. (See Chapter 6: Fostering Positive Interdependence.) These roles may involve the practice of cooperative skills or be necessary for the completion of the learning task.

(c) *Create individual accountability:* Each student must be responsible for learning the material and for helping other group members. A common way of ensuring individual accountability is to have group members sign the group's worksheet in order to indicate that they agree with and understand the answers.

(d) *Set criteria for success:* You should clearly communicate to your students what they are expected to learn (both academic and cooperative skill objectives) and how they are expected to learn it. Students must understand the goals of the day's activities before they begin, as well as the criteria for success. Students need to comprehend how they are reliant on their group members, the way the roles and task division will function, and how they will be evaluated.

(e) *Explain expected behaviors:* As outlined earlier, students must be taught the types of behaviors that will facilitate group learning and must understand that you expect them to display those behaviors.

Step 4. Monitor and process: While students are engaged in their group work, you need to guide group processes. You should be continually monitoring groups as they work and evaluating their effectiveness. Circulate among the groups, making sure that each student understands the material and is on task. When necessary, you should be prepared to intervene. Your role here is that of group facili-

tator. You may decide to help the group deal with an ongoing problem at the time it occurs, if it will not be too disruptive. Or you may choose to wait and mention the problem during the group discussion following the cooperative learning session. If several groups are experiencing the same type of difficulty, you may schedule a whole-class, problem-solving discussion on that topic.

Step 5. Evaluate outcomes: Group members should be evaluated on their ability to work together, as well as on their academic work. Therefore, plan to evaluate both (a) group functioning and (b) academic work

(a) *Academic work:* You can evaluate students individually or as a group for their achievement of academic goals. To encourage individual accountability in Learning Together, the Johnsons recommend that you calculate the group mark based on individual group members' contributions to the group product or task. This can help motivate all group members to participate to the best of their ability. You should be careful to consider the differing ability levels of group members when deciding how to assign group grades so that the evaluation procedure is perceived as fair and equitable for all members, and peer support for less able students does not develop into undue peer pressure.

(b) *Group functioning:* Students should discuss how effectively they are working together to achieve academic goals and master interpersonal and cooperative skills during group processing sessions. These sessions are usually held at the completion of each group activity. Decide what skills to focus on by examining your students' abilities and your objectives. Then observe, or have group members observe, those skills in action during group work. These observations can be informal, anecdotal notes taken as you circulate among the groups, or they can be structured checklists or rating scales focusing on particular skills (see Chapter 9: Evaluating and Reflecting). The information gained from the observations is communicated to group members and used in the group processing discussion. Finally, have group members set goals for attaining specific cooperative skills in future sessions. You may want to give special recognition to those groups whose members worked well together and to those who improved their collaborative skills.

Illustrative Example of Learning Together

Level and subject: Grade-five language arts

Content: The novel *Sara, Plain and Tall*

Objectives: To critically read the novel in order to discuss it and answer questions concerning characters, theme, symbolism, action, and so on. To practice the cooperative skill of criticizing ideas not people.

Materials: Individual copies of the worksheet for each student and one copy as the partner worksheet for each pair (see Exhibit 13.3).

Procedure:

Step 1. Select a lesson: After students read *Sara, Plain and Tall*, structure a focused discussion for pair interaction.

Step 2. Make decisions:

(a) *Group size and* (b) *Assigning students to groups:* Assign students to heterogeneous pairs according to ability.

(c) *Time spent in groups:* One class period.

(d) *Room arrangement:* Students form pairs by moving chairs together.

(e) *Materials for each pair:* Give students two individual copies of the worksheet and one partner copy.

Step 3. Set the lesson:

(a) *Task:* Explain the task as follows: Students will read Question 1. Individually, they will write

············· Exhibit 13.3 **Sample Worksheet for Learning Together Illustrative Example** ·············

SARA, PLAIN AND TALL

Worksheet

Partners' names _____

1. List the four main characters in the story.
   _____
   _____

2. What things did Sara miss from her home?
   _____
   _____

3. What could you do to make a person feel at home while he or she was staying at your house?
   _____
   _____

4. How do you know that the children wanted Sara to stay?
   _____
   _____

5. How was the prairie like the ocean?
   _____
   _____

6. Do you think Sara should have stayed or returned to Maine? Why?
   _____
   _____

down a response on their own worksheets. They will discuss their answers with their partners. Together, students will create a new answer. The Recorder will write the combined answer on the partner worksheet. A Checker will make sure both students in the pair understand the answers. Roles will be reversed for the next question.

(b) *Positive interdependence:* Assign the roles of Checker, and Recorder. Make sure that students understand their responsibilities before the activity begins. The goal of each pair is to answer the questions individually, discuss the answers, and come up with a joint response. Students are taught the skill of criticizing ideas not people using a T-chart.

(c) *Individual accountability:* Explain that each student is responsible for explaining the joint answers.

(d) *Criteria for success:* Emphasize that all questions are understood and answered by each student.

(e) *Specific behaviors expected:* Explain that students should develop social skills in explaining, elaborating, paraphrasing, synthesizing ideas, and active listening. Students should demonstrate behaviors appropriate to these skills.

Step 4. Monitor and process:

(a) *Evidence of expected behaviors:* Students should exhibit the behaviors appropriate to the social skills outlined in Step 3.

(b) *Observation form:* Use informal monitoring. Circulate from pair to pair and observe for the use of expected social skills. Listen for any problems that the pairs may encounter. Intervene to assist them with problems they may be having with the content or with the social skills they are expected to use.

·················· EXHIBIT 13.4 **Analysis of Learning Together Illustrative Example** ··················

Grade and subject: Grade-five language arts	
Content: The novel *Sara, Plain and Tall*	
Group task: Using rotating roles, pairs answer questions on partner worksheet.	
Grouping • Students are assigned to heterogeneous pairs. • Pairs are selected by the teacher based on ability. • Pairs work together for a single class period.	**Positive Interdependence** • Goal: To create one set of combined answers from the pair. • Reward: Partner worksheet answers contribute to grade. • Role: Assigned roles of Checker and Recorder.
Individual Accountability • Each student has to write an answer for each question before the discussion begins. • Each student is responsible for the pair's combined answer. • Each student is responsible for a particular role in the pair.	**Interpersonal and Cognitive Skills** • Direct teaching, using T-charts, of the skill of criticizing ideas not people. • Guided practice of this skill during the activity.
Evaluation and Reflection • Each student is evaluated on his or her individual answers and on the pair's combined answer. • There is an individual test on the content of the novel. • Pairs reflect upon their contributions using a self- and teammate evaluation form.	**Extension Activity** • Students who complete the task before other pairs could help other pairs. • Pairs who have completed the task could combine all the answers and then give a short oral presentation to the class.

(c) *Plans for processing (feedback):* Provide feedback for task problems or for difficulties students may have with using the social skills.

Step 5. Evaluate outcomes:

(a) *Task achievement:* Grade individual and joint answers. Individual answers contribute to a student's individual grade, and the joint answers contribute to each student's grade for effort and participation on his or her next report card. After students have finished the novel, prepare a test to be completed by students individually. Each student's score becomes part of his or her individual grade on the report card.

(b) *Group functioning:* Use the Group Reflection Form (Exhibit 9.4) to assess students' social skills. Each student also completes a self- and teammate evaluation form to assess his or her ability to criticize ideas not people.

An analysis of the important features of this illustrative example is presented in Exhibit 13.4.

SUMMARY

In this chapter, we have outlined the fundamental aspects of Learning Together. This approach has five elements: positive interdependence, face-to-face promotive interaction, individual accountability, interpersonal and group skills, and group processing. Teachers using this method combine these elements in various ways to teach a wide range of content. Learning Together emphasizes the importance of learning, practicing, and internalizing social collaborative skills for effective group interaction. Johnson, Johnson, and Johnson Holubec (1993) have suggested that teachers trained in Learning Together become instructional "mechanics" who should be able to fix any problems they encounter.

REFLECTION ACTIVITIES

1. What emphasis do you place on the learning of interpersonal skills? Elaborate on your ideas and discuss them with a colleague.

2. Think of an objective for an academic task and structure a lesson cooperatively following the steps outlined in this chapter. Share your lesson with someone else who is exploring the Learning Together approach.

3. Compare the analysis of the illustrative example for Learning Together with the analysis of the illustrative example for TGT in Chapter 11. In what ways are the two methods similar and in what way do they differ?

Cathie Archbould

CHAPTER 14

Group Project Methods

Are Co-op Co-op and Group Investigation appropriate methods for the content that I want my students to learn?

•

What motivates students to cooperate and learn in these methods?

•

How are the basic components of cooperative learning structured in these methods?

•

What steps should I follow to implement Co-op Co-op and Group Investigation?

In group project methods such as Co-op Co-op (Kagan, 1985, 1992) and Group Investigation (Sharan and Hertz-Lazarowitz, 1980; Sharan and Sharan, 1992), knowledge is not viewed as the input and storage of facts, but rather as "the cognitive product emerging from our interaction with the environment, both inanimate and social" (Sharan and Hertz-Lazarowitz, 1980). Group project methods also build on intrinsic motivation and encourage the development of cooperative skills and appreciation for others' contributions. Teachers who implement Co-op Co-op or Group Investigation methods support interpersonal communication in their classrooms and value the affective-social dimensions of learning. In this chapter, we will show you how to implement these methods and we will provide an illustrative example of each.

SIMILARITIES BETWEEN CO-OP CO-OP AND GROUP INVESTIGATION

Co-op Co-op and Group Investigation are best suited for *multifaceted tasks*, such as large projects that will challenge teams of students. This encourages meaningful exchanges of ideas and independent judgments essential to the development of higher-level thinking skills. Within the general task and topic area set by the teacher, students determine and coordinate their class, group, and individual learning goals. Individual students then collaborate within small groups to produce their group's contribution to the class's learning goal. The learning goal set by the students becomes the primary source of positive interdependence. Extrinsic rewards are not usually necessary, since satisfying the intrinsic desire to learn and achieving the common goal motivates students.

Students are required to plan, coordinate, and evaluate their learning with their peers, resolve differences of opinion, independently seek answers to their questions from a variety of sources, and communicate their knowledge in a meaningful and interesting format. Students participate in teambuilding and interpersonal skill training activities to develop a strong sense of group identity and commitment.

In both group project methods, you as the teacher maintain an important role as resource person and facilitator of groups, but you are no longer the sole source of knowledge and director of learning. You promote student autonomy through modeling behavior and interacting with the groups. You circulate among the groups, check that they are managing their work, and provide guidance in overcoming difficulties they encounter.

Both methods begin with a general discussion of the topics so that students' curiosity is heightened, and they can explore possible topics for further study. It is important *not* to impose predetermined topics but rather to encourage students to delve into the unknown, to discover and express a "need to know," and to experience that they, with others, can define an area of exploration.

Students are encouraged to capitalize on each other's strengths and talents when formulating the approaches and procedures they will each use to investigate their topics. In preparation of the projects, students may do library research, interviews, experiments, and so on, depending on the nature of the subject being covered. Students will become more involved and take ownership of their learning if they are working toward a common goal that requires the *application* of their learning, rather than the demonstration on a test of how much information they have accumulated.

Groups should be encouraged to be creative in the design of their projects or presentations. Presentations should require the integration of the individual group members' work to produce debates, demonstrations, learning centers, or skits. You may need to provide training in various presentation skills, such as public speaking and using audiovisual equipment. Taking the time to develop these skills will help make the reports a more educational and interesting experience.

Students, in fact, become teachers during their presentations. This is a new and challenging role that gives them experience in organizing and summarizing complex material and communicating it in an effective manner. These presentations can be intellectually and emotionally rewarding for students. You should make it clear to teams that the classroom is theirs for the time of the presentations and that they can reorganize it to suit their presentations.

Group project methods challenge you to be innovative in evaluating your students. The evaluation should assess what process students used in carrying out the investigation, how they approached a problem for their group project, what higher-level thinking skills they used in analytical and problem-solving discussions, and how they applied their knowledge to new situations and questions. Both peer and self-assessment are usually components of the evaluation process.

Both Co-op Co-op and Group Investigation have been described as "advanced" cooperative learning methods because they make great demands of the students. Consequently, you may want to consider using these group project methods when you are certain that students have already had successful experiences with more structured cooperative learning methods. As you will see, Group Investigation and Co-op Co-op share many principles, techniques, and similarities in their implementation steps.

Implementation of Co-op Co-op

Although Co-op Co-op is a flexible technique, the inclusion of the following ten steps increases the likelihood of a successful experience for both you and your students. Kagan (1985, 1992) provided guidelines for these steps, and each is summarized below.

Step 1. Student-centered class discussion: An initial set of readings, anecdotes, pictures, or experiences should introduce the topic so that students' interests are stimulated. You should then lead a class discussion in which students discover and express their curiosity. Together you will create a list of topics for further study.

Step 2. Assigning students to teams: There are various options for assigning students to teams. If the goal is to encourage individual intellectual development based on preestablished, intrinsic interests, students may select teams on the basis of the topic they most want to explore. If, on the other hand, you want to encourage students to interact with peers of differing abilities or perspectives, you should assign students to teams maximizing heterogeneity.

Step 3. Teambuilding and cooperative skill development: Kagan recommended that team members participate in teambuilding and cooperative skill training exercises to develop a sense of team identity and effective communication skills. We suggest that you also have team members reflect regularly during Co-op Co-op on the effectiveness of their collaboration. This not only helps develop cooperative skills, it also encourages members to assess and modify, if necessary, the strategies they have adopted to complete their project.

Step 4. Team topic selection: List the topics your students considered to be of most interest during the class discussion. Each team then discusses these topics and selects one to explore further. Each team should be encouraged to select a topic that addresses the interests of the whole class and one the team can identify with. Should two or more teams select the same topic, encourage them to reach a compromise by either dividing the topic or choosing another.

Step 5. Mini-topic selection: During this step, the members of each team discuss their team's topic and select a mini-topic for individual exploration. You may have to take a more directive role here and help students select manageable mini-topics.

Step 6. Mini-topic preparation: Give students time to work individually on their mini-topics. Team members should share references and resources and

have a group discussion about the individual progress of each member.

Step 7. Mini-topic presentations: Each team member gives a formal presentation of the mini-topic to his or her team. Team members should be encouraged to take different roles during these presentations (e.g., Moderator, Secretary, Critic, Timekeeper, etc.). A time limit should be given for each presentation, including time for questions, group discussion, and feedback from team members.

Step 8. Preparation of team presentations: Each team prepares a class presentation by integrating the mini-topics so that the presentation will be more than just a sum of the mini-topics. Encourage between-team cooperation during this preparation phase by suggesting that teams ask for feedback or help from other teams if they think that doing so will aid their presentations.

Step 9. Team presentations: Turn the classroom over to teams during their presentations. The Timekeeper, who is not a member of the presenting team, could hold up a card when the team has only a few minutes left for its presentation. You can suggest that teams include question-and-answer periods as part of their presentations. After each presentation, you may also hold a class feedback session to explore effective preparation and presentation strategies that may help teams in future Co-op Co-op units.

Step 10. Evaluation: You should include all students in determining the evaluation. Since students differ in their interests and abilities, not all of them need to make equal contributions; however, each student must make a unique contribution to the team effort. A three-level method of evaluation is usually recommended for Co-op Co-op: (1) team members evaluate individual contributions to the team effort; (2) the entire class evaluates team presentations; and (3) the teacher evaluates each student's individual write-up of the mini-topic. These evaluations may or may not be used to assign grades; Co-op Co-op works well under a wide range of grading schemes.

Scheduling Co-op Co-op

There are several ways in which you can incorporate Co-op Co-op into your classes, ranging from short-duration activities to the more usual group project. For example, you can periodically assign one-day Co-op Co-op mini-topics, where students work together to make team presentations of about five minutes. You may also incorporate Co-op Co-op into a traditional classroom structure. For example, you can have students work on their Co-op Co-op projects one or two days a week for four to five weeks, and devote the remaining days to whole-class instruction. Another interesting way of incorporating Co-op Co-op into your classes is to schedule a two-week intensive project at the end of each term rather than a traditional review session. This allows students to extend, reinforce, and integrate the knowledge they have gained during the term.

Illustrative Example of Co-op Co-op

This senior high-school history activity would be carried out at the end of a unit on the Second World War, after students have developed a basic understanding of the main events of the war. The activity challenges students to go beyond the dates and events to explore the reactions and motives of North Americans from varied ethnic origins.

Level and subject: Senior high-school twentieth-century history

Content: Understanding the perspectives on the Second World War of different ethnic groups in North America.

Objectives: To develop an understanding of the Second World War from the perspectives of racially, religiously, and ethnically distinct groups in North America. To develop skills in active listening and constructive criticism.

Materials: Documentation on the Second World War, showing varied perspectives and including excerpts from newspapers, filmstrips, and archival records of the period.

Procedure:

Step 1. Student-centered class discussion: Lead a class discussion about the various ethnic groups living in North America at the time of the Second World War. Bring in excerpts from newspapers and magazines that present the viewpoints of these groups to stimulate discussion. (For example, include documentation about people of German, Italian, Japanese, British, and Jewish origin.) On the board, list the ethnic groups that students are most interested in exploring and any possible explanations for the perspectives of these groups. Also list any questions students may have generated during the discussion. Encourage students to suggest additional topics that they could explore within an investigation of an ethnic group (e.g., the status and influence of the group or its perspective on events that occurred in Europe or Asia).

Step 2. Assigning students to teams: Prepare different colored sets of paper. (Each set should contain four or five slips of paper. You will need seven sets for a class of 28 to 35 students.) Randomly distribute these slips of paper to your students. Have students write down the name of a movie they have seen or a book they have read about the Second World War. Students then form teams with others who have the same colored slips of paper.

Step 3. Teambuilding and cooperative skill development: Use the Name Card activity from Chapter 4: Classbuilding and Teambuilding. Have students use the roles of Speaker, Prober, and Recorder to describe their movies or books, ask questions, and take notes. Based on their discussion notes, encourage students to identify a common theme on which to base a team name. Students then reflect on the activity, list the skills they used to help them exchange ideas, and set specific goals for skills, such as active listening, that they can work on during their next Co-op Co-op meeting.

Step 4. Team topic selection: Turn your students' attention back to the list of ethnic groups they came up with in Step 1. Each team chooses the ethnic group it would like to explore further. One member from each team signs his or her team's name next to the topic on the board. (Encourage teams to have a second choice in case another team selects the same ethnic group.)

Step 5. Mini-topic selection: During the class discussion in Step 1, students suggested additional topics they could explore in conjunction with the ethnic groups. To decide on their mini-topics, team members refer to their notes from the class discussion, consult reference material on the ethnic group they have chosen, and discuss which mini-topic each individual will investigate.

Step 6. Mini-topic preparation: Each student individually researches his or her mini-topic and prepares a presentation. Some students may wish to conduct interviews with members of specific ethnic groups or veterans of the war. Others may rely more on library sources. Give students ten minutes at the beginning of each class to conduct group discussions about the progress of individual team members.

Step 7. Mini-topic presentations: Students present their mini-topics to their teams, rotating the roles of Speaker, Timekeeper, Encourager, and Prober. Ask all students to give feedback on the mini-topic presentations.

Step 8. Preparation of team presentations: Each team prepares its presentation by amalgamating the mini-topics researched by team members. Encourage students to be innovative in the way they make their presentations. For example, a team might decide to act out a skit with characters from the ethnic group it has studied. During this step, teams would write a script, assign acting roles and backstage jobs, and rehearse.

Step 9. Team presentations: Give each team fifteen minutes for its presentation, followed by five minutes for a question-and-answer period.

Step 10. Evaluation: Following each presentation, allow five minutes for feedback and team evaluation. After all the teams have given their presentations, have the class reflect on the learning process and set goals for the next Co-op Co-op project. You could use the following three types of evaluation to help determine the total grade for the project.

- Each student privately completes a Teammate and Self-Evaluation form (see Chapter 9: Evaluating and Reflecting).

- The class completes team Presentation Evaluation forms (also see Chapter 9).

- You assess each student's write-up on his or her mini-topic and his or her performance during the team presentation.

Exhibit 14.1 presents an analysis of this illustrative example of Co-op Co-op.

Implementation of Group Investigation

Group Investigation consists of a series of six steps that are presented below. As with other cooperative learning methods, you may need to adapt some aspects of the approach to make it more suitable for your students' experience and abilities.

Step 1. Identifying the topic and organizing students into groups: Students scan sources, propose topics, and categorize suggestions to produce a small number of topics. Students then join a group of three to six members that will study the topic of their choice. Group composition is based primarily on interest in the topic, but as much as possible encourage heterogeneous groups.

Step 2. Planning the learning task: Members of each group discuss the group topic and determine the aspects of the topic they will investigate, alone or in pairs. Each group devotes time to its own organization, the formulation of a research problem, and the planning of its course of action. Three questions should guide these discussions: What do we study? How do we study it? Why do we study it?

Step 3. Investigating the topic: Each group carries out the plans it developed in Step 2, including the projects or tasks of individual group members. Set a time limit for completion of the investigation, but remain flexible. It is best if students proceed until most of the work is completed.

During this step, group members will need to cooperate closely in collecting and analyzing their information, evaluating and integrating diverse ideas and perspectives, and reaching conclusions. You should not underestimate the complexity of skills required here. You may need to provide training in the social and cognitive skills necessary for effective group work.

Step 4. Preparing the final report: Toward the end of the investigation in Step 3, ask each group to appoint one representative to a steering committee. The committee will follow up on the progress of all the groups, ensure that every students is involved, hear each group's plan for its report, and coordinate the schedule of presentations and materials needed.

Encourage groups to focus on the major ideas and conclusions of their investigations and to use creative formats for their presentations, such as audiovisual presentations, learning stations, or dramatizations. Each student should have a role in the group's final report.

Step 5. Presenting the final report: In presenting their final report, students assume the role of teacher. If students do not know how to make effective presentations, you will have to provide instruction in presentation skills.

Step 6. Evaluation: Your evaluation should assess how students approached the problem for investigation, the process they used to carry out the investigation, the higher-level thinking skills they used, and their ability to apply their knowledge. The best way to evaluate students on these bases is by observing students while they work with their peers. You could also have students reconstruct their process of investigation, mapping out the different steps they followed in their work.

You should also involve students in evaluating what they have learned through teammate evalua-

·················· EXHIBIT 14.1 **Analysis of Co-op Co-op Illustrative Example** ··················

Grade and subject: Senior high-school twentieth-century history
Content: Perspectives on the Second World War of different ethnic groups in North America
Group task: Research and prepare a presentation on a group topic.

Grouping	Positive Interdependence
• Four to five students are assigned to each team. • Teams have a mix of students of different ethnic origin and upbringing to encourage multiple perspectives. • Teams are randomly assigned using colored slips of paper. • Teams stay together for the duration of Co-op Co-op.	• Goal: To give a team presentation. • Role: Each member is assigned roles in teambuilding and mini-topic presentations. • Task: Each member completes a mini-topic as part of the group topic. • Resources: Students are encouraged to share resources within and between groups. • Reward: Teams are assessed by other groups on their team presentations. • Identity: Each team selects a group name based on commonalities discovered during the teambuilder.
Individual Accountability	**Interpersonal and Cognitive Skills**
• Each member completes a mini-topic presentation and write-up. • Each member has a role in the team presentation. • Team members evaluate each other's efforts and contributions to their team's progress.	• Teams select skills and set goals for skill development. • Students practice listening, probing, and encouraging through structured roles. • Teams and the class meet regularly to reflect on group process and progress.
Evaluation and Reflection	**Extension Activity**
• Students give within-team formative feedback on mini-topic presentations. • The teacher assesses mini-topic write-ups. • The class evaluates team presentations. • Team members evaluate the efforts and contributions of team members to the group.	• Teams that finish early can brainstorm questions about other teams' topics. (The teacher can assess these questions for depth of understanding and other qualities for team bonus points. This will encourage the development of questioning skills—an important cognitive skill for lifelong learning.)

tion, self-evaluation, steering committee feedback, and whole-class comments. To evaluate content learning, groups could be asked to compose questions on the most important ideas they presented to the class and evaluate their classmates' responses.

Illustrative Example of Group Investigation

Level and subject: Junior high-school physical education

Content: Cooperation in sports and physical activities

Objectives: To analyze the features that distinguish cooperative and competitive sports and games. To evaluate when each is appropriate. To create several cooperative sports or games by inventing modifications to make competitive sports or games more cooperative. To engage in cooperation and develop cooperative skills.

Materials: Books, magazines, posters, and photographs of sports and games.

Procedures:

Step 1. Identifying the topic and organizing students into groups: Tell your students that the class will be exploring a variety of sports and games and the role that cooperation plays in those sports and games. Allow students some time to scan the materials you have brought and elicit from them different types of sports and games they would be interested in investigating. Have students write down on a piece of paper two they would be interested in exploring. Have them group together with two to four others who made similar selections.

Step 2. Planning the learning task: Have students discuss in their groups what questions they have about cooperation in sports or what topics they will explore and how they will communicate or present this information to others at the end of their investigation, perhaps by creating a new cooperative game and teaching it to the class. Provide students with a clear time limit for completing the investigation and help them choose manageable tasks. Part way through this process, you may want students to present a group progress report, via a steering committee, where one representative from each group presents that group's ideas about their investigation into cooperative games to the class (see example in Chapter 5: Grouping Students). Have groups give you a plan of their investigation, including the roles or tasks of each member.

Step 3. Investigating the topic: While the groups are carrying out their plan, observe and monitor their progress and interaction. Set aside time for groups to reflect regularly on their progress, to provide each other with suggestions and assistance, and to coordinate the information they are gathering about cooperation in sports.

Step 4. Preparing the final report: When you meet with the steering committee that coordinates the final reports, encourage students to consider creative formats for their presentations on cooperation in sports and each group member's contribution in the presentation. Before the presentations begin in Step 5, have each member complete the Group Productivity Reflection Form (see Chapter 9: Evaluating and Reflecting) and submit it to you.

Step 5. Presenting the final report: During the presentation, encourage the class to be supportive and provide assistance if requested. For example, some groups may elect to teach the class their cooperative versions of competitive games. Alternatively, groups may collaborate to produce a book of cooperative games. In this case, these groups may present their book to other groups for feedback. Classmates should be urged to participate actively and to provide constructive feedback.

Step 6. Evaluation: Conduct formative evaluation and feedback sessions at various steps throughout the investigation. In addition, keep a log of your own observations during Steps 2, 3, and 4. Collect each team's plan of their investigation from Step 2 and the Group Productivity Reflection Forms completed by the groups at the end of Step 4. In Step 5, have students complete a Presentation Evaluation form (see Chapter 9: Evaluating and Reflecting) following each presentation. Then conduct a brief question period and feedback session on the presentation.

Exhibit 14.2 presents an analysis of this illustrative example of Group Investigation.

Summary

Group project methods, such as Co-op Co-op and Group Investigation, foster learning through stimulating intrinsic interest and self-directed goals. For these methods to work to their fullest, you must be prepared to give your students the freedom to explore their topic with minimal guidance. Too much teacher control will inhibit the process of discovery that these methods are designed to promote.

Co-op Co-op and Group Investigation differ from traditional group projects by their attention to cooperative learning structures, particularly positive interdependence and individual accountability. By including these two critical components of cooperative learning, these methods minimize problems of unequal participation and lack of accountability typically experienced in group projects.

Reflection Activities

1. Consider the content you teach in your class. What aspects could be explored by the students

EXHIBIT 14.2 **Analysis of Group Investigation Illustrative Example**

Grade and subject: Junior high-school physical education	
Content: Cooperation in sports and physical activities	
Group task: Investigate cooperation in sports and games.	
Grouping • Three to five students form each group. • Students join groups according to their interest in the topic. • Groups stay together for the duration of investigation.	**Positive Interdependence** • Goal: To give a group presentation. • Task: Each member completes a task determined by the group in the plan for the investigation. • Resource: Students are encouraged to share resources within and between groups. • Reward: Groups are assessed by other groups on their presentation.
Individual Accountability • Each member completes a part of the investigation. • Each member has a role in the group presentation. • Group members evaluate each other's efforts and contributions to their group's presentation.	**Interpersonal and Cognitive Skills** • Groups meet regularly to reflect on group process and progress. • The teacher observes the functioning of the group and provides training in interpersonal and cognitive skills as needed.
Evaluation and Reflection • The group reflects on process and progress for formative feedback at regular intervals during the investigation. • The teacher observes and assesses the students' interpersonal and academic performance during the investigation. • Students do peer and self-evaluation of their efforts and contributions to the group investigation. • Classmates reflect on and the teacher evaluates group presentations.	**Extension Activity** • Groups that finish early can analyze the cooperative sports created to determine the types of positive interdependence that they employ.

through group project methods? What aspects would not be appropriate for these methods? Why?

2. Are these methods consistent with your approach to teaching and learning? What modifications would you make either to your own teaching style or to these methods if you used

them in your classroom? What results would you predict?

3. What do you see as the major differences between Co-op Co-op and Group Investigation? Which would work best for you and your students?

Cathie Archbould

The Structural Approach

HOW CAN I INTEGRATE A VARIETY OF SHORTER
COOPERATIVE ACTIVITIES INTO MY TEACHING?

•

HOW DOES THE STRUCTURAL APPROACH HELP ME
EXPAND MY REPERTOIRE OF GROUP ACTIVITIES?

•

WHAT IS THE DIFFERENCE BETWEEN A STRUCTURE
AND AN ACTIVITY?

•

WHAT TYPES OF STRUCTURES MAKE UP A MULTI-
STRUCTURAL LESSON?

•

HOW ARE THE PRINCIPLES OF COOPERATIVE
LEARNING INCORPORATED IN THIS METHOD?

The Structural Approach was developed by Kagan (1993) to provide teachers with a flexible, eclectic method of implementing cooperative learning in their classrooms. Most cooperative learning methods provide one basic design for organizing the classroom, and focus primarily on the development of a specific type of learning (e.g., social-interaction skills, higher-level thinking skills, or acquisition of facts). In contrast, the Structural Approach offers a repertoire of content-free activity structures that teachers can select from, apply to their content area, and sequence to create a complete lesson. This flexibility allows teachers to foster the types of skills that students need the most or that are most appropriate for a given lesson or topic.

Kagan's development of the Structural Approach grew out of his experience with training teachers in cooperative learning. He found that teachers were better able to grasp the somewhat abstract principles of positive interdependence and individual accountability when they were illustrated with concrete activities that highlighted the steps, or structure. Because the steps of the activity were presented as distinct from the content of the activity, teachers left the workshop equipped with clear step-by-step procedures (structures) that they could apply to the teaching of any subject.

At first glance, it may appear that this is a "cookbook" approach to cooperative learning—follow the steps and your class will be learning cooperatively. However, underlying the Structural Approach is a solid foundation of cooperative learning principles. Kagan outlines four basic principles in his approach. In addition to positive interdependence and individual accountability, he includes *simultaneous interaction*, and equal participation. *Simultaneous interaction* increases the amount of active participation through the use of group work. For example, in a whole-class discussion, only one in a class of thirty-two students is speaking at a given time. Many students may never speak at all, and some may not even be listening. During four-member group discussions, eight students (one per group) are speaking simultaneously, and in paired discussions, fifteen students are expressing themselves at any one time. *Equal participation* emphasizes the need to ensure that everyone in the group contributes. Thus, applying a structure in which each group member contributes an idea in turn (Round Robin), will likely result in more equal participation than would occur in an open-group discussion.

DEFINITIONS

A key concept of the Structural Approach is the *structure* as a unit of lesson design. Kagan defines structure as "a content-free way of organizing social interaction in the classroom, . . . involving a series of steps or elements" (1992, 5:2). For example, Think-Pair-Share is a three-step structure in which students "think" individually about a question posed by the teacher (Step 1); "pair" up with a neighboring student and discuss their ideas together (Step 2); and "share" the ideas discussed in pairs with the entire class (Step 3). Think-Pair-Share is one example of a relatively simple cooperative alternative to the traditional whole-class, question-answer structure. It encourages increased participation, since all students are given the opportunity to discuss and communicate their knowledge, and it can be considerably less threatening for less able students.

Each *element* of a structure defines the action taking place (e.g., discussing, writing), who is doing the action (e.g., an individual, the teacher, a team), and who is the recipient of the action, if anyone (e.g., a partner, the class). Thus, the elements provide a way of describing the type of learning and interaction taking place in the classroom (Kagan and Kagan, 1992). A teacher may decide to begin with some direct instruction (Teacher Instructs Class), followed by a group discussion on an assigned topic (Teams Discuss), and a summary presentation by one member of each group (Individual Presents to Class). Reorganizing, adding, or substituting elements in a lesson can have considerable impact. Consider a teacher who notices that not all group members are actively participating during the Teams Discuss step. To ensure greater positive interdependence and individual accountability, the teacher decides to replace the Teams Discuss element with a series of Individuals Share with Teammates (Round Robin structure).

You may find it useful to think of elements as bones that combine to create a structure. The structure, in turn, is the skeleton to which you can apply diverse subject matter to create a specific activity. When you combine a structure with content, you have created what Kagan calls an *activity*. For example, Think-Pair-Share can be applied in virtually any content area. Once you decide that the topic for Think-Pair-Share will be "to develop criteria for classifying animals," you have created an activity for your biology class in which individuals think about the criteria, discuss their ideas in pairs, and present their criteria to the class. See Chapter 4: Classbuilding and Teambuilding for a description of how the Think-Pair-Share structure can be used to help students get to know one another better.

An entire lesson can be conceived of as a series of structures. For example, a teacher may begin the lesson with Direct Instruction, followed by a Think-Pair-Share on a particular issue addressed in the instruction, and then conclude with a Send-a-Problem (see Chapter 8: Developing Interpersonal and Cognitive Skills), in which groups author content questions, exchange questions with other groups, respond to the questions they receive, and verify other groups' responses to their own questions. This *lesson design* becomes an actual lesson when you decide what subject matter you will apply the design to.

Kagan (1993), in collaboration with teachers, has compiled dozens of cooperative structures. The creativity of this method begins when you consider your lesson content and objectives and select which series of structures will help you accomplish your goals. To assist you in this task, Kagan has classified his structures according to their usefulness in generating specific types of academic, cognitive, and interpersonal development. Exhibit 15.1 defines each category and provides an example of a structure within each one. Some of these structures are described in this chapter or in the examples of earlier chapters of this book. Potentially, there are an infinite number of structures that you, other teachers, and instructional designers can continue to develop. Examples include structures that have been developed at the Centre for the Study of Classroom Processes, Concordia University, such as Match and Master Marathon, described in Chapter 8: Developing Interpersonal and Cognitive Skills, and Communication Cube, described in Chapter 4: Classbuilding and Teambuilding.

Implementation of the Structural Approach

Kagan's Structural Approach has a number of advantages for implementation. If you are new to cooperative learning, you can experiment with some of the simpler structures initially, adding new structures to your repertoire one at a time. As you and your students become more comfortable and experienced with cooperative groups, you may choose to implement more complex structures and create integrated lessons based on a sequence of structures. Once you have a solid understanding of the principles and elements that make up a cooperative structure, you may even begin to design your own structures. Thus, the Structural Approach allows you to customize instruction according to your own teaching styles and goals, your students' learning styles and needs, and the curriculum content.

While each multi-structural cooperative lesson is unique, Kagan (1993) recommends that it should include a motivational introduction, clearly defined goals and processes, practice opportunities, and teacher-directed closure. Each of the structures compiled by Kagan contains clearly delineated steps; however, it is your responsibility to decide on the global structure of the multi-structural lesson plan. In designing a multi-structural lesson, the following three steps are crucial.

Step 1. Determining the objectives: The first step in planning any lesson is deciding on your objectives. When using the Structural Approach, you should consider not only the academic goals, but the cognitive and interpersonal skill development goals as well. These goals form the basis upon which structures are selected and sequenced.

Step 2. Selecting and sequencing structures: Each structure should be carefully analyzed in terms of the types of skills it is most effective in promoting. These include cognitive skills (e.g., comprehension, analysis, synthesis), and interpersonal skills (e.g., active listening, conflict resolution). Structures also need to be evaluated for their usefulness in specific curricular areas, or in the achievement of certain academic objectives. With this knowledge, you can then select structures that best meet the objectives you set for the lesson. If these issues are overlooked, problems may arise because the selected structure may not be appropriate for the academic, cognitive, and social objectives you want to achieve. Be careful, for example, not to ask students to hold a group discussion on high-consensus material for which there is only one correct answer.

You should also assess the appropriateness of the structure in terms of the stage of the lesson (e.g., motivational introduction, reflection) and in terms of the sequencing of structures within the lesson. There should be a progression in the lesson so that each structure builds on the learning experiences of the previous ones. Some structures may be selected primarily for their ability to develop prerequisite skills for subsequent activities. Teambuilding structures, for example, may be used to create an appropriate climate for later collaboration on more academic tasks.

Step 3. Structuring and destructuring group work: When cooperative learning is new either to you or your students, it is wise to closely structure the group work, clearly outlining for students the steps

······· EXHIBIT 15.1 **Classification and Examples of Structures** ·······

- **Classbuilding:** structures that help create a positive classroom climate conducive to cooperation and appreciation of others (e.g., Inside-Outside Circle).
- **Teambuilding:** structures that build a sense of group identity, an appreciation of individual differences, and mutual support (e.g., Uncommon Commonalities, see Chapter 4: Classbuilding and Teambuilding).
- **Communication skills:** structures that develop interpersonal communication skills (e.g., Think-Pair-Share, see Chapter 4: Classbuilding and Teambuilding).

- **Mastery:** structures used to practice specific skills, acquire, review, and memorize facts or high-consensus content (e.g., Numbered Heads Together).
- **Thinking skills:** structures appropriate for generating questions and ideas, revising understanding, exploring interrelationships among ideas, analyzing complex concepts, and encouraging inductive and deductive reasoning (e.g., Word-Webbing, see Chapter 8: Developing Interpersonal and Cognitive Skills).
- **Information sharing:** structures that facilitate information sharing within and between teams to support teambuilding, classbuilding, exchange of multiple ideas, constructive feedback, and higher-level thinking (e.g., Round Robin).

Source: Adapted from S. Kagan, *Cooperative Learning: Resources for Teachers*, San Juan Capistrano, California: Resources for Teachers, 1992. Copyright © 1992 by Spencer Kagan. Used by permission.

of each structure and the expected behaviors. As students become more skilled in cooperative group work, you may wish to provide less structure. Progressive destructuring offers greater opportunities for students to internalize cooperation and to develop higher-level thinking, interpersonal skills, and autonomy. When working toward this goal, you must take care to include more time for students to reflect on how effectively they have structured their own interactions and on how they can improve their participation and collaboration next time. You must help students take on this responsibility and not expect that it will happen naturally.

Illustrative Example of the Structural Approach

Level and subject: Primary grades, personal and social development

Content: Learning about myself and my peers

Objectives: To contribute to a group project. To develop a positive sense of self. To begin to develop an awareness of the differences and similarities between people. To learn to take turns and listen carefully.

Materials: Sheets of paper with the outline of a large star in the middle of each sheet, markers or crayons, and a stapler.

Procedure:

Before beginning this lesson, talk about cooperation and the types of skills children will need (e.g., turn-taking, active listening). We recommend that you model the skills and steps of each structure with two children to illustrate the instructions to the class.

This lesson plan comprises a sequence of four structures. Students begin with a classbuilding structure, engage in a teambuilding structure, participate in an information-sharing structure, and end with a closure classbuilding structure.

Structure 1. Inside-Outside Circle:

Step 1. Number off the children using the numbers 1 and 2 alternately.

Step 2. Ask all number 1 children to make a circle in the middle of the room facing outward.

Step 3. Ask each number 2 child to stand facing a number 1 child, forming two concentric circles with each child facing another.

Step 4. Give a dialogue prompt such as, "Tell your partner about your favorite animal" (food, hobby, color).

Step 5. Partners then share their response to the prompt.

Step 6. After the prompt, tell children in the outside circle to move clockwise past three children and to face their new partners.

Children repeat the process with a new prompt until they have had a chance to share with multiple partners.

Structure 2. Simultaneous Rally Table:

Step 1. Tell children they are going to make a book about themselves and their classmates. To begin, each child will work with the last partner he or she had from Inside-Outside Circle.

Step 2. Give each child a piece of paper with a large star drawn on it. Each child writes his or her name in the center of the star.

Step 3. Give children the first dialogue prompt from Inside-Outside Circle and ask them to share their responses with their partners. Each child then draws a picture in one point of the star to represent his or her own response. (Older children may also want to write a sentence or two in the point.)

Step 4. Partners then exchange sheets.

Step 5. Give the second dialogue prompt. Partners again exchange responses and each child draws a picture in a second point of the star to represent his or her *partner's* response.

Step 6. Partners exchange sheets and repeat the process with a third, fourth, and fifth prompt.

Structure 3. Round Robin Partner Share:

Step 1. Each pair combines with another pair to form groups of four.

Step 2. In Round Robin, each child, in turn, presents his or her partner using the star as a visual cue.

Structure 4. Closure Classbuilding:

Step 1. When all children have finished presenting their partners to their groups, you and the children can assemble the class book. (Don't forget to include an authors' page.)

Step 2. Place the book in the book corner. Authors can take turns taking the book home to show their families.

Step 3. Assemble all the children in a circle. Discuss how they cooperated and the skills they used during the lesson.

Exhibit 15.2 presents an analysis of the elements of the Structural Approach in this lesson.

·············· EXHIBIT 15.2 **Analysis of the Structural Approach Illustrative Example** ················

Grade and subject: Primary grades, personal and social development

Content: Awareness of self and others

Group Task: Complete drawings on stars based on your own and your partner's interests and assemble them into a class book.

Grouping	Positive Interdependence
• Students are combined in randomly matched pairs (Inside-Outside Circle; Rally Table). • Student pairs combine to form groups of four (Round Robin Partner Share).	• Goal: To complete stars and create a class book. • Task: Each child adds a drawing to his or her star and to the star of his or her partner. • Resource: Partners share the star sheets.
Individual Accountability	Interpersonal and Cognitive Skills
• Each child must contribute illustrations to both stars (Rally Table). • Each child must present his or her partner to another pair (Round Robin Partner Share).	• The teacher introduces skills needed during pair work and models the skills with two children. • The teacher observes for the use of skills and intervenes to reinforce appropriate behaviors.
Evaluation and Reflection	Extension Activity
• An assessment of each child's contribution is added to his or her evaluation portfolio. • All students in the class discuss how well they cooperated and the skills they used (Closure Classbuilding).	• Pairs that finish early could talk about other things they like within each category.

SUMMARY

In this chapter, you have seen how the Structural Approach offers teachers concrete step-by-step activity plans, or structures, in which the principles of interdependence, individual accountability, simultaneous interaction, and equal participation are incorporated. After setting the objectives of a lesson, you can select structures appropriate to those objectives and sequence them to create an integrated, multi-structural lesson. As you develop more expertise in cooperative learning and the Structural Approach, you can begin to modify the elements that make up the structures, and even design new structures yourself to meet specific needs.

REFLECTION ACTIVITIES

1. Use the structures outlined in the illustrative example to create a lesson in your subject area.

2. Consider your own approach to lesson planning. Could you use this method effectively in teaching your students? Why or why not?

3. Design a Match and Master Marathon (Activity 8.4) to review course material. What structures would you use to introduce and follow up this activity to create a multistructural lesson?

Cathie Archbould

CHAPTER

16

Cooperative Concept Mapping

WHAT ARE THE INSTRUCTIONAL GOALS OF
COOPERATIVE CONCEPT MAPPING?

•

WHAT LEARNING MATERIAL IS COOPERATIVE
CONCEPT MAPPING WELL SUITED FOR?

•

WHAT ARE THE IMPORTANT ELEMENTS OF A
CONCEPT MAP?

•

HOW ARE POSITIVE INTERDEPENDENCE AND
INDIVIDUAL ACCOUNTABILITY STRUCTURED
IN THIS METHOD?

•

WHAT INTERPERSONAL AND COGNITIVE SKILLS ARE
REQUIRED FOR COOPERATIVE CONCEPT MAPPING?

Cooperative Concept Mapping, developed at the Centre for the Study of Classroom Processes, Concordia University, Montreal (Dedic, Rosenfield, d'Apollonia, and De Simone, 1994), was originally designed to alleviate some of the comprehension difficulties faced by college science students. Educators and researchers have pointed out that students often equate understanding with rote memorization. Consequently, they are able neither to apply concepts and principles to the real world nor to forge connections among ideas.

Cooperative Concept Mapping is a combination of two strategies—cooperative learning and concept mapping—in which students work in small groups clarifying and elaborating their understanding of a text passage or lecture. Cooperative Concept Mapping is based on the belief that students arrive at an understanding of concepts by discussing them with their peers, by connecting new ideas to what they already know, by actively generating new ideas, and by incorporating these ideas into coherent mental schemas.

Concept mapping, also called networking, is a text comprehension strategy (McGagg and Dansereau, 1991; Novak and Gowin, 1984) that helps students construct visual representations (concept maps) of verbal information. Concept mapping requires students to identify important ideas, discern the relationships between the ideas, and represent the knowledge in the form of a two-dimensional node-link-node visual representation. Concepts are displayed in nodes (boxes or circles) that are connected by specific links, indicating the nature of the relationships between concepts. These links often have arrowheads showing the direction of the relationship. Concept maps are often hierarchical; that is, the general or more inclusive concepts are at the top of the concept map, and the specific or less inclusive concepts are arranged beneath them. The entire map functions as a visual representation of the relationships among the ideas in the text, or lecture.

In Cooperative Concept Mapping, students discuss the material that will be mapped to develop a preliminary understanding of the concepts. Subsequently, they individually construct a concept map either in class or as an assignment. Team members then regroup to compare and discuss their maps. This exchange of ideas elaborates and refines students' understanding, thus allowing them either to integrate the multiple perspectives into a collective concept map or to revise their individual maps to take other perspectives into account. The combination of concept mapping, which emphasizes the internal reconstruction of knowledge, and cooperative learning, which facilitates the communication and sharing of knowledge, enhances meaningful conceptual understanding.

IMPLEMENTATION

Cooperative Concept Mapping can be integrated into an entire course or used as an independent class activity. In this chapter, we will describe Cooperative Concept Mapping in its most complete form, as an integrated, term-long implementation. In this application, Cooperative Concept Mapping is especially useful for promoting meaningful learning, since you and your students develop greater commitment and take the time to develop greater expertise in applying this strategy to learning.

Before committing to a full-fledged implementation of this sort, however, you may wish to experiment with Cooperative Concept Mapping as an independent class activity. You can do so by assigning students to random groups of three or four, by selecting a manageable text passage of several hundred words, and by proceeding with Steps 6 to 10, which we will describe below.

Cooperative Concept Mapping alternates individual preparation and tasks with group discussion and refinement, building both positive interdependence and individual accountability into the process. For example, outcome interdependence is ensured by having students develop, in the final stages, a single group map. In addition, means interdependence is structured by having students combine their individually constructed concept maps into a group map or by assigning specific roles during group discussions and tasks. Individual accountability for contributing to the group task is supported by having each student identify main ideas and draft maps in preparation for group discussions.

An Integrated Term-Long Implementation

Cooperative Concept Mapping can be used as a complex teaching and learning strategy that is integrated with the curriculum and implemented during an entire course. Used in this manner, it emphasizes learning as a process and involves you and your students in a strong commitment to more meaningful, conceptual learning. You may find it necessary to cut back on the breadth of topics you cover in order to devote more time to developing thinking skills and enhancing the depth of students' understanding.

There are ten steps to term-long implementation of Cooperative Concept Mapping: (1) integrating course curriculum; (2) orienting students; (3) assigning students to groups; (4) developing interpersonal and cognitive skills; (5) whole-class instruction and modeling concept mapping; (6) identifying main ideas (individually); (7) categorizing related ideas (in groups); (8) drafting concept maps (individually); (9) revising and using concept maps (in groups); and (10) feedback and evaluation. Although we describe this implementation in separate steps, there isn't a fixed sequence. You may need to return to previous steps as required throughout the term. For example, you may reintroduce skills training whenever a group or the class is experiencing difficulty.

Step 1. Integrating course curriculum: Using the textbook for the course, your knowledge of the content, or a course syllabus, select the concepts within each topic you wish to include in your course. Group the concepts into clusters or categories to serve as an organizational framework for integrating your course with the Cooperative Concept Mapping method. Determine the relationships among the concepts and decide which ones to emphasize. We also recommend that you prepare general concept maps of the domain. This process will help you and your students recognize the similarity of concepts across topics and the potential for transfer of problem-solving strategies. Such recognition will also allow you to cut back on the amount of time you devote to redundant content, leaving additional time for more active learning through Cooperative Concept Mapping.

Use this framework when preparing instructional objectives, lectures, questions, assignments, tests, and so on. In this way, you will integrate the strategy with the course content, and students will perceive that *how* the content is interrelated is as important as *what* the content is. Moreover, they will experience the strategy as an integral part of the course and not as an added frill.

Step 2. Orienting students: Many students come to class with the belief that success, particularly in the sciences, depends on rote learning and the acquisition of basic facts and procedures. Typically, these students are used to devoting their time to memorizing facts and practicing routine procedures for problem solving. This approach to learning is usually reinforced by the type of demands made by teachers on students through course assignments and examinations. Effective use of the Cooperative Concept Mapping method requires that students change this attitude to learning. They must become more active, self-regulated learners and come to value higher-level conceptual understanding. Initially, you may need to motivate them to change. You can encourage students to become actively engaged by relating the content to past and future activities, to their daily lives, and to the "real world."

Students may also be accustomed to working individually or in competition with other students when learning course material. Their past experience may initially interfere with their effectiveness in interacting with others. Therefore, at the outset, you may want to discuss with your students the importance of developing cooperative skills as a career objective and as a means to promote more meaningful learning.

Specify both the collaborative and cognitive skills you wish your students to acquire. Be sure to design your assignments and examinations so that this type of learning occurs. Communicate these goals in such a way that your students can see their relevance to their future academic success. In these ways, your students may make these goals their own.

Step 3. Assigning students to groups: At the beginning of the course, assign students to three- or four-member groups. Since students will be engaged in complex cognitive tasks, students with extreme differences in ability may find it more difficult to work together effectively. More able students may take over the task and be unwilling to provide thorough explanations for their reasoning. Similarly, less able students may become frustrated or threatened by their inability to contribute. They may lose motivation and may not actively engage in the task. On the other hand, heterogeneity encourages discussion and the formulation of alternative points of view. Therefore, we recommend moderately heterogeneous groups. In instances where classes vary widely in ability, we have found that dividing the class into two strata on the basis of ability and prior performance and then assigning students to heterogeneous teams within each stratum works well.

Step 4. Developing interpersonal and cognitive skills: To apply Cooperative Concept Mapping effectively, students require certain interpersonal and cognitive skills, as well as prerequisite domain-specific knowledge. Specific strategies for developing these skills are provided in Chapter 8: Developing Interpersonal and Cognitive Skills. Some skill development may be carried out before Cooperative Concept Mapping begins, but it should be emphasized during the steps below.

In addition, students must have some knowledge of the content area before concept mapping begins. Prior to exploring the content in greater depth, they need to have at least a superficial understanding of the basic facts and vocabulary required for discussion. Preparing students for this may also include remedial coverage of content from earlier courses.

Step 5. Whole-class instruction and modeling concept mapping: Since Cooperative Concept Mapping is a complex cognitive task, you will need to ensure that students understand the concept mapping process. In your lecture, model how you would think about the topic and construct a concept map along with the class. That is, think aloud by asking rhetorical questions, providing partial answers, recapitulating related ideas, and so on. Subsequently, draw students' attention to the mental processes that you have modeled. Invite students to participate in the modeling activity by pausing and waiting for their input. Participant modeling, where teacher and students co-construct a concept map representing the topic, is an essential component of Cooperative Concept Mapping. Initially, you will provide much of the scaffolding necessary for the conceptualization, then gradually withdraw your contribution, providing corrective feedback when absolutely necessary. Thus, students learn not only what the course content is but also how to contribute to the development of ideas in the domain.

Step 6. Identifying main ideas (individually): Students need to have some domain-specific skills and knowledge to construct meaning from text. They need to know the terminology, be able to distinguish between relevant and irrelevant concepts, summarize text, and so on. Assign pertinent textbook passages or other materials as homework. Ask students to read the text and select the main ideas by highlighting them, listing them, or writing them on Post-it notes.

Step 7. Categorizing related ideas (in groups): Ask students to get into their groups to check that everyone has done the assigned homework. Have them review and summarize the content, pose and answer questions on the content, and compare their lists of selected main ideas. Have the groups reduce the number of ideas by grouping closely related ideas and summarizing the "chunks" to create more global concepts. Encourage students to question and justify each other's categorizations.

Step 8. Drafting concept maps (individually): Ask students to individually prepare a draft of a concept map based on either a text passage or their understanding of an assigned topic. Particularly at the outset, the text passage should be only moderate in length so that the concept map will have about ten to fifteen nodes, organized into four or five clusters with three or four different relationships. The text passage should be sufficiently complex so that different representations reflecting individuals' understanding are possible.

Ask students to draft a concept map using the instructions in Exhibit 16.1.

Encourage students to invest enough time to verify the coherency and accuracy of their maps. Tell your students that they should be prepared to explain their maps to others. These individual concept maps can be completed either in class or as a homework assignment.

Step 9. Revising and using concept maps (in groups): Have students get into their groups to compare their individual concept maps. Through the process of explaining their maps to each other, students refine their understanding of the content. Finally, students agree on a final group concept map. You can then ask them to use the maps to solve problems or to integrate the maps with prior maps to build a "super-concept map" of the entire course. You could also ask the different groups to post and compare their maps. Encourage group members to discuss the differences they noted in the maps, paying particular attention to how the concepts were related.

Step 10. Feedback and evaluation: Provide feedback on both cooperative learning and concept mapping. This feedback can be given either by you or by the students themselves. For example, at the end of a class, students can reflect on how they worked together and on what they learned. Such reflections can be brief and provide a sense of accomplishment and closure.

When giving feedback on concept mapping, probe for the rationale behind a given concept map rather than merely correct it. In this manner, you will emphasize the process of developing a concept map rather than only the end product.

Make sure that the test items and problems on midterm and final exams test high-level understanding. Reliance on factual recall or the application of standard procedures to fixed problems undermines

·················· EXHIBIT 16.1 **Instructions for Drafting Individual Concept Maps** ··················

1. Read the text or consider the content that you want to map.

2. Decide on the important ideas or concepts and list them.

3. Choose the most important idea or concept. Draw a box at the top of the page. Inside the box write a word or short phrase that represents this concept. This box and its content is called a "node."

4. Rank the other concepts in order of importance and construct nodes for each of them. Make sure that nodes for concepts of equal importance are placed at the same level horizontally. In this manner, you create a visual structure in which ideas or concepts of equal importance are placed along the same horizontal line. Nodes for concepts of lesser importance should be placed below those of more importance.

5. Consider each concept and ask yourself how this concept is related to other concepts. Attempt to express this relationship in words (e.g., "cause" is a relationship between the concepts of "bacteria" and "illness").

6. For each relationship between two concepts, draw a line connecting the nodes representing the concepts. We call these lines "links." Label each link with words that describe the relationship between the two concepts it connects. Continue this process until all relationships are in place. You may need to rearrange the concepts to minimize the number of links that cross one another. As you rearrange your map, you will find that the concepts that are closely related will cluster in your map. (Because of the need to rearrange, some people find it useful to use Post-it notes as the nodes.)

7. Draw arrowheads on the links to indicate the direction of each relationship. For example:

   | bacteria | —causes→ | illness |

8. Examine your map and the text or the content that you wanted to map. Ask yourself, "Is there anything missing?" "Is there anything that needs to be changed?" Read the map to yourself. Does it make sense to you?

---

the strategy. Such questions can be answered by rote and make genuine understanding superfluous.

Illustrative Example of Cooperative Concept Mapping

Level and subject: College physics

Content: Mechanics—Work-Energy Theorem

Objectives: To develop an understanding of the concepts of work and various forms of energy. To relate work to change in the form of energy. To relate the work-energy theorem to real-life observations.

Materials: Physics textbook, Post-it notes (optional)

Procedure:

Step 1. Integrating course curriculum: Examine the topics covered in the mechanics course using your textbook, course syllabus, and objectives. The list of topics constitutes the framework for designing your Cooperative Concept Mapping implementation. A mechanics course typically covers kinematics, dynamics, Work-Energy Theorem, conservation of energy, conservation of linear momentum, rotational kinematics and dynamics, conservation of the angular momentum, and gravitation.

Look for common problem-solving strategies and concepts that will help you relate one topic to another. Reduce the amount of time you spend on redundant concepts or applications by teaching your students to recognize these patterns and to transfer strategies. This will allow you to devote more time to in-depth understanding through Cooperative Concept Mapping.

For this example, we will illustrate the use of Cooperative Concept Mapping to explore the Work-Energy Theorem and the Law of Conservation of Energy. Both of these laws involve concepts that are abstract and difficult to grasp. Therefore, Cooperative Concept Mapping helps students revise their misconceptions and misunderstandings.

Step 2. Orienting students: You can encourage your students to become more actively engaged in higher-level conceptual understanding by stating a principle (e.g., work is related to the transfer of energy) and asking students to come up with real-life observations (e.g., a sliding object comes to a stop). Another strategy is to ask students what they already know about "work" and then relate your explanations to their examples.

When introducing cooperative learning, you can demonstrate the relevance of learning to work effectively with others to your students by distributing current job ads in engineering, medicine, and technology that stipulate the ability to work well with others and to communicate effectively as qualifications. You can also make references to sport teams, rock bands, medical teams, shuttle crews, and so on, leading a discussion on what makes these teams effective.

Step 3. Assigning students to groups: Students in this introductory college physics course are given a standardized physics test and then ranked on the basis of their performance. Alternatively, you can use prior marks from similar courses as the basis for your ranking. Assign students to heterogeneous groups of four using the procedure described under STAD in Chapter 11: Student Team Learning Methods. If the class varies widely in ability or prior knowledge, first divide students into two groups and assign each subgroup of students using the same procedure. Ask students to come up with a group name appropriate for a team of physicists. Students remain in the same groups for the duration of the term.

Step 4. Developing interpersonal and cognitive skills: Monitor the groups as they work, and intervene to help groups that are experiencing problems. Have students complete the Group Productivity Reflection Form (see Chapter 9: Evaluating and Reflecting) at regular intervals to draw their attention to effective group-work skills.

In order to develop depth of knowledge through elaboration, students need to question their understanding of both the concepts and their applications. Initially, students ask trivial questions (e.g., "How did you calculate this ratio?"). Guide students in distinguishing between trivial questions and those that probe understanding. (See Chapter 8: Developing Interpersonal and Cognitive Skills.)

Step 5. Whole-class instruction and modeling concept mapping: To model the Cooperative Concept Map-

ping process, introduce the topic by writing out the proposition illustrated in Exhibit 16.2, Phase 1.

Model thinking about this topic by asking yourself questions aloud, such as, "What does *transfer* as opposed to *transformation* of energy mean?" Invite your students' participation by pausing for such elaborations as, "Transfer means energy moves from one particle to another" and "Transformation means a change of one form to another." Incorporate these thoughts into your map as in Exhibit 16.2, Phase 2.

To probe the issue further, ask your students to provide an example of the *transformation of energy* (e.g., a free-falling object) and the *transfer of energy* (e.g., the motion of an object on a horizontal surface with friction). Often students fail to recognize that the motion of an object on a horizontal surface with friction can also be considered an example of transformation. Instead, they think it is only an example of transfer of energy. Record these competing propositions on the map using links labeled with question marks as in Exhibit 16.2, Phase 3.

Encourage your students to elaborate upon both propositions. Taking the perspective of an object *in isolation*, they may suggest that the object loses kinetic energy (slows down) because of the work done by friction (transfer). Taking the perspective of an object as part of a *surface-object system*, students may suggest that the loss of the object's kinetic energy is due to work done by friction and leads to an increase of internal energy of the system because both the object and the surface get warmer (transformation). The final concept map is drawn to incorporate both perspectives (see Exhibit 16.3).

This process models both the construction of a concept map and the elaborative discussion that leads to refinement of the concept map and deeper understanding. While students are engaged in Cooperative Concept Mapping, observe the groups and encourage them to use the process you have modeled.

Step 6. Identifying main ideas (individually): A free-falling object can also be perceived as either an isolated object or as a part of a more complex system that includes both the object and the ground. Ask students to explore these two perspectives. They should identify important concepts involved in each of the perspectives (e.g., work done by gravity, gravitational potential energy, earth-object system).

Step 7. Categorizing related ideas (in groups): Ask your students to get into their groups to discuss how this example could be used to illustrate both the transformation of energy and the transfer of energy. Encourage agreement on the important concepts involved.

Step 8. Drafting concept maps (individually): Ask your students to individually construct a concept map that incorporates both perspectives following the example of Exhibits 16.2 and 16.3. This can be done either in class, if time permits, or at home as part of the homework assignment.

Step 9. Revising and using concept maps (in groups): In groups, have students go over their individual concept maps and compare them with those of other group members. Assign four problems and ask students to analyze each using their concept maps as a guide. Have students decide which perspective

is most useful for a given problem, using their concept map to justify their decision. Subsequently, students should revise their concept maps and agree on a group concept map.

Step 10. Feedback and evaluation: While the groups are working together, circulate and observe their interactions. Are they on task? Are the groups asking for and giving elaborated explanations? Are they using proper questioning skills? Are they demonstrating effective interpersonal skills? Have students discuss their responses to the Group Productivity Reflection Form (see Step 4).

Collect the students' concept maps and give feedback on them. Make sure the important concepts are in nodes, the links between the concepts are appropriately labeled, and there is a coherent structure. Rather than revising students' maps yourself, pose probing questions in writing, such as, "Why did you link gravity with kinetic energy?" Students should then revise their maps in response to your feedback and resubmit them.

·············· Exhibit 16.2 **Modeling the Phases in the Construction of a Concept Map** ···············

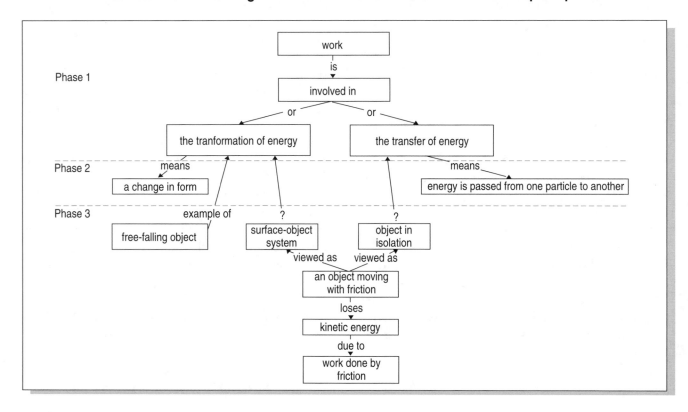

To encourage your students to persist in meaningful learning, make sure that your final exam elicits conceptual understanding of the content rather than rote recall or application of procedures. For instance, ask students to describe an event from their own lives that could be analyzed and explained using the two perspectives developed in the concept map in the illustrative example. Ask them to analyze the event using both perspectives and to draw a concept map integrating the two perspectives.

An analysis of the important features of the illustrative example of Cooperative Concept Mapping is presented in Exhibit 16.4.

SUMMARY

Cooperative Concept Mapping was designed by members of the Centre for the Study of Classroom Processes at Concordia University in Montreal to promote deeper and more meaningful understanding of science. It is a complex strategy that combines elements of cooperative learning with those of concept mapping. Students work together in small groups, assisting each other to think about how concepts are related and thus constructing a deeper understanding of the topic.

Cooperative Concept Mapping is a comprehension strategy in which learners identify the main ideas within a content area (individually), categorize related ideas and analyze how these ideas are related to their prior knowledge (in groups), draft concept maps to visually represent the relationships among the ideas (individually), and revise and use the concept maps, thus reflecting refinements in their understanding (in groups).

You can implement Cooperative Concept Mapping as an independent classroom activity or as a comprehensive teaching and learning method throughout the whole term. This method comple-

EXHIBIT 16.3 **The Final Concept Map**

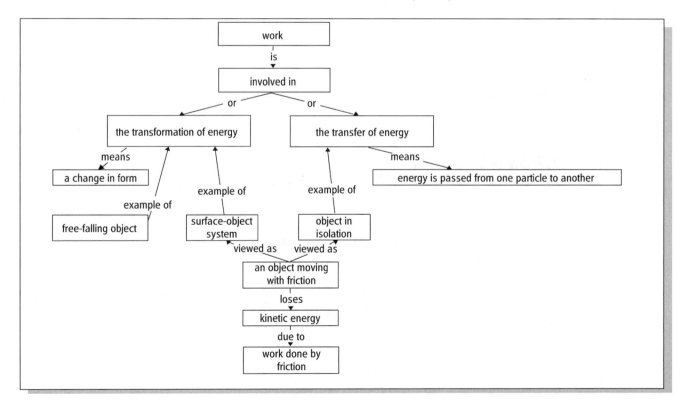

·········· EXHIBIT 16.4 **Analysis of the Cooperative Concept Mapping Illustrative Example** ············

Grade and Subject: College physics	
Content: Mechanics—Work-Energy Theorem	
Group task: Use a concept map to analyze the motion of a free-falling object from two perspectives using the conservation of energy law.	
Grouping • Students are assigned to groups of four. • The ability grouping of each group is moderately heterogeneous. • Groups stay together for the duration of term.	**Positive Interdependence** • Goal: To prepare an integrated concept map. • Resource: Students share their maps to refine their understanding. • Identity: Students develop a team name.
Individual Accountability • Group members do individual maps to prepare for group discussion. • Each member's map is incorporated into a group map. • Individual contributions to the group map are submitted for feedback.	**Interpersonal and Cognitive Skills** • Students explain and justify their perspectives. • Students use elaborated questioning.
Evaluation and Reflection • Group members complete the Group Productivity Reflection Form. • The final exam reflects conceptual understanding rather than recall by rote.	**Extension Activity** • Groups create a physics problem based on real life to evaluate understanding of energy transformations. The problem may be used as a test item.

ments and enriches traditional lectures by giving students the opportunity to construct and refine their understanding of the content.

REFLECTION ACTIVITIES

1. Work with a partner. First, individually construct a concept map of Vygotsky's perspective of cognitive development as explained in Chapter 1: Learning and Motivation. Then, meet to compare and contrast your concept maps. Revise your understanding (and your concept map) by discussing similarities and differences.

2. Select a content area in which you currently teach or are interested in teaching. Construct a concept map of the major topics and use the concept map to identify common features across these topics, as described in Step 1 of Cooperative Concept Mapping. How will this influence your strategy in teaching this content?

3. Prepare a Cooperative Concept Mapping activity to assign to students. It should include the objectives, materials (e.g., text passage), instructions for individual and group work, and feedback criteria. Identify which steps in your activity promote positive interdependence and individual accountability.

Other Peer Interaction Methods

Cathie Archbould

WHAT ARE COLLABORATIVE LEARNING, TRIBES,
GROUP WORK FOR MULTIPLE ABILITIES,
COOPERATIVE SCRIPTS, AND TUTORING?

•

WHAT METHODS ARE APPROPRIATE FOR CLASSES IN
WHICH STUDENTS HAVE A WIDE RANGE OF
ABILITIES?

•

WHAT METHOD PROMOTES INTERACTION BETWEEN
CHILDREN IN DIFFERENT GRADES?

•

IF I WANT TO FOCUS ON GROUP DYNAMICS AND
SOCIAL SUPPORT WHAT METHOD SHOULD I USE?

There are many other methods that use peer interaction to promote learning. Some can only be used with specific curricula, others are more generic. In this chapter, we will briefly describe several of these methods to provide you with an even broader range of ways to structure your classes. But even these brief descriptions do not exhaust the possibilities. There are a variety of other methods, some excellent textbooks and materials, and trainers available to assist you and your school. Many of the resources not described here are listed in Appendix B: Selected Resources.

Not all methods summarized in this chapter employ all of the elements of cooperative learning. But each of the methods we will discuss employs some of these elements. These methods reflect very different beliefs about the characteristics of students and what education should be like. Some, like Cooperative Scripts, are extremely structured; while others, like Collaborative Learning, give students a great deal of autonomy. As we have emphasized throughout this book, you should analyze the context of instruction carefully and choose methods that correspond to your beliefs about education, the characteristics of your students, the curriculum that you teach, and so on.

COLLABORATIVE LEARNING

Collaborative learning is not simply another cooperative learning method. It is an approach to small-group instruction that grew out of a different theoretical and philosophical basis than did most cooperative learning methods. Proponents of collaborative learning want to restructure the power relationships within schools, making them more egalitarian (Pradl, 1991). They advocate a more democratic process, giving students more power than in traditional instruction.

The collaborative approach has been most popular in Britain, Australia, and New Zealand. But it has also been supported by some educators in North America, particularly those who teach language arts. Collaborative learning uses less structure than other cooperative methods and relies more on students' intrinsic interest in cooperative tasks. It emphasizes the role of purposeful talk in promoting learning and a climate of openness and shared responsibility between teacher and students.

There is more student autonomy in the collaborative approach than in most other cooperative learning approaches. Students are usually permitted to decide with whom they will work, rather than being assigned to heterogeneous groups, as most cooperative methods call for. Together, the teacher and the students discuss what will be learned and how it will be learned. In the Collaborative Learning method, the teacher does not make those decisions alone and then attempt to stimulate students' interest in participating (Boomer, 1990).

Most often, the collaborative approach takes the form of group projects. The groups, in consultation with the teacher, decide which specific topics they will study and how to divide the tasks for their projects. There is also between-group cooperation. Groups share the resources they discover with other groups that may find them useful. As Collaborative Learning is not a specific instructional method, there are no specific step-by-step instructions for its implementation. However, Reid, Forrestal, and Cook (1984) developed a set of guidelines for implementing collaborative group projects that we believe you will find useful.

Students begin by forming their own groups of four to six members. Sometimes, they base their selection of group members on shared interest in a particular topic. The framework for this group work incorporates five stages: input, exploration, reshaping, presentation, and reflection.

1. The *input* stage is an initial experience, such as a field trip, that engages students and forms the basis for further learning. After the teacher has introduced the general topic, each group negotiates with him or her to determine the specific topic they will cover.

2. During the *exploration* phase, students investigate their topic in various ways (e.g., group discussion or library research). Students have quite a bit of freedom in deciding how they will gather the information necessary to complete the project.

3. In the *reshaping* stage, students actively work to transform the new information to arrive at a deeper understanding of the concepts. The teacher encourages students to consider creative ways to express their new knowledge.

4. In the *presentation* stage, students present what they have learned to an audience of interested individuals, such as parents or other classes. Students should try to actively engage the audience so that they might learn the information, too.

5. In the *reflection* stage, students think carefully about how and what they have learned during group work. Reflection should increase students' sense of involvement with their own learning and should encourage them to provide feedback about the process that the teacher can incorporate into the design of future activities.

TRIBES

Developed by Jeanne Gibbs (1987, 1994), Tribes is based on principles of social psychology and on group development theory. It is designed to foster a supportive peer climate and sense of community in the classroom and school. Consequently, careful attention is given to teambuilding and classbuilding activities—referred to as inclusion activities—and to communication and conflict management skill development. Tribes cultivates an environment in which every student feels included and valued. This supportive social climate encourages an academic climate in which planning, a sense of responsibility, problem-solving, and achievement are promoted.

In Tribes, groups of five or six students work together daily on cooperative activities assigned by the teacher throughout an entire year. During this time, these long-term support groups progress through three stages of group development: inclusion, influence, and affection ("community"). These stages correspond roughly to Tuckman's forming, storming, and performing stages (Tuckman and Jensen, 1977), respectively. (See Chapter 2: Group Processes and Productivity.) A teacher trained in the Tribes method acts as facilitator during these stages by modeling positive class norms, observing group interactions, and conducting activities consistent with each stage.

During the *inclusion* stage, students get to know each other and learn to feel comfortable in their groups. At this time, the teacher conducts team-building and positive class norm activities to create a relaxed and caring environment for learning.

During the *influence* stage, students usually need to assert themselves and affect group decisions. Recognizing this, the teacher conducts activities in which students develop interpersonal and conflict management skills. These activities encourage students to value differences of opinion and to appreciate the richness such diversity can bring to the group.

The *affection* stage is reached when the group works together effectively in a caring, supportive climate. Group members will have developed a strong sense of esteem for themselves and others, and will help one another to achieve their goals.

GROUP WORK FOR MULTIPLE ABILITIES

Elizabeth Cohen, director of the Program for Complex Instruction at Stanford, developed an approach to cooperative learning that is especially useful in classrooms of students with diverse backgrounds. In multiethnic classrooms, language and cultural minority students often have a lower status compared to other classmates. Such status problems can create negative expectations for success that lead to underperforming and demotivated learners. To overcome these problems, Cohen (1994a) emphasizes redesigning both the curriculum and the methods of instruction to be inclusive and culturally neutral. Unlike most cooperative learning techniques, where the status of high-ability students is reinforced through their roles as tutors in heterogeneous groups, Cohen recommends designing demanding tasks that emphasize a broad range of skills and abilities, thus optimizing opportunities for all students to contribute.

In a typical application, students in heterogeneous groups work at complex tasks requiring a broad range of abilities. For example, technical, political, and organizational aspects of activities should be highlighted and valued, along with the academic aspects. Students are trained to complete these complex tasks by drawing on the diverse skills of each group member.

Teachers publicly acknowledge students when they employ any of these skills, thereby enhancing the status of students who are typically derided by others because they are not the high academic achievers in the class. Teachers are trained to delegate authority, to become more like facilitators, and to deal effectively with status problems.

COOPERATIVE SCRIPTS

Cooperative Scripts is one of the learning strategies developed by Dansereau and his colleagues (Dansereau, 1985; McDonald, Dansereau, Garland, Holley, and Collins, 1979) to enhance the text-comprehension skills of college students. Dansereau and his colleagues have studied the benefits of training students in specific information-processing skills, such as extraction of main ideas and relationships, memorization, recall, and application of textual information. Most of the research using these strategies was carried out under controlled laboratory conditions using volunteer college students who obtained course credit for their participation. However, these strategies can be adapted for classroom instruction across different academic levels and content areas.

Cooperative Scripts is based on information-processing theories of learning. The role of peers in this strategy is to provide effective modeling, rehearsal, elaboration, and so on. Thus, peers function as trainers and coaches. There is little, if any, emphasis on social skills training or peer support.

Cooperative Scripts is designed to help learners clarify their understanding and to facilitate the storage and retrieval of information in memory. Pairs of students read and recall a written passage as outlined in the steps that follow:

Step 1. Curricular materials: Divide a 2,500-word passage into 500-word segments. You can use the same passage for all student pairs or choose different material for each pair.

Step 2. Assigning students to pairs: Students form pairs. There are no restrictions as to how students are assigned or to the duration of the pairs.

Step 3. Group work: Give each student pair two copies of the text. Each student takes a turn playing the role of Recaller or Listener. (Students can flip a coin to decide who goes first as Recaller.)

(a) Both students silently read the first 500-word segment.

(b) The Recaller summarizes aloud what he or she has read as completely as possible without looking at the passage. The Recaller tries to include all of the important facts and ideas.

(c) After the Recaller has finished, the Listener, while looking at the passage:

- corrects the Recaller's summary by mentioning any important information the Recaller may have left out and points out any ideas that have been summarized incorrectly.

- helps the Recaller memorize the material better by suggesting memory aids.

(d) The students switch roles. They read the next 500-word segment and repeat Steps (a) to (c) until they have read and summarized the entire text.

TUTORING

Tutoring is broadly defined as an individual teaching approach in which one person teaches another. Both people can be either of similar abilities or ages (peer tutoring) or of different abilities or ages (cross-age tutoring).

With the rise of the one-room schoolhouse, in which children of different ages and abilities shared one space and one teacher, tutoring became a common practice. More knowledgeable (and often older) students would instruct less knowledgeable (and often younger) students. Because the teacher did not have much time to review material, tutors were given this responsibility. Such tutorials were a necessary supplement to the teacher's lessons. As one-room schoolhouses disappeared, and children of similar ages were grouped by grade level, there was less need to have children assist one another. Teaching functions became the sole responsibility of the teacher.

There are numerous reasons for the re-implementation of tutoring practices. First, as classrooms have increased in size and as children with special needs have been integrated into regular classrooms, it has become impossible for a teacher to attend to the individual needs of all students. Second, budgetary cutbacks have made it difficult for school administrators to hire professional assistance. Third, as a teaching and learning process, tutoring provides the tutor with an opportunity to verbalize material, rehearsing and clarifying his or her own understanding, while instructing another student. Fourth, the tutor is typically closer in age and experience to the tutee than is the adult teacher and may relate better to the tutee's cognitive framework and language level.

Classwide Peer Tutoring (Carta, Dinwiddie, Kohler, Delquardi, and Greenwood, 1984) involves pairing all students in the classroom to work together at the same time. Like most tutoring methods, Classwide Peer Tutoring is aimed at further developing skills or rehearsing information already presented by the teacher.

Cross-age tutoring brings students from higher grades together with students from lower grades to work on a one-to-one basis. In cross-age tutoring, students from different grades usually work together once a week for an extended period. Often the older students read to the younger ones and help them work on projects.

Some guidelines to keep in mind when implementing a tutoring program include the following:

1. The degree to which a lesson is structured should depend upon the age, ability, and motivation of the students involved. Both the tutor and tutee must be aware of what is expected of them during any given lesson. More motivated, capable, or older students can be given the opportunity to decide what they think they need to teach and learn.

2. Tutoring should last long enough to have an effect. Too many interruptions or too lengthy a program may strain the tutor and tutee without additional gain.

3. Tutors need to be trained in appropriate interpersonal skills, such as giving feedback in a non-threatening manner, listening, being patient, and handling conflicts constructively. Tutees may also benefit from training in how to ask questions, how to explain difficulties to tutors, how to get help, and sometimes how to offer help.

4. The training of tutors should not end once the tutoring begins. Identifying problems tutors may have and working through them are necessary to ensure that time is not wasted and that gains are made.

5. Teachers should interact daily with every pair. Depending on the level of the tutor and tutee, teachers or other professionals should monitor these relationships and offer feedback and reinforcement to maintain the interest of both students.

6. Staff and administrative support is essential. Tutoring must be supported as an integral component of the school's curricula.

SUMMARY

In this chapter, we have provided brief descriptions of other strategies that employ interpersonal interaction. These methods include Collaborative Learning, Tribes, Group Work for Multiple Abilities, Cooperative Scripts, and Tutoring. Not all of these methods employ all of the elements of cooperative learning, but all of them have students working together in effective ways for particular situations. Collaborative Learning emphasizes student autonomy and democratic decision making in the classroom. Tribes focuses on long-term support groups and how to facilitate group development. Group Work for Multiple Abilities is concerned with providing all students with equal opportunities to contribute by drawing upon many different abilities and skills in a single group task. Cooperative Scripts is designed to enhance understanding and recall of textual information. Lastly, Tutoring encourages learning through peer teaching among students. As a teacher, your job is to determine which methods are appropriate for your students, your curriculum, and your setting.

REFLECTION ACTIVITIES

1. Divide your class in half. One half analyzes a poem using Collaborative Learning and the other half analyzes the same poem using the Learning Together method. Compare the results.

2. Think of a time when you tutored someone in a subject. Did you benefit from that experience? Explain why or why not.

3. Choose one of the methods described in this chapter and look back at the elements of cooperative learning outlined in Part Two: Implementation. What elements are missing? Is the method weaker as a result or is there another mechanism to compensate?

Mr. Sedar has been teaching chemistry for fifteen years at Wildwood Collegiate. At first, he was bothered by the unwillingness of some students to try to learn. These students found chemistry a waste of time. Eventually, Mr. Sedar stopped worrying about these students and took comfort in those few who were really interested in studying chemistry.

One day, the new principal of Wildwood Collegiate urged teachers to try cooperative learning in their classrooms. Mr. Sedar tried this new approach and was surprised to find that more students were involved in and excited about chemistry. They were actually talking with each other and really learning. But along with these positive changes, new problems developed. It seemed as if the class as a whole was learning in greater depth but the pace was slower. Mr. Sedar even had to drop certain topics from his schedule and was spending a lot less time presenting facts and ideas to the whole class.

The parents of one of the brightest students, Nick, complained that Nick was not learning as much as he did when Mr. Sedar was teaching chemistry in the usual manner. Worse, Nick's grade actually depended on how one of the slowest students in the class was doing.

Nick's parents demanded that things change immediately. "You are ruining our son's chances of going to medical school," they said. "How can he compete with other applicants when you are holding him back like this? School is a place that is supposed to recognize the skills and accomplishments of each individual student. What you are doing goes against that philosophy."

Especially in North America, there are strongly held beliefs that competition is a necessary form of interaction for life in the "real world." Accordingly, the educational system reflects this reality and recognizes and encourages the student who attempts to compete with peers to be the best, to overcome obstacles, and to deal with adversity in order to achieve. But are these beliefs correct? In Exhibit A.1, Johnson and Johnson (1974) describe the four myths about the benefits of competition and conclude that they are largely false.

Research on group processes and the effects of social facilitation on individual performance dates back to the nineteenth century (Triplett, 1897). Questions about group work have been posed by social psychologists interested in understanding group dynamics, by industrial psychologists interested in enhancing worker productivity and job satisfaction, and by educational psychologists interested in promoting student learning and motivation. But what does the accumulated evidence tell us about the effectiveness of cooperation, especially when used to enhance students' learning?

In this appendix, we summarize the evidence regarding the overall effectiveness of cooperative learning in promoting productivity and achievement and other outcomes, including social support and self-esteem. We also briefly summarize reviews on more specialized topics in cooperative learning, such as applications to computer-assisted instruction, college teaching, and so on.

EARLY NARRATIVE REVIEWS

A narrative review is an organized and critical summary of research on a topic written in prose form. Narrative reviews often use the frequency or consistency of findings to determine, for example, whether a classroom implementation is effective or not. As interest grew in the area of goal and reward structures—cooperative, competitive, and individualistic—and especially in the application of the research findings to practice, reviews of the literature began to appear (Miller and Hamblin, 1963; Johnson and Johnson, 1974; Slavin, 1977; Michaels, 1977; Sharan, 1980; Slavin, 1980). But the findings of these reviews were not always uniform. In fact, the early narrative reviews were sometimes contradictory.

What can one conclude about the effects of cooperative learning based on these early narrative reviews? First, it is apparent that the reviews reach different conclusions about the effectiveness of cooperation in promoting increased productivity and achievement. Second, the reviews are much more consistent in establishing the positive effects of cooperative learning on affective and interpersonal outcomes. Third, in the case of either cognitive or noncognitive outcomes, the magnitude of the effects to be expected is unclear—not only when, but how much does cooperative learning promote achievement, self-esteem, and social skills?

Why Are the Narrative Reviews Contradictory?

There are several reasons that may explain why the reviews reached different conclusions about achievement and productivity effects. First, the reviews explored different questions about the effectiveness of cooperation. Some explored differences among reward structures, while others explored differences among cooperative learning methods compared to traditional instruction. Second, the reviews differed in scope. Some included both classroom research and laboratory studies of reward structures, while others limited their analysis to classroom applications lasting two or more weeks. In addition, the number of studies available for inclusion, especially classroom applications, increased significantly from the earliest reviews to the later ones. Third, the reviews differed in the extent to which individual versus group post-test measures of productivity or achievement were included. Some included achievement measures that had a substantial number of group measures of performance, which cannot be used to ascertain whether the individual gained from the experience of working with others. Fourth, the reviews were selective in the research cited. For example, Michaels's analysis (1977) of reward structures was based on ten studies, while Slavin's review (1980) included 28 studies. Only a single study was common to both reviews.

···················· EXHIBIT A.1 **Four Myths about Competition** ····················

- The first myth is that our society is highly competitive and that a student must be able to function in a "survival of the fittest" world. The truth is that the vast majority of human interaction, in our society as well as in all other societies, is not competitive but cooperative interaction.... Competition is a very, very small part of interacting with other individuals in our society and probably not a very important type of human interaction....

- The second myth concerning competition is that achievement, success, drive, ambition, and motivation depend upon successfully competing with other individuals. This is not the case: a competitive goal structure does not yield higher achievement than a cooperative goal structure.... Competition will by and large decrease achievement rather than increase it. Competition is threatening and discouraging to those who believe they cannot win and many students will withdraw or only half try in competitive situations....

- A third myth about competition is that competition builds character and toughens the young for life in the "real world".... There is ... no evidence that competition builds character and toughens the individual for success in future competition; on the contrary, there is evidence that competition does just the opposite....

- Finally, there is a myth that students prefer competitive structures.... Children seem to enjoy competitive reward structures as long as they are winning and as long as they exhibit some mastery of the task.... A series of more recent studies have found that students prefer cooperatively structured instructional situations to competitive ones....

Source: Adapted from D. W. Johnson and R. T. Johnson, "Instructional Goal Structures: Cooperative, Competitive, or Individualistic," in *Review of Educational Research* 44 (1974): 217–19. Copyright © 1974 by the American Educational Research Association.

META-ANALYSIS: RECENT QUANTITATIVE REVIEWS
•••

The research on classroom goal and reward structures and cooperative learning was not the only area where reviews reached different conclusions about research—this was a growing, endemic problem in many areas of science but especially in the social sciences. These different conclusions sometimes sparked debate among researchers which contributed to further studies being conducted and the growth of the area. But for practitioners especially, the division of opinions expressed in the reviews was more often a source of frustration and cynicism.

Then in 1976, Gene Glass had a better idea. He suggested that literature reviews should be undertaken with the same care and thoroughness as primary research. And like primary research, the methodology of the research review should be described in sufficient detail so that the careful reader would be able to replicate it exactly.

Equally important, Glass suggested that the results of individual studies should be converted to a common metric, or effect size, so the results of different studies could be combined. The effect-size measure has the unique advantage of providing an estimate of the size of a treatment or application and answering the question, How much of a difference does this make?

Especially in applied areas like education, knowledge of effect sizes is important. Educators must constantly evaluate whether to undertake a new classroom implementation. Knowing the size of the potential benefit helps in the decision process.

•••••••••••••••••• Exhibit A.2 **Results of Two Meta-Analyses on Cooperative Learning** ••••••••••••••••••
and Productivity/Achievement[1]

Comparison	Average Effect Size	Standard Deviation	Number of Comparisons	Percent Positive (Percent Negative)	Percentile Rank Advantage	Expected Test Advantage
Johnson and Johnson (1989)						
Cooperation vs. Competition	+0.67	0.93	129	55% (08%)	24.86%	6.70
Cooperation vs. Individualistic	+0.64	0.79	184	51% (06%)	23.89%	6.40
Competition vs. Individualistic	+0.30	0.77	38	35% (16%)	11.79%	3.00
Slavin (1989)						
Cooperation vs. Controls	+0.21	—	57	72% (15%)	8.71%	2.10

Data sources: Johnson, D.W., and Johnson, R.T. (1989), *Cooperation and Competition: Theory and Research*, Edina, Minn.: Interaction Book Co., p. 41. Slavin, R.E. (1989), Cooperative Learning and Student Achievement. In R.E. Slavin (ed.), *School and Classroom Organization*, Hillsdale, N.J.: Erlbaum, pp. 129–156. (Data are extracted from p. 147.)

[1]Key to Table

Number of comparisons is the number of study findings used to calculate the average effect size.

Percent positive is the percent of the study findings showing a positive result. *Percent negative* is the percent of study findings showing a negative result.

Percentile rank advantage is the standing of one group relative to the other. For example, the percentile rank advantage of the cooperative group relative to the competitive group would place the average (50th%) cooperative member above 74.86% of the members of the competitive group.

Expected test advantage is based on a hypothetical examination with a mean of 70.00 and a standard deviation of 10.00. For example, the expected test advantage of 6.70 means the cooperative group would average 76.70 on a test where the competitive group would average 70.00.

After the reviewer has calculated effect sizes for individual studies, the results are combined. The reviewer is then ready to ask questions about the collection of studies. For example, what is the average effect size for the studies? Are the results uniform or do they vary considerably from study to study? What factors explain the variability in study findings?

Does Cooperative Learning Enhance Students' Learning?

Since the early 1980s, both the Johnsons and Slavin have expanded and refined their original quantitative reviews (Johnson, Maruyama, Johnson, Nelson, and Skon, 1981; Slavin, 1983a). The updated review by Johnson and Johnson (1989a) was based on the findings reported in 475 studies, including all types of outcomes: achievement, social, and affective. In contrast, Slavin's updated review (1989a), which used stricter inclusion criteria (e.g., methodological quality, germaneness to primary and secondary school classrooms), was based on the findings reported in only 60 studies. The findings of these two reviews for productivity and achievement are summarized in Exhibit A.2.

The results of the review conducted by the Johnsons suggest that cooperative goal structures have moderately large positive effects on productivity and achievement compared to either competitive or individualistic goal structures. The average effect sizes exceed +0.60; the percentile advantage for cooperation is about 24 percent. This means that students in classes using cooperative learning would score on average six points higher on a hypothetical, common examination (mean = 70.00, standard deviation = 10.00) than would students in classes where competitive or individualistic goal structures were used. Furthermore, very few of the studies (8 percent or less) showed results in which either competitive or individualistic goal structures were superior to cooperative goal structures.

The results of the more selective review conducted by Slavin also found positive effects for cooperative learning methods compared to control conditions. The overall effect size (+0.21) was modest, resulting in a percentile rank advantage of

almost 9 percent and a test advantage of slightly more than two points. Furthermore, the majority of the studies (72 percent) favored cooperative learning methods. Only a fraction (15 percent) had evidence favoring the control methods.

Thus, two quantitative reviews using very different inclusion criteria both concluded that cooperation benefits productivity and achievement. However, the reviewers disagreed in their estimates of how much of the benefit was due to cooperation.

Which Cooperative Learning Methods Work Best?

Perhaps understandably, the sharpest disagreement seems to be over which cooperative learning method works best. The different findings are presented in Exhibit A.3. Both reviews indicate that the Student Team Learning methods (TGT, STAD, TAI, CIRC) developed or advocated by Slavin and his associates generally produce positive effects on achievement. The average effect size for these methods reported by Johnson and Johnson (1989a) was +0.37; Slavin (1989a) reported an average effect size of +0.30.

In contrast, the reviewers reached opposite conclusions about other cooperative learning methods. For example, the Johnsons found that studies ostensibly employing pure cooperation (including Group Investigation and their own method, Learning Together), without any form of inter-team competition or group reward for individual achievement, produced an average effect size of +0.71. Meanwhile, Slavin found that methods other than Student Team Learning and Jigsaw produced effects that averaged almost zero (+0.02).

A COMPROMISE POSITION

There is little question that Slavin's Student Team Learning methods promote student achievement over the short term. These methods are highly structured, are very prescriptive in their implementation, and are especially effective at promoting the achievement of lower-level cognitive skills, such as knowledge and comprehension of basic facts and principles. It is arguably the case that these types of

·············· EXHIBIT A.3 **Results of Two Meta-Analyses on Effects of Cooperative Learning** ··············
Methods on Productivity/Achievement

Comparison	Average Effect Size	Standard Deviation	Number of Comparisons
Johnson and Johnson (1989) Cooperative vs. Competitive Goal Structures			
TGT	+0.39	0.19	4
STAD	+0.37	0.33	9
TAI	+0.35	0.11	3
Above Methods = Student Team Learning (STL)	+0.37	—	16
Jigsaw	+0.46	1.11	7
Overall Mixed (STL + Jigsaw)	+0.40	0.62	23
Overall Pure	+0.71	1.01	96
Slavin (1989) Cooperative Learning vs. Control Methods			
TGT	+0.38	—	7
STAD	+0.27	—	18
TAI/CIRC	+0.21	—	7
Above Methods = Student Team Learning (STL)	+0.30	—	32
Jigsaw	+0.04	—	4
STL + Jigsaw	+0.27	—	36
Learning Together (LT)	+0.00	—	7
Group Investigation (GI)	+0.12	—	5
Other	+0.06	—	3
LT + GI + Other	+0.02	—	15

Data sources: Johnson, D.W., and Johnson, R.T. (1989), *Cooperation and Competition: Theory and Research,* Edina, Minn.: Interaction Book Co., p. 41. Slavin, R.E. (1989), Cooperative Learning and Student Achievement, In R.E. Slavin (ed.). *School and Classroom Organization,* Hillsdale, N.J.: Erlbaum, pp. 129–156. (Data are extracted from p. 147.)

achievement form the bulk of classroom learning. It is also arguably the case that the achievement of lower-level skills is most often and most easily assessed on class tests and on many standardized achievement tests, making it easier to obtain significant results. Finally, these methods better lend themselves to short-term classroom experimentation.

In contrast to the Student Team Learning methods, other methods of cooperative learning, including Group Investigation and Learning Together, are more loosely structured, are less prescriptive, and are often used to promote higher levels of cognitive functioning over the long term. It is not altogether surprising then that when you examine the classroom studies exclusively cited by Slavin (1989a), these other methods appear less effective. It is also apparent that more extensive research is required on the long-term impacts of cooperative learning, especially as the different methods impact on both lower-level achievement and higher-level reasoning.

The effect size of $+0.71$ reported by Johnson and Johnson (1989a) for the pure cooperative learning methods includes findings from classroom studies of brief duration and laboratory research; the near-zero effect size reported by Slavin (1989a) excludes these findings. It seems inappropriate to completely disregard the carefully controlled, but artificial laboratory research, as Slavin did, on the basis that it *may* not generalize to real classrooms. First, laboratory research may test specific theoretical propositions under carefully controlled conditions that are extremely difficult to study experimentally in classrooms (Johnson and Johnson, 1989b), but may very well apply to them. Such research can help identify the underlying mechanisms responsible for the benefits of cooperative learning. However, to include these studies in a review requires an explanation of which theoretical mechanisms are being explored.

Second, the question of generalizing these results is a difficult one and can never be decided in a simple way. For example, what makes an inner-city Baltimore class of tenth graders learning language arts resemble a rural Minnesota class of third graders learning mathematics? Even research conducted in actual classrooms can be criticized for problems with generalization, too. Brief, controlled experiments

cannot be dismissed as evidence on cooperative learning unless you establish, through theory and experimentation, that certain classroom conditions substantially modify the results from laboratory research. For example, some may question the generalization of laboratory research to classrooms because subjects in laboratory experiments often begin working together as strangers and only participate for short periods as a team. This familiarity hypothesis can be studied experimentally, of course, and its effects estimated. To the extent that teammate familiarity improves group cohesiveness, the laboratory research may be inaccurate—*under*estimating the effects of goal structures in classrooms.

What Facilitates the Effectiveness of Cooperative Learning?

As an additional feature of his meta-analysis, Slavin (1989a) organized the studies according to whether group goals (or rewards) and individual accountability were employed. He included studies that used varying combinations of group goals and individual accountability. As Exhibit A.4 shows, the most effective cooperative learning techniques employ both group goals and individual accountability.

EFFECTS ON NONCOGNITIVE OUTCOMES

Teachers use cooperative learning for a variety of reasons. Some instructors are excited about students learning together because of the gains in academic achievement that often accrue. Others are enthused about cooperative learning because it promotes the development of students' interpersonal and verbal skills and their self-esteem.

While there has been some debate over which methods of cooperative learning best promote students' learning, and the extent and determining factors of these benefits, there is virtually no disagreement that cooperative learning promotes noncognitive outcomes. The results from the meta-analysis by Johnson and Johnson (1989a) for several noncognitive outcomes are summarized in Exhibit A.5.

These data reveal the general tendency for cooperative structures to produce meaningfully large effects on attitudes toward the subject matter and learning, attraction toward and liking of peers, feelings of social support, and positive self-concept and self-esteem. Students who learn in cooperative groups like both the subjects they are learning and school more, get along better with their classmates and teachers, feel that they have support from their classmates and teachers, and feel good about themselves as learners.

There are no other classroom strategies that can claim both so much research evidence and such large effects on attitudinal and affective outcomes. Nevertheless, you should be aware that these findings represent average effects; individual findings vary. For example, about 10 percent of the published research on attitudes toward task had effect sizes as large as +1.20 favoring cooperation, but another 10 percent had effect sizes about 0.00. Not every implementation of cooperative learning will be successful. Not every student is certain to react positively.

WHAT ABOUT COOPERATIVE LEARNING AND . . .?

The use of cooperative learning has mushroomed in the last decade. More and more teachers are sup-

plementing their whole-class instruction with small-group learning techniques. With the rise in popularity of cooperative learning, the approach has been used and researched widely. While classroom applications have concentrated on primary and secondary schools, cooperative learning has been used successfully in early childhood education and increasingly in postsecondary education. Teachers use it to instruct every imaginable type of subject matter from academic subjects, such as language arts, mathematics, and science, to commercial or trade courses. Cooperative learning has been used with adult learners, gifted students, and the academically handicapped. Successful cooperative learning implementations have occurred in destreamed and integrated classrooms, with computer-assisted instruction, and with language-minority students.

To give the reader a better understanding of these applications, we have listed and summarized below some of the *reviews* of research on more specialized uses of cooperative learning.

Mathematics

Davidson (1985, 1989, 1991) reviewed the research on cooperative learning in mathematics. In 36 of 78 experimental studies, cooperative learning promoted superior student achievement compared to comparison procedures. In only two of the 78 studies did cooperative learning students do worse than con-

················ EXHIBIT A.4 **Influence of Group Goals and Individual Accountability** ················
on Student Achievement

Condition	Number of Findings	Average Effect Size	Percentile Rank Advantage	Expected Test Advantage
Group Goals and Individual Accountability	32	+0.30	11.79%	3.00
Group Goals Only	8	+0.04	1.60%	0.40
Individual Accountability Only	9	+0.12	4.78%	1.20
No Group Goals or Individual Accountability	2	+0.05	1.99%	0.50

Data source: Slavin, R.E. (1989), Cooperative Learning and Student Achievement. In R.E. Slavin (ed.), *School and Classroom Organization,* Hillsdale, N.J.: Erlbaum, pp. 129–156. (Data from table p. 147.)

trol students. Johnson and Johnson (1989a) found average effect sizes of + 0.60 or higher on mathematics tasks when cooperative goal structures were compared with competitive or individualistic ones.

Verbal Skills

Winitsky (1991) reviewed research in social studies and related subject areas, such as reading, language arts, and English. She concluded that the findings strongly support the conclusion that cooperative task and reward structures promote achievement, positive behavior, and affective outcomes. Johnson and Johnson (1989a) found average effect sizes of + 0.60 or higher on verbal tasks when cooperative goal structures were compared with competitive or individualistic ones.

·············· EXHIBIT A.5 **Influence of Goal Structures on Noncognitive Outcomes** ···············

Comparison	Average Effect Size	Standard Deviation	Number of Comparisons	Percentile Rank Advantage
Attitudes toward Task				
Cooperative vs. Competitive	+ 0.57	0.62	54	21.57%
Cooperative vs. Individualistic	+ 0.42	0.62	38	16.28%
Competitive vs. Individualistic	+ 0.15	0.64	12	5.96%
Interpersonal Attraction				
Cooperative vs. Competitive	+ 0.66	0.49	93	24.54%
Cooperative vs. Individualistic	+ 0.60	0.58	60	22.57%
Competitive vs. Individualistic	+ 0.08	0.70	15	3.19%
Social Support				
Cooperative vs. Competitive	+ 0.62	0.44	84	23.24%
Cooperative vs. Individualistic	+ 0.70	0.45	72	25.80%
Competitive vs. Individualistic	− 0.13	0.36	19	− 5.17%
Self-Esteem				
Cooperative vs. Competitive	+ 0.58	0.56	56	21.90%
Cooperative vs. Individualistic	+ 0.44	0.40	38	17.00%
Competitive vs. Individualistic	− 0.23	0.42	19	− 9.10%

Data sources: Johnson, D.W., and Johnson, R.T. (1989), *Cooperation and Competition: Theory and Research,* Edina, Minn.: Interaction Book Co., pp. 85, 120, 123, 133, and 156.

Computer-Based Instruction

Rysavy and Sales (1991) reviewed the research on the effects of cooperative computer-based instruction (CBI). The studies either showed positive effects of cooperative CBI on achievement or no significant differences.

Secondary Schools

Newmann and Thompson (1987) examined cooperative learning and student achievement for students in grades seven through twelve. Twenty-five of 37 study findings (68 percent) showed a significant positive effect favoring cooperative learning methods over control methods.

College Instruction

Johnson and Johnson (1993, under review) identified over 120 studies of goal structures and individual college student achievement. In these studies, cooperative structures promoted higher achievement than either competitive or individualistic goal structures. The average effect sizes exceeded +0.50. In addition, college students learning cooperatively also benefited in terms of liking of the subject matter, peer support, and self-esteem.

Native Students

Swisher (1990) concluded that the literature about the cooperative nature of native culture is sufficient for practitioners to use cooperative learning. However, more research is needed; the effects of specific cooperative learning methods have not been researched or reported to any great extent.

Language-Minority Students

Most of the research on language-minority students has involved Mexican-American children in the Southwest of the United States. But according to Slavin (April, 1990c), this research tends to suffer from poor methodological quality. Findings related to achievement are mixed. Effects seem generally positive, but not a single study shows convincing, solid effects on the learning of language-minority students.

Cross-Ethnic Classrooms

School desegregation is based on the assumption that placing students with various ethnic backgrounds in the same school and classroom will facilitate positive attitudes and relationships among the students. Considerable research has been directed at determining whether and to what extent classroom goal structures affect interpersonal attraction in cross-ethnic and desegregated classrooms. Reviews (Johnson, Johnson, and Maruyama, 1983; Johnson and Johnson, 1989a) suggest that cooperative goal structures are superior to both competitive goal structures (average effect size = +0.52) and individualistic ones (average effect size = +0.44) in promoting positive interethnic relationships.

Mainstreamed Classrooms

The Johnsons (Johnson, Johnson, and Maruyama, 1983; Johnson and Johnson, 1989a) also summarized the studies on mainstreaming and showed the superiority of cooperative learning in promoting interpersonal attraction in classrooms containing students with mild disabilities or handicaps (average effect sizes > +0.60).

However, the achievement effects of cooperative learning for mainstreamed students with mild learning disabilities has been the subject of some debate. Tateyama-Sniezek (1990) found twelve studies but suggested that the findings across studies were inconsistent. Stevens and Slavin (1991) (see also Margolis and Freund, 1991) reinterpreted the findings of Tateyama-Sniezek according to whether the studies used cooperative learning with or without group goals and individual accountability. The four studies that used these elements had an average effect size for handicapped students' achievement of +0.48.

Gifted Students

Should gifted students be educated in their own classrooms or be more fully integrated into the regular classroom stream? What are the effects of cooperative learning on talented students? On the one hand, proponents of the integration of gifted students argue that the needs of talented students are best met by helping others through cooperative learning strategies in the heterogeneous classroom (Slavin, 1990a). On the other hand, critics argue that advanced courses already exist that produce clear, positive effects for talented students (Robinson, 1990a, 1990b; Mills and Tangherlini, 1992) and that placing talented students in cooperative, heterogeneous groups is a form of exploitation.

Slavin's review (1990a) found that high achievers achieve significantly more in cooperative classrooms than in traditional classrooms, and proportionally the same as medium- and low-ability students. In contrast, Robinson (1990a) suggested that the majority of the studies used basic skill measures to define student achievement. In the few studies where higher-level learning outcomes were assessed, there was no achievement advantage for talented students placed in cooperative learning groups.

SUMMARY

There have been hundreds of studies exploring the effects of working and learning under cooperative, competitive, or individualistic goal structures. There is little doubt that cooperative learning produces superior results when the objective is the promotion of positive attitudes and feelings toward learning, classmates, and self. While early narrative reviews reached conflicting conclusions, more recent quantitative reviews of the literature show generally positive effects of cooperative goal structures on achievement.

However, there remains some dispute about which of several cooperative learning methods are most effective at promoting students' achievement. There are two elements that appear especially important in promoting effective group work for the purposes of enhanced student learning. Student teams should be provided with, or asked to develop, clearly articulated group goals, and students should be individually accountable for their own accomplishments within the team. Finally, cooperative learning is now being implemented widely. Most of these implementations show encouraging evidence of the effectiveness of cooperative learning in varied contexts.

REFLECTION ACTIVITIES

1. Write a letter to your school board explaining why you would like funding to collaborate with researchers at your local university in examining the effects of cooperative learning in your school. Discuss what research questions would be explored and how carefully designed studies would answer them. Also include a statement of your hypotheses as based on the research evidence summarized in this appendix.

2. On the basis of the evidence presented here, you are asked by your colleagues to recommend a method of cooperative learning. What questions would you ask your colleagues to clarify their instructional objectives? What method would you recommend for each of their possible responses?

3. What would you recommend to your school about its policies regarding integration? Working with a partner, each of you choose a different perspective and present your arguments: (a) a teacher with ethnically diverse students and (b) a teacher with academically diverse students.

••••••••• *Appendix B* SELECTED RESOURCES

COMPILED BY ANNE WADE, INFORMATION SPECIALIST,
CENTRE FOR THE STUDY OF CLASSROOM PROCESSES,
CONCORDIA UNIVERSITY

An exhaustive list of published material on cooperative learning would constitute several books in itself. In fact, the Centre for the Study of Classroom Processes, Concordia University has compiled a comprehensive bibliography and electronic database with over 10,000 records on cooperative learning. A selection of recent citations has been published by the University Press of America (Wade, Abrami, Poulsen, and Chambers, 1995).

This chapter, therefore, provides only a selective list of some of the current books, periodicals, and nonprint material available to researchers, educators, and others interested in learning more about cooperative learning. Additionally, some of the well-known, but older, items have been included, if there are no current editions of the specific work.

This chapter has been arranged with the following divisions: Scholarly Books; Practical Teaching Guides: General Sources of Information; Practical Teaching Guides: Specific Methods; Practical Teaching Guides: Selected Topics; Periodicals; Videocassettes; Sports and Games; and Computer Software.

•••••••• SCHOLARLY BOOKS
•••••••••••••••••••••••••••••••••••

Adams, D., Carlson, H., and Hamm, M. 1990. **Cooperative learning and educational media: Collaborating with technology and each other.** Englewood Cliffs, NJ: Educational Technology.

Brandt, R.S. (ed.). 1991. **Cooperative learning and the collaborative school: Readings from *Educational Leadership*.** Alexandria, VA: Association for Supervision and Curriculum Development.

Brubacher, M., Payne, R., and Rickett, K. 1990. **Perspectives on small group learning.** Oakville, ON: Rubicon Publishing.

Cohen, E.G. 1994. **Designing groupwork: Strategies for the heterogeneous classroom.** 2nd ed. New York: Teachers College Press.

Cooperative learning: Resource guide 1993. Special issue 12(4). International Association for the Study of Cooperation in Education.

Davidson, N. and Worsham, T. (eds.). 1992. **Enhancing thinking through cooperative learning.** New York: Teachers College Press.

Freinet, C. 1990. **Cooperative learning and social change: Selected writings of Celestin Freinet.** Our schools/Ourselves, no. 7. Toronto, ON: Ontario Institute for Studies in Education Press.

Galton, M. and Williamson, J. 1992. **Group work in the primary classroom.** New York: Routledge.

Hamm, M. 1992. **The collaborative dimensions of learning: Cultural diversity and restructuring schools with cooperative learning.** Norwood, VA: Ablex.

Hertz-Lazarowitz, R. and Davidson, J. 1990. **Six mirrors of the classroom: A pathway to cooperative learning.** Westlake Village, CA: Joan B. Davidson.

Hertz-Lazarowitz, R. and Miller, N. (eds.). 1992. **Interaction in cooperative groups: The theoretical anatomy of group learning.** New York: Cambridge University Press.

Hinde, R.A. and Groebel, J. (eds.). 1991. **Cooperation and prosocial behavior.** New York: Cambridge University Press.

Johnson, D.W. 1991. **Human relations and your career: A guide to interpersonal skills.** Edina, MN: Interaction Book.

Johnson, D.W. and Johnson, F.P. 1994. **Joining together: Group theory and group skills.** 5th ed. Needham Heights, MA: Allyn and Bacon.

Johnson, D.W. and Johnson, R.T. 1989. **Cooperation and competition: Theory and research.** Edina, MN: Interaction Book.

Johnson, D.W. and Johnson, R.T. 1989. **Leading the cooperative school.** Edina, MN: Interaction Book.

Johnson, D.W. and Johnson, R.T. 1994. **Learning together and alone: Cooperative, competitive, and individualistic learning.** 4th ed. Needham Heights, MA: Allyn and Bacon.

Johnson, D.W., Johnson, R.T., and Johnson Holubec, E. 1993. **Circles of learning: Cooperation in the classroom.** 4th ed. Edina, MN: Interaction Book.

Kohn, A. 1992. **No contest: The case against competition.** Boston: Houghton Mifflin.

Kohn, A. 1993. **Punished by rewards: The trouble with gold stars, incentive plans, A's, praise, and other bribes.** Boston: Houghton Mifflin.

Petersen, J. and Digby, A. (eds.). 1994. **Cooperative learning in secondary schools: Theory and practice.** New York: Garland.

Schmuck, R.A. and Schmuck, P.A. 1993. **Group processes in the classroom.** 6th ed. Palatine, IL: Skylight Publishing.

Sharan, S. 1984. **Cooperative learning in the classroom: Research in desegregated schools.** Hillsdale, NJ: Lawrence Erlbaum Associates.

Sharan, S. 1990. **Cooperative learning: Theory and research.** New York: Praeger.

Sharan, S., Hare, P., Webb, C.D., and Hertz-Lazarowitz, R. 1980. **Cooperation in education.** Prova, UT: Brigham Young University Press.

Sharan, S. and Shachar, H. 1988. **Language and learning in the cooperative classroom.** New York: Springer-Verlag.

Sharan, S. and Sharan, Y. 1976. **Small group teaching.** Englewood Cliffs, NJ: Educational Technology.

Slavin, R.E. 1983. **Cooperative learning.** Research on Teaching Monograph Series. New York: Longman.

Slavin, R.E. 1989. **School and classroom organization.** Hillsdale, NJ: Lawrence Erlbaum Associates.

Slavin, R.E. 1990. **Cooperative learning: Theory, research and practice.** Needham Heights, MA: Allyn and Bacon.

Slavin, R.E., Sharan, S., Kagan, S., Hertz-Lazarowitz, R., Webb, C., and Schmuck, R. (eds.). 1985. **Learning to cooperate, cooperating to learn.** New York: Plenum Press.

Totten, S., Sills, T., Digby, A., and Russ, P. 1991. **Cooperative learning: A guide to the research.** Garland bibliographies in contemporary education, no. 12. New York: Garland.

Wade, A., Abrami, P.C., Poulsen, C., and Chambers, B. 1995. **Current resources in cooperative learning.** Lanham, MD: University Press of America.

Webb, N.M. (ed.). 1989. Peer interaction, problem-solving and cognition: Multidisciplinary perspectives. Theme issue of **International Journal of Educational Research, 13,** San Francisco: Pergamon Press.

PRACTICAL TEACHING GUIDES: GENERAL SOURCES OF INFORMATION

For workshop information on cooperative learning in the United States, you may wish to consult Manning, P. (ed.). **Cooperative learning: Staff Development Directory.** Available from IASCE, Box 1582, Santa Cruz, CA 95061–1582.

Albert, L. 1989. **A teacher's guide to cooperative discipline.** Circle Pines, MN: American Guidance Service.

Archibald M.S. and McDonald, P. 1990. **Tools for the cooperative classroom.** Palatine, IL: Skylight Publishing.

Barnes, D. 1989. **Building a cooperative learning classroom.** Pacifica, CA: Laguna Salada Union School District.

Bass, M.B. and Clark, E. 1992. **Starter kit for cooperative thematic instruction.** Willits, CA: ITA Pub.

Bellanca, J. 1990. **The cooperative think tank: Practical techniques to teach thinking in the cooperative classroom.** Palatine, IL: Skylight Publishing.

Bellanca, J. 1992. **The cooperative think tank II: Graphic organizers to teach thinking in the cooperative classroom.** Palatine, IL: Skylight Publishing.

Bellanca, J. and Fogarty, R. 1991. **Blueprints for thinking in the cooperative classroom.** Palatine, IL: Skylight Publishing.

Bennett, B., Rolheiser-Bennett, C., and Stevahn, L. 1991. **Cooperative learning: Where heart meets mind.** Toronto, ON: Educational Connections.

Brandt, R.S. (ed.). 1989/90. Cooperative learning. Special issue of **Educational Leadership** 47(4).

Breedan, T. and Mosley, J. 1993. **The cooperative learning companion.** Palatine, IL: Skylight Publishing.

Breedan, T. and Mosley, J. 1993. **The middle grades teacher's handbook for cooperative learning.** Palatine, IL: Skylight Publishing.

Brown, M. 1990. **Activities for cooperative learning.** Huntington Beach, CA: Teacher Created Materials.

Brown, M. 1990. **All about cooperative learning.** Huntington Beach, CA: Teacher Created Materials.

Burke, K. 1992. **What to do with the kid who . . .: Developing cooperation, self-discipline, and responsibility in the classroom.** Palatine, IL: Skylight Publishing.

Cantlon, T. 1989. **Structuring the classroom successfully for cooperative learning.** Portland, OR: Prestige Publishers/C and M Education Consultants.

Cantlon, T. 1991. **The first four weeks of cooperative learning: Activities and materials.** Portland, OR: Prestige Publishers.

Clarke, J., Wideman, R., and Eadie, S. 1990. **Together we learn.** Scarborough, ON: Prentice-Hall.

Cowie, H. and Rudduck, J. 1988/90. **Learning together, working together.** Wetherby, West Yorkshire: BP Educational Service. (This series includes Vol.1: Co-operative group work: An overview; Vol.2: School and classroom studies; Vol.3: Co-operative learning traditions and transitions; and Vol.4: Co-operative groupwork in the multi-ethnic classroom.)

Dalton, J. 1992. **Adventures in thinking: Creative thinking and co-operative talk in small groups.** South Melbourne, Australia: Thomas Nelson.

Davies, A., Cameron, C., and Politano, C. 1992. **Co-operative learning.** Building connections. Winnipeg, MB: Peguis.

DeAvila, E. and Duncan, S. 1986. **Finding out/Descubrimiento curricular materials.** Northvale, NJ: Santillana Publishing.

Dishon, D. and O'Leary, P.W. 1984. **A guidebook for cooperative learning: A technique for creating more effective schools.** Holmes Beach, FL: Learning.

Ellis, S.S. and Whalen, S.F. 1990. **Cooperative learning: Getting started.** Jefferson City, MO: Scholastic.

Falsetto, N., Montalban, C., and Tyler, P. 1989. **Cooperative learning in the middle schools.** Tampa, FL: Wiles, Bondi and Associates.

Farmer, L.S. 1991. **Cooperative learning activities in the library media center.** Englewood, CO: Libraries Unlimited.

Finney, S. 1991. **Together I can: Increasing personal growth and creating lifelong learners through cooperative learning.** Spring Valley, CA: Innerchoice Publishing.

Forte, I. and Mackenzie, J. 1992. **The cooperative learning guide and planning pack for primary grades: Thematic projects and activities.** Nashville, TN: Incentive Publications.

Forte, I. and Schurr, S. 1992. **The cooperative learning guide and planning pack for middle grades: Thematic projects and activities.** Nashville, TN: Incentive Publications.

Gibbs, J. 1994. **Tribes: A process for social development and cooperative learning.** Santa Rosa, CA: Center Source Publications.

Graves, N. and Graves, T. 1990. **Tips for teachers and trainers.** Santa Cruz, CA: Cooperative College of California.

Holt, D.D. (ed.). 1993. **Cooperative learning: A response to linguistic and cultural diversity.** Washington, DC: Delta Systems.

Larson, C.C. and LaFasto, F.M. 1989. **Teamwork: What must go right/What can go wrong.** Newbury Park, CA: Sage Publications.

Lincoln County Board of Education. 1993. **Growing collaboratively: Breaking barriers, building bridges.** Scarborough, ON: Prentice-Hall.

Lyman, L. 1993. **Cooperative learning in the elementary classroom.** Analysis and action series. Washington, DC: NEA Professional Library.

Male, M. and Anderson, M. (eds.). 1990. **Fitting in: Cooperative learning in the mainstream classroom.** San Francisco: Majo Press.

McCabe, M.E. and Rhoades, J. 1988. **The nurturing classroom: Developing self-esteem, thinking skills, and responsibility through simple cooperation.** Sacramento, CA: ITA Publications.

Meyers, M. 1993. **Teaching to diversity: Teaching and learning in the multi-ethnic classroom.** Toronto, ON: Irwin Pub.

Putnam, J. (ed.). 1993. **Cooperative learning and strategies for inclusion: Celebrating diversity in the classroom** (Children, youth, and change series). Baltimore, MD: P.H. Brookes.

Reid, J., Forrestal, P., and Cook, J. 1989. **Small group learning in the classroom.** rev. ed. Portsmouth, NH: Heinemann Educational Books.

Rhoades, J. and McCabe, M.E. 1992. **The cooperative classroom: Social and academic activities**. Bloomington, IA: National Educational Service.

Rhoades, J. and McCabe, M. 1992. **Outcome-based learning: A teacher's guide to restructuring the classroom**. Sacramento, CA: ITA Publications.

Rhoades, J. and McCabe, M.E. (eds.). 1993. **Lessons from Cherry Creek: A handbook in simple cooperation**. Sacramento, CA: ITA Publications.

Rottier, J. and Ogan, B.J. 1991. **Cooperative learning in middle-level schools**. Washington, DC: National Education Association.

Roy, P. 1990. **Students learning together**. Richfield, MN: Patricia Roy.

Rybak, S. 1992. **Cooperative learning throughout the curriculum: Together we learn better**. Carthage, IL: Good Apple.

Scearce, C. 1993. **100 ways to build teams**. Palatine, IL: Skylight Publishing.

Schniedewind, N. and Davidson, E. 1987. **Cooperative learning, cooperative lives**. Dubuque, IA: W.C. Brown.

Schniedewind, N. and Davidson, E. 1983. **Open minds to equality: A sourcebook of learning activities to promote race, sex, class and age equity**. Old Tappan, NJ: Prentice-Hall.

Sharan, S. (ed.). 1994. **Handbook of cooperative learning methods**. Westport, CT: Greenwood Publishing.

Smith, A.H.E. and Mabrey, J. 1990. **Team up: Activities for cooperative learning K–6**. Bloomington, IN: National Educational Service.

Sonius, D. 1992. **Superbook of cooperative learning**. Palatine, IL: Skylight.

Thousand, J.S., Villa, R.A., and Nevin, A.I. (eds.). 1994. **Creativity and collaborative learning: A practical guide to empowering students and teachers**. Baltimore, MD: P.H. Brookes Publishing.

Tiberius, R. 1990. **Small group teaching: A troubleshooting guide**. Toronto, ON: Ontario Institute for Studies in Education Press.

Williams, R.B. 1993. **More than 50 ways to build team consensus**. Palatine, IL: IRI/Skylight Publishing.

Winget, P. 1992. **Integrating the core curriculum through cooperative learning: Lesson plans for teachers**. Sacramento, CA: Resources in Special Education.

PRACTICAL TEACHING GUIDES: SPECIFIC METHODS

(See also the section on videocassettes.)

Co-op Co-op

Kagan, S. 1985. Co-op Co-op: A flexible cooperative learning technique. In R. Slavin, S. Sharan, S. Kagan, R. Hertz-Lazarowitz, C. Webb, and R. Schmuck (eds.), **Learning to cooperate, cooperating to learn**. New York: Plenum.

Kagan, S. 1993. **Cooperative learning**. San Juan Capistrano, CA: Kagan Cooperative Learning.

For workshop information, contact:

Kagan's Cooperative Learning Co., 27128 Paseo Espada, Suite 602, San Juan Capistrano, CA 92675; Tel: 800–933-2667; Fax: 714–248–9662.

Group Investigation

Sharan, S. and Hertz-Lazarowitz, R. 1980. A group-investigation method of cooperative learning in the classroom. In S. Sharan, P. Hare, C.D. Webb, and R. Hertz-Lazarowitz (eds.), **Cooperation in education**. Provo, UT: Brigham Young University Press.

Sharan, Y. and Sharan, S. 1992. **Expanding cooperative learning through group investigation**. New York: Teachers College Press.

For workshop information, contact:

Yael or Schlomo Sharan, 12 Oppenheimer St., Ramat-Aviv, Tel Aviv, 69395 Israel; Tel: 011–972–3-418478; Fax: 011–972–3-641–0895.

Jigsaw

Aronson, E., Blaney, N., Stephan, C., Sikes, J., and Snapp, M. 1978. **The jigsaw classroom**. Beverly Hills, CA: Sage Publications (out of print).

Aronson, E. and Goode, E. 1980. Training teachers to implement jigsaw learning: A manual for teachers. In S. Sharan, P. Hare, C.D. Webb, and R. Hertz-Lazarowitz (eds.), **Cooperation in education**. Provo, UT: Brigham Young University Press.

Coelho, E. 1991. **Jigsaw**. Markham, ON: Pippin Publishing.

Coelho, E. and Winer, L. 1991. **Jigsaw plus**. Markham, ON: Pippin Publishing.

Coelho, E., Winer, L., and Winn-Bell Olsen, J. 1989. **All sides of the issue: Activities for cooperative jigsaw groups**. Des Moines, IA: Prentice-Hall.

Learning Together

Johnson, D.W. and Johnson, R.T. 1991. **Cooperative learning lesson plans**. Edina, MN: Interaction Book.

Johnson, D.W. and Johnson, R.T. 1992. **Teaching students to be peacemakers**. Edina, MN: Interaction Book.

Johnson, D.W. and Johnson, R.T. 1994. **Learning together and alone: Cooperative, competitive, and individualistic learning**. 4th ed. Needham Heights, MA: Allyn and Bacon.

Johnson, D.W. and Johnson, R.T. 1993. **Positive interdependence: The heart of cooperative learning**. Edina, MN: Interaction Book.

Johnson, D.W. and Johnson, R.T. (eds.). 1992. **Creative controversy: Intellectual challenge in the classroom**. Edina, MN: Interaction Book.

Johnson, D.W., Johnson, R.T., and Bartlett, J.K. 1991. **Our mediation notebook**. Edina, MN: Interaction Book.

Johnson, D.W., Johnson, R.T., Bartlett, J.K., and Johnson, L.M. 1988. **Our cooperative classroom**. Edina, MN: Interaction Book.

Johnson, D.W., Johnson, R.T., and Holubec, E.J. 1992. **Advanced cooperative learning**. Edina, MN: Interaction Book.

Johnson, D.W., Johnson, R.T., and Holubec, E.J. 1993. **Cooperation in the classroom**. 6th. ed. Edina, MN: Interaction Book.

Johnson, R.T. and Johnson, D.W. 1985. **Cooperative learning: Warm-ups, grouping strategies and group activities**. Edina, MN: Interaction Book.

Johnson, R.T., Johnson, D.W., and Holubec, E.J. (eds.). 1987. **Structuring cooperative learning: Lesson plans for teachers**. Edina, MN: Interaction Book.

For workshop information, contact:

Cooperative Learning Center, 202 Pattee Hall, 150 Pillsbury Drive SE, Minneapolis, MN 55455; Tel: 612–624–7031.

Structural Approach

Kagan, M. and Kagan, S. 1992. **Advanced cooperative learning**. San Juan Capistrano, CA: Kagan Cooperative Learning.

Kagan, M. and Kagan, S. 1992. **Advanced co-op learning kit: The element deck**. San Juan Capistrano, CA: Kagan Cooperative Learning.

Kagan, M. and Kagan, S. 1992. **Playing with elements: Fun advanced work, all grades and subjects**. San Juan Capistrano, CA: Kagan Cooperative Learning.

Kagan, S. 1992. **Cooperative learning structures**. San Juan Capistrano, CA: Kagan Cooperative Learning.

Kagan, S. 1992. **Cooperative lesson designs and lesson planning**. San Juan Capistrano, CA: Kagan Cooperative Learning.

Kagan, S. 1992. **Co-op across the curriculum**. San Juan Capistrano, CA: Kagan Cooperative Learning.

Kagan, S. 1992. **Co-op facilitator's handbook**. San Juan Capistrano, CA: Kagan Cooperative Learning.

Kagan, S. 1993. **Cooperative learning**. San Juan Capistrano, CA: Kagan Cooperative Learning.

Shaw, V. 1992. **Community building in the classroom**. San Juan Capistrano, CA: Kagan Cooperative Learning.

Wiederhold, C. 1990. **Cooperative learning and critical thinking: The question matrix**. San Juan Capistrano, CA: Resources for Teachers.

Wiederhold, C. 1990. **Q-materials packet**. San Juan Capistrano, CA: Resources for Teachers.

For workshop information, contact:

Kagan's Cooperative Learning Co., 27128 Paseo Espada, Suite 602, San Juan Capistrano, CA 92675; Tel: 800–933–2667; Fax: 714–248–9662.

Student Team Learning

Slavin, R.E. 1986. **Using student team learning**. 3rd ed. Baltimore, MD: Johns Hopkins University.

Slavin, R. 1990. **Cooperative learning: Theory, research, and practice**. Englewood Cliffs, NJ: Prentice-Hall.

Slavin, R.E. 1991. **Student team learning: A practical guide to cooperative learning.** 3rd ed. West Haven, CT: Professional Library, National Education Association.

Slavin, R.E., Leavey, M., and Madden, N.A. 1982. **TAI mathematics: Team assisted individualization** (teacher's manual). rev. ed. Baltimore, MD: Center for the Organization of Schools, Johns Hopkins University.

Stevens, R.J., Madden, N.A., Slavin, R.E., and Farnish, A.M. 1986. **Cooperative integrated reading and composition: A brief overview of the CIRC program.** Baltimore, MD: Johns Hopkins University.

For workshop information, contact:

The Johns Hopkins Team Learning Project, 3505 North Charles St., Baltimore, MD 21218; Tel: 410–516–0370.

PRACTICAL TEACHING GUIDES: SELECTED TOPICS

Young Children

Adcock, D. and Segal, M. 1983. **Play together grow together: A cooperative curriculum for teachers of young children.** White Plains, NY: Mailman Family Press.

Carroll, J.A. and Seaton, M. 1992. **Cooperative learning throughout the year: Helping young children work together.** Carthage, IL: Good Apple.

Chambers, B., Patten, M., Schaeff, J., and Wilson-Mau, D. 1993. **Kids can cooperate: Interactive activities for young children.** Montreal, PQ: Concordia University, Centre for the Study of Classroom Processes. (Revised edition to be published in 1995 by Harcourt Brace.)

Curran, L. 1990. **Cooperative learning lessons for little ones.** San Juan Capistrano, CA: Resources for Teachers.

Foyle, M.C. and others. 1991. **Cooperative learning in the early childhood classrooms.** Washington, DC: National Education Association.

College Instruction

Cooper, J., Prescott, S., Cook, L., Smith, L., Mueck, R., and Cuseo, J. 1990. **Cooperative learning and college instruction: Effective use of student learning teams.** Long Beach, CA: California State University Foundation on behalf of California State University Institute for Teaching and Learning, Office of the Chancellor.

Goodsell, A., Maher, M., and Tinto, V. (eds.). 1992. **Collaborative learning: A sourcebook for higher education.** University Park, PA: National Center on Postsecondary Teaching, Learning, and Assessment.

Johnson, D.W., Johnson, R.T., and Smith, K.A. 1991. **Active learning: Cooperation in the college classroom.** Edina, MN: Interaction Book.

Johnson, D.W., Johnson, R.T., and Smith, K.A. 1992. **Cooperative learning: Increasing college faculty instructional productivity.** Washington, DC: George Washington University.

Meyers, C. and Jones, T.B. 1993. **Promoting active learning: Strategies for the college classroom.** San Francisco: Jossey-Bass.

Computers

Anderson, M. 1990. **Partnerships: Developing teamwork at the computer.** Arlington, VA: MAJO Press.

Male, M., Johnson, R., Johnson, D., and Anderson, M. 1985. **Cooperative learning and computers: An activity guide for teachers.** 4th ed. Minneapolis, MN: Cooperative Learning Project, University of Minnesota.

McDonald, P. 1992. **Cooperation at the computer: A handbook for using software with cooperative learning books.** Palatine, IL: Skylight.

Willing, K.R. and Girard, S. 1990. **Learning together: Computer-integrated classrooms.** Markham, ON: Pembroke.

Language Arts

Bourman, A. 1989. **61 cooperative learning activities: Thinking, writing, and speaking skills.** Portland, ME: J. Weston Walch.

Brown, M. 1990. **Writing and cooperative learning.** Huntington Beach, CA: Teacher Created Materials.

Curran, L. 1992. **Cooperative lessons for little ones: Language arts edition.** San Juan Capistrano, CA: Kagan Cooperative Learning.

High, J. 1993. **Second language learning through cooperative learning**. San Juan Capistrano, CA: Kagan Cooperative Learning.

Hill, S. and Hamcock, J. 1993. **Reading and writing communities: Co-operative literacy learning in the classroom**. Winnipeg, MB: Peguis.

Kessler, C. (ed.). 1992. **Cooperative language learning: A teacher's resource book**. Englewood Cliffs, NJ: Prentice-Hall Regents.

McCabe, M.E. and Rhoades, J. 1993. **Language arts and simple cooperation: Reading and writing across the curriculum**. Sacramento, CA: ITA Publications.

Molyneux, L. 1991. **Cooperative learning reading and success: Step by step activities**. Canandaigua, NY: Trellis Books.

Neaman, M. 1992. **Literature circles: Cooperative learning for grades 3–8**. Englewood Cliffs, NJ: Teacher Ideas Press.

Stone, J. 1991. **Cooperative learning and language arts: A multi-structural approach**. San Juan Capistrano, CA: Resources for Teachers.

Whisler, N. and Williams, J. 1990. **Literature and cooperative learning: Pathway to literacy**. Sacramento, CA: Literature CO-OP.

Writing and cooperative learning. 1992. Huntington Beach, CA: Teacher Created Materials.

Mathematics

Andrini, B. and Kagan, S. 1989. **Cooperative learning and mathematics: A multi-structural approach**. San Juan Capistrano, CA: Resources for Teachers.

Burns, M. 1992. **About teaching mathematics: A K–8 resource**. Sausalito, CA: Math Solutions Publications.

Burns, M. 1992. **Math by all means: Multiplication grade 3**. Palo Alto, CA: Dale Seymour.

Curran, L. (in press). **Cooperative learning math lessons for little ones**. San Juan Capistrano, CA: Resources for Teachers.

Davidson, N. (ed.). 1989. **Cooperative learning in mathematics: A handbook for teachers**. Reading, MA: Addison-Wesley.

Dolan, D. and Williamson, J. 1992. **Mathematics activities for elementary school teachers: A problem solving approach**. Palo Alto, CA: Dale Seymour.

Johnson, D. 1992. **Every minute counts: Making your math class work**. Palo Alto, CA: Dale Seymour.

Johnson, D.W. and Johnson, R.T. (eds.). 1991. **Learning mathematics and cooperative learning: Lesson plans for teachers**. Edina, MN: Interaction Book.

Parker, R. 1993. **Mathematical power: Lessons from a classroom**. Portsmouth, NH: Heinemann.

Robertson, L. 1993. **Fraction fun through cooperative learning**. San Juan Capistrano, CA: Kagan Cooperative Learning. [Also available: **The Fraction spinners** and **The Fraction manipulatives.** Curriculum material.]

Weissglass, J. 1990. **Exploring elementary mathematics: A small-group approach for teaching**. Dubuque, IA: Kendall/Hunt.

Science

Berman, S. 1992. **Catch them thinking in science**. Palatine, IL: Skylight Publishing.

Hassard, J. 1990. **Science experiences: Cooperative learning and the teaching of science**. New York: Addison-Wesley.

Hassard, J. 1991. **Using cooperative learning to enhance your science instruction**. Atlanta, GA: Georgia State University.

Lungren, L. 1992. **Cooperative learning with biology: An everyday experience**. Blacklick, OH: Macmillan/McGraw-Hill.

Social Studies

Alberts, M., Caldwell, J., and Schmidt, C. 1990. **Lesson plans for cooperative learning: Secondary social studies**. Monticello, MN: Learning Incentives.

Stahl, R. 1993. **Cooperative learning in social studies**. Reading, MA: Addison-Wesley.

Stahl, R. and Van Sickle, R. (eds.). 1992. **Cooperative learning in the social studies classroom**. New York: NCSS Publications.

PERIODICALS

Computer Supported Cooperative Work: An International Journal, available from Kluwer Academic Publishers Group, P.O. Box 358, Accord Station, Hingham, MA 02018–0358.

Cooperation Unlimited, available from Pat Wilson O'Leary and Dee Dishon, P.O. Box 68, Portage, MI 49081.

Cooperative Learning: A Magazine for Cooperation in Education, available from IASCE, Box 1582, Santa Cruz, CA 95061–1582. (This is the quarterly publication of the International Association for the Study of Cooperation in Education.)

Cooperative Learning and College Teaching, available from New Forums Press, P.O. Box 876, Stillwater, OK 74076.

Cooperative Link, available from 202 Pattee Hall, University of Minnesota, Minneapolis, MN 55455.

VIDEOCASSETTES

Available from the **Association for Supervision and Curriculum Development**, 1250 North Pitt Street, Alexandria, VA 22314; Tel: 703–549–9110.

Cooperative learning series. Includes a comprehensive series of five videotapes (20–42 minutes each) that demonstrate how cooperative learning works in elementary, middle, and secondary classrooms, using the Learning Together and Student Team Learning models.

Available from **Cuisenaire Co. of America**, 12 Church St., Box D, New Rochelle, NY 10802; Tel: 800–237–3142.

Mathematics: With manipulatives. Marilyn Burns's six skill-building videos demonstrate how to use manipulative materials in both small, cooperative groups and whole-class settings. Grades K–6.

Mathematics: For middle schools. Three twenty-minute, skill-building videos address specific aspects of middle school mathematics instruction, using Burns's hands-on problem-solving approach with manipulatives and students working together in small groups, and engaging whole-class discussion. Grades 6–8.

Mathematics: Teaching for Understanding. These skill-building videos demonstrate teacher-led, whole-class instruction, students working together in small groups with manipulatives, and verbal and written communication. Grades K–8.

Available from **Educational Activities, Inc.**, Box 392, Department El, Freeport, NY 11520. Tel: 800–645–3739.

Cooperative learning from a student's point of view. These seven skill-building interactive videotapes include student worksheets, problem-solving activities, and a detailed teacher's manual and reference guide. Grades K–adult.

Available from **Interaction Book Company**: 7208 Cornelia Drive, Edina, MN 55435; Tel: 612–831–9500.

Belonging. This video describes how handicapped students can be mainstreamed in a classroom in which the teacher is using cooperative learning (27 min). Grades K–adult.

Circles of learning. This video presents procedures for structuring cooperative lessons (32 min). Grades K–adult.

Controversy in the classroom. This video shows grade-five and -six students reenacting a structured cooperative controversy (12 min).

Positive interdependence: The heart of cooperative learning. This video shows how to structure positive interdependence (15 min). Grades K–adult.

Teaching students to be peacemakers. This video presents the steps involved in training students to negotiate wise solutions to interpersonal conflicts and to mediate classmates' conflicts. It is a good introduction to peer mediation programs (10 min).

Available from **Kagan Cooperative Learning Co.**: 27134 Paseo Espada, Suite 302, San Juan Capistrano, CA 92765. Tel: 800-WEE-COOP.

Co-op co-op. This skill-building video developed by Spencer Kagan is designed to assist teachers in implementing the Co-op Co-op method (30 min). Grades K–adult.

Fairy tale express. Jeanne Stone demonstrates a multistructural language arts lesson from her book **Cooperative learning and language arts** (19 min). Grades K–adult.

Foundations of cooperative learning. Kagan surveys the research and theoretical underpinnings of cooperative learning (58 min).

Just a sample. Beth Andrini demonstrates a multi-structural mathematics lesson from her book **Cooperative learning and mathematics** (33 min). Grades K–adult.

Numbered heads together. This video has been developed to assist teachers in implementing the Numbered Heads structure (30 min). Grades K–adult.

Pairs check. This video presents an in-depth look at the rationale and practice of Pairs Check and a step-by-step guide on how to introduce this structure into your classroom (30 min).

We can talk. This video is designed to acquaint teachers with ways to increase language development through cooperative learning (45 min).

Available from the **Metropolitan Toronto School Board**, Educational Resources Department, 45 York Mills Road, Willowdale, ON, M2P 1B6

Together we learn. This video program explores initial questions teachers may have regarding cooperative learning (23 min). Grades K–adult.

Available from the **Team Learning Project**, The Johns Hopkins University, 3505 N. Charles Street, Baltimore, MD 21218. Tel: 301–338–7570.

Cooperative integrated reading and composition (CIRC). This 22-minute video is designed to acquaint viewers with CIRC, the specific Student Team Learning method for language arts instruction. Eight years and up.

Student Team Learning. Robert Slavin and colleagues developed this 20-minute video to introduce viewers to several Student Team Learning procedures including STAD, TGT, and Jigsaw II. Grades K–adult.

Team Accelerated Instruction (TAI). This video introduces viewers to TAI for use in elementary mathematics (30 min). Eight years and up.

Available from **Teachers College Press,** 1234 Amsterdam Avenue, New York, NY 10027.

Status treatments for the classroom. This video accompanies the second edition of **Designing groupwork: Strategies for the heterogeneous classroom**. It explains the origins of status problems and the rationale for status treatments for diverse classrooms using cooperative learning.

SPORTS AND GAMES

Cooperative games are available from the following sources.

Animal Town, P.O. Box 485, Healdsburg, CA 95448 Tel: 800–445–8642.

Family Pastimes, R.R.4, Perth, ON, K7H 3C6. Tel: 613–267–4819.

Several are available from **Kagan Cooperative Learning Co.**, 27134 Paseo Espada, Suite 302, San Juan Capistrano, CA 92765. Tel: 800-WEE-COOP.

Sports and Games Books

Brown, M. 1992. **Great games for cooperative learning.** Huntington Beach, CA: Teacher Created Materials.

Deacove, J. 1978. **Sports manual of non-competitive games.** Perth, ON: Family Pastimes.

Deacove, J. 1987. **Co-op games manual.** Perth, ON: Family Pastimes.

Deacove, J. 1987. **Co-op marble games.** Perth, ON: Family Pastimes.

Deacove, J. 1987. **Co-op parlor games.** Perth, ON: Family Pastimes.

Deacove, J. 1990. **Games manual of non-competitive games.** Perth, ON: Family Pastimes.

Fluegelman, A. 1981. **More new games.** Healdsburg, CA: Animal Town.

Hill, S. 1993. **Games that work: Co-operative games and activities for the primary school classroom.** Winnipeg, MB: Peguis.

LeFevre, D.N. 1988. **New games for the whole family.** Healdsburg, CA: Animal Town.

Orlick, T. 1978. **The cooperative sports and games book.** New York: Pantheon Books.

Orlick, T. 1981. **The second cooperative sports and games book.** Sacramento, CA: ITA Publications.

Sobel, J. 1983. **Everybody wins: Non-competitive games for young children.** Healdsburg, CA: Animal Town.

Turner, L.F. and Turner, S. 1989. **Alternative sports and games for the new physical education.** Needham Heights, MA: Ginn Press.

COMPUTER SOFTWARE

Available from **Humanities Software**, P.O. Box 950, 408 Columbia St., Ste. 222, Hood River, OR 97031; Tel: 800–245–6737.

Write on!: Elementary collection. 1992. Steps in the writing process are internalized as students brainstorm, draft, revise, edit, and publish their expository and creative writing. Includes the following series: Elementary literature; Elementary novels; Language enrichment; Elementary poetry and songs; Elementary skills; The five senses; and Seasons and holidays. Available for Apple II, Macintosh, and IBM. Grades 3–6.

Write on!: Intermediate collection. 1992. Literature-based writing activities and the power of word processing provide a combination that engages adolescent minds and encourages them to practice, develop, and integrate their skills. Includes the following series: Novels series I; Novels series II; Building word power; Poetry; Skills; You are the editor; Essay writing; and Writer's voice. Available for Apple II, Macintosh, and IBM. Grades 6–9.

Write on!: Primary collection. 1992. Small groups of youngsters, a teacher at the keyboard, and the Write On! software promote joyful learning. Includes the following series: Wild imaginings in literature; Literature about my world; Literature about me; Adventuring with literature; and Language development, patterns, and songs. Available for Apple II, Macintosh, and IBM. Grades K–3.

Write on!: Secondary collection. 1992. Students think, write, and read about ideas that matter to them to improve their reflective and communication skills and to help them make appropriate decisions. Includes the following series: Classics series I, Classics series II; Poetry; Life skills; You are the editor; Writing; and Writer's voice. Available for Apple II, Macintosh, and IBM. Grades 9–12.

Available from **Skylight Publishing**, 200 E. Wood St., Ste. 274, Palatine, IL 60067; Tel: 800–348–4474.

McDonald, P. (1988). **Perception**. This program focuses on concept development, concept demonstration, hypothesis testing, and logic/problem-solving skills. Ideally suited to cooperative groups, it includes both pre- and post-disk lessons. Available for Apple. Grades 3–5.

Available from **Tom Synder Productions,** 80 Coolidge Hill Rd., Watertown, MA 02172–2817; Tel: 800–342–0236.

Choices choices. 1992. Based on the **Decisions, decisions series**, these programs provide a structured context that teaches important critical thinking skills. Available for Apple II and IBM. Grades K–5.

Decisions, decisions. 1993. This series combines role-playing, debate, decision making, and critical thinking in a simulation designed for groups of students.

Complete pack includes: Colonization, Immigration, Revolutionary wars, Budget process, Foreign policy, Urbanization, Environment, Television, On the campaign trail, Prejudice, and Substance abuse. 11 disks. Available for Apple II, Macintosh, and IBM. Grades 5–12.

The great ocean rescue. 1993. Working in cooperative teams of scientific experts, students must analyze actual visual information from the videodisk to solve the problem. Available for CAV videodisk. Grades 5–8.

The great solar system rescue. 1993. Small groups of students make up teams of experts searching for lost probes in the solar system. Available for CAV videodisk. Grades 5–8.

Group grammar. 1993. This program's special group approach gets students working together and wanting to know more about parts of speech. Available for Apple II and IBM. Grades 5–12.

The graph club with Fizz and Martina. 1993. This program uses the power of cooperative learning to spur students to read, write, create and interpret picture, bar, pie, and line graphs in a multitude of fun, motivating activities. Available for Macintosh. Grades K–3.

Innerbody works. 1992. Inspire students to learn the interconnections between and the functions of human body systems with this database that simulates a voyage through the body. It can be used by one big group, by a single player, or by a small team. Available for Apple IIGS, Macintosh, and IBM. Grades 4–12.

International inspirer. 1993. Students must work together to interpret international data to aid in their search for oil producers, energy consumers, agricultural countries, and urbanized populations. Available for Apple, Macintosh, and IBM. Grades 5–12.

The little shoppers kit. 1992. This program sets up a classroom-store situation to introduce elementary students to math skills and money denominations. Students will quickly see how they have to work cooperatively to make the store run smoothly. Available for Apple II. Grades K–4.

National inspirer. 1993. Groups of students travel throughout the United States. in search of important resources and commodities. Available for Apple II and IBM. Grades 5–12.

The other side. 1993. Students work in groups to resolve disputes in a world where interests and values conflict. Available for Apple II. Grades 5–12.

Our town meeting. 1993. Teams of students armed with town surveys, revenue projections and cost estimates lobby for town improvement projects. Available for Apple II and IBM. Grades 5–12.

Reading magic library plus. 1992. This series presents one-of-a-kind interactive storybooks that let students step into the shoes of lovable heroes, choosing what will happen next. The series builds vocabulary and problem-solving skills in a whole-language context. The group management feature helps teachers create mixed-level reading groups. Available for Macintosh. Grades K–3.

Smart choices. 1992. This program allows students to observe and practice positive decision-making strategies. This role-playing simulation has students confront peer pressure, responsible versus irresponsible behavior, and relationships with authority. Available for Apple II, Macintosh, and IBM. Grades 4–12.

Snooper troops. 1992. These detective games build deductive reasoning skills, while helping students learn to analyze clues, classify and organize information, and develop vocabulary and language skills. Students are encouraged to work as a team, devising group strategies and sharing clues that help them solve these mysteries. Available for Apple II. Grades 4–6.

Available from **Wings for Learning**, 12140 Horseshoe Way, Richmond, BC V7A 4V5; Tel: 800–321–7511.

The learn about series. 1992. This series provides a basis for integrated cooperative learning tasks. Students learn science, mathematics, and relational concepts. It includes the following packages: Learn about lights in the night sky; Learn about dinosaurs; Learn about the human body; Learn about plants; Learn about animals; and Learn about insects. Six disks for IBM or Macintosh. Grades K–3.

The geometric supposer series. 1992. This series provides activities for cooperative group work that encourages students to reflect upon geometric relationships, to share data to formulate definitions, and to express observations and generalizations. Available for IBM and Macintosh. Age level: 14–18.

References

Abrami, P.C., Chambers, B., d'Apollonia, S., Farrell, M., and De Simone, C. July, 1990. **Failing groups: The relationship between team learning outcome, attributional style, and student achievement.** Paper presented at the biannual meeting of the International Association for the Study of Cooperation in Education, Baltimore, MD.

Abrami, P.C., Chambers, B., d'Apollonia, S., Farrell, M., and De Simone, C. 1992. Group outcome: The relationship between group learning outcome, attributional style, academic achievement, and self-concept. **Contemporary Educational Psychology** 17:201–210.

Abrami, P.C., Chambers, B., Poulsen, C., Kouros, C., Farrell, M., and d'Apollonia, S. 1994. Positive social interdependence and classroom climate. **Genetic, Social, and General Psychology Monographs** 120:327–346.

Abrami, P.C., Cohen, P.A., and d'Apollonia, S. 1988. Implementation problems in meta-analysis. **Review of Educational Research** 58:151–179.

Ames, C. 1981. Competitive versus cooperative reward structures: The influence of individual and group performance factors on achievement attributions and affect. **American Educational Research Journal** 18:273–287.

Ames, C. 1984. Competitive, cooperative, and individualistic goal structures: A cognitive-motivational analysis. In R.E. Ames and C. Ames, **Research on motivation in education.** Vol. 1. **Student motivation**, 177–207. Orlando, FL: Academic Press.

Aronson, E., Blaney, N., Stephan, C., Sikes, J., and Snapp, M. 1978. **The jigsaw classroom.** Beverly Hills, CA: Sage Publications.

Aronson, E. and Goode, E. 1980. Training teachers to implement jigsaw learning: A manual for teachers. In S. Sharan, P. Hare, C.D. Webb, and R. Hertz-Lazarowitz (eds.), **Cooperation in education.** Provo, UT: Brigham Young University Press.

Atkinson, J. 1964. **An introduction to motivation.** Princeton, NJ: Van Nostrand.

Bellanca, J. 1990. **The cooperative think tank: Practical techniques to teach thinking in the cooperative classroom.** Palatine, IL: Skylight Publishing.

Bellanca, J. and Fogarty, R. 1991. **Blueprints for thinking in the cooperative classroom.** Palatine, IL: Skylight Publishing.

Bennett, B., Rolheiser-Bennett, C., and Stevahn, L. 1991. **Cooperative learning: Where heart meets mind.** Toronto, ON: Educational Connections.

Bloom, B.S., Englehart, M.D., Furst, E.J., Hill, W.H., and Krathwohl, D.R. 1974. **The taxonomy of educational objectives: Affective and cognitive domains.** New York: David McKay.

Bloom, G. 1990. Empowering the student. In M. Bradshaw, R. Payne, and K. Rickett (eds.), **Perspectives on small group learning**, 42–51. Oakville, Ont.: Rubicon Publishing.

Boomer, G. 1990. Empowering the student. In M. Brubaker, R. Payne, and K. Rickett (eds.), **Perspectives on small group learning: Theory and practice**, 42–51. Oakville, Ont.: Rubicon Publishing.

Brickner, M.A., Harkins, S.G., and Ostram, T.M. 1986. Effects of personal involvement: Thought provoking implications for social loafing. **Journal of Personality and Social Psychology** 37:515–521.

Carta, J.J., Dinwiddie, G., Kohler, F., Delquardi, J., and Greenwood, C.R. 1984. **The juniper gardens peer tutoring programs for spelling, reading, and math (version 1): Teachers' manual.** Kansas City, KS: Juniper Gardens Children's Project, Bureau of Child Research, University of Kansas.

Cartwright, D. 1968. The nature of group cohesiveness. In D. Cartwright and A. Zander (eds.). **Group dynamics: Research and theory**, 91–109. Third edition. New York: Harper and Row.

Chambers, B. and Abrami, P.C. 1991. The relationship between student team learning outcomes and achievement, causal attributions, and affect. **Journal of Educational Psychology** 83:140–146.

Chambers, B., Patten, M., Schaeff, J., and Wilson-Mau, D. 1993. **Kids can cooperate: Interactive activities for young children**. Montreal, PQ: Concordia University, Centre for the Study of Classroom Processes. (Revised edition to be published in 1995 by Harcourt Brace.)

Clarke, J. 1991. The hidden treasure of co-operative learning. **Cooperative Learning** 12(1):2–3.

Clarke, J., Wideman, R., and Eadie, S. 1990. **Together we learn**. Scarborough, ON: Prentice-Hall.

Coelho, E. and Winer, L. 1991. **Jigsaw plus**. Markham, ON: Pippin Publishing.

Cohen, E. 1994a. **Designing groupwork: Strategies for the heterogeneous classroom**. 2nd ed. New York: Teachers College Press.

Cohen, E. 1994b. Restructuring the classroom: Conditions for productive small groups. **Review of Educational Research** 64:1–35.

Curran, L. 1990. **Cooperative learning lessons for little ones: Literature-based language arts and social skills**. San Juan Capistrano, CA: Resources for Teachers.

Damon, W. 1984. Peer education: The untapped potential. **Journal of Applied Developmental Psychology** 5:331–343.

Dansereau, D.F. 1985. Learning strategy research. In J.W. Segal, S.F. Chipman, and R. Glaser (eds.), **Thinking and learning skills: Vol. 1. Relating instruction to research,** 209–239. Hillsdale, NJ: Erlbaum.

Davidson, N. 1985. Small-group learning and teaching in mathematics: A selective review of the research. In R.E. Slavin, S. Sharan, S. Kagan, R. Hertz-Lazarowitz, C. Webb, and R. Schmuck (eds.), **Learning to cooperate, cooperating to learn,** 211–230. New York: Plenum.

Davidson, N. 1989. Cooperative learning and mathematics achievement: A research review. **Cooperative Learning** 10:15–16.

Davidson, N. 1991. An overview of research on cooperative learning related to mathematics. **Journal for Research in Mathematics Education** 22:362–365.

DeAvila, E. and Duncan, S. 1986. **Finding out/ Descubrimiento curricular materials**. Northvale, NJ: Santillana Publishing.

de Charms, R. 1976. **Enhancing motivation: Change in the classroom**. New York: Irvington.

Dedic, H., Rosenfield, S., d'Apollonia, S., and De Simone, C. 1994. **Using Cooperative Concept Mapping in college science classes**. Cooperative Learning and College Teaching 4:12–15.

DeVries, D.L., Slavin, R.E., Fennessey, G.M., Edwards, K.J., and Lombardo, M.M. 1980. **Teams-Games-Tournaments: The Team Learning Approach**. Englewood Cliffs, NJ: Educational Technology Publications.

Dishon, D. and O'Leary, P.W. 1984. **A guidebook for cooperative learning: A technique for creating more effective schools**. Holmes Beach, FL: Learning.

Fisher, C.W. and Berliner, D.C. (eds.). 1985. **Perspectives on instructional time**. White Plains, NY: Longman.

Forsyth, D.R. 1990. **Group dynamics**. 2nd ed. Pacific Grove, CA: Brooks/Cole Publishing.

Fox, D. and Lorge, I. 1962. The relative quality of decisions written by individuals and by groups as the available time for problem solving is increased. **Journal of Social Psychology** 57:227–242.

Gibb, J.R. 1978. **Trust: A new view of personality and organizational development**. Los Angeles, CA: The Guild of Tutors.

Gibbs, G., Habeshaw, S., and Habeshaw, T. 1989. **53 Interesting ways of helping your students to study**. Bristol, England: Technical and Educational Services.

Gibbs, J. 1987. **Tribes: A process for social development and cooperative learning**. Santa Rosa, CA: Center Source Publications.

Gibbs, J. 1994. **Tribes: A process for social development and cooperative learning**. Santa Rosa, CA: Center Source Publications.

Glass, G.V. 1976. Primary, secondary, and meta-analysis of research. **Educational Researcher** 5:3–8.

Graves, T. 1991. The controversy over group rewards in the classroom. **Educational Leadership** 48:77–79.

Graves, T. 1993. Teacher Feature: Engineering professor Karl Smith at the University of Minnesota. **Cooperative Learning** 13(3):12–16.

Harkins, S.G. 1987. Social loafing and social facilitation. **Journal of Experimental Social Psychology** 23:1–18.

Harkins, S.G. and Petty, R.E. 1982. Effects of task difficulty and task uniqueness on social loafing. **Journal of Personality and Social Psychology** 43:1214–1229.

Hayes, L. 1976. The use of group contingencies for behavioral control: A review. **Psychological Bulletin** 83:628–648.

Hertz-Lazarowitz, R. and Shachar, H. 1990. Teachers' verbal behavior in cooperative and whole-class instruction. In S. Sharan (ed.), **Cooperative learning: Theory and research**. New York: Praeger.

Jackson, J. and Williams, K. 1988. **A review and theoretical analysis of social loafing**. Bronx, NY: Fordham University.

Johnson, D.W. 1993. **Reaching out: Interpersonal effectiveness and self-actualization**. 5th ed. Englewood Cliffs, NJ: Prentice-Hall.

Johnson, D.W. and Johnson, F.P. 1991. **Joining together: Group theory and group skills**. Englewood Cliffs, NJ: Prentice-Hall.

Johnson, D.W. and Johnson, R.T. 1974. Instructional goal structures: Cooperative, competitive, or individualistic. **Review of Educational Research**. 44:213–240.

Johnson, D.W. and Johnson, R.T. 1987. **Learning together and alone: Cooperation, competition, and individualization**. 2nd ed. Englewood Cliffs, NJ: Prentice-Hall.

Johnson, D.W. and Johnson, R.T. 1989a. **Cooperation and competition: Theory and research**. Edina, MN: Interaction Book.

Johnson, D.W. and Johnson, R.T. 1989b. Toward a cooperative effort: A response to Slavin. **Educational Leadership**. 46:80–81.

Johnson, D.W. and Johnson, R.T. 1990. **Cooperation in the classroom**. Edina, MN: Interaction Book.

Johnson, D.W. and Johnson, R.T. 1992a. Encouraging thinking through constructive controversy. In N. Davidson and T. Worsham (eds.), **Enhancing thinking through cooperative learning**. New York: Teachers College Press.

Johnson, D.W. and Johnson, R.T. 1992b. Positive interdependence: Key to effective cooperation. In R. Hertz-Lazarowitz and N. Miller (eds.), **Interaction in cooperative groups: The theoretical anatomy of group learning**, 174–199. New York: Cambridge University Press.

Johnson, D.W. and Johnson, R.T. 1992c. **Positive interdependence: The heart of cooperative learning**. Edina, MN: Interaction Book.

Johnson, D.W. and Johnson, R.T. 1993a. What we know about cooperative learning at the college level. **Cooperative Learning** 13(3):17–18.

Johnson, D.W. and Johnson, R.T. 1993. **Cooperative, competitive, and individualistic procedures for educating adults: A comparative analysis.** Manuscript submitted for publication.

Johnson, D.W. and Johnson, R.T. 1994. **Learning together and alone: Cooperative, competitive, and individualistic learning.** 4th ed. Boston, MA: Allyn and Bacon.

Johnson, D.W., Johnson, R.T., and Johnson Holubec, E.J. 1992. **Advanced cooperative learning**. Edina, MN: Interaction Book.

Johnson, D.W., Johnson, R.T., and Johnson Holubec, E.J. 1993. **Cooperation in the classroom**. 6th. ed. Edina, MN: Interaction Book.

Johnson, D.W., Johnson, R.T., Holubec, E.J., and Roy, P. 1984. **Circles of Learning.** Alexandria, VI: Association for Supervision and Curriculum Development.

Johnson, D.W., Johnson, R., and Maruyama, G. 1983. Interdependence and interpersonal attraction among heterogeneous and homogeneous individuals: A theoretical formulation and meta-analysis of the research. **Review of Educational Research** 53:5–54.

Johnson, D.W., Johnson, R.T., Stanne, M.B., and Garibaldi, A. 1990. Impact of group processing on achievement in cooperative groups. **Journal of Social Psychology** 130:507–516.

Johnson, D.W., Maruyama, G., Johnson, R., Nelson, D., and Skon, L. 1981. Effects of cooperative, competitive, and individualistic goal structures on achievement: A meta-analysis. **Psychological Bulletin**. 89:47–62.

Kagan, M. and Kagan, S. 1992. **Advanced cooperative learning: Playing with elements**. San Juan Capistrano, CA: Kagan Cooperative Learning.

Kagan, S. 1985. Co-op Co-op: A flexible cooperative learning technique. In R. Slavin, S. Sharan, S. Kagan, R. Hertz-Lazarowitz, C. Webb, and R. Schmuck (eds.), **Learning to cooperate, cooperating to learn**. New York: Plenum.

Kagan, S. 1990. **Cooperative learning: Resources for teachers.** San Juan Capistrano, CA: Resources for Teachers.

Kagan, S. 1992. **Cooperative Learning: Resources for teachers**. San Juan Capistrano, CA: Resources for Teachers.

Kagan, S. 1993. **Cooperative learning**. San Juan Capistrano, CA: Kagan Cooperative Learning.

Kerr, N.L. 1983. Motivation losses in small groups: A social dilemma analysis. **Journal of Personality and Social Psychology** 45:819–828.

Kohn, A. 1986. **No contest: The case against competition.** Boston: Houghton Mifflin.

Kohn, A. 1991a. Group grade grubbing versus cooperative learning. **Educational Leadership** 48:83–87.

Kohn, A. 1991b. Don't spoil the promise of cooperative learning: Response to Slavin. **Educational Leadership** 48:93–94.

Kohn, A. 1993. **Punished by rewards: The trouble with gold stars, incentive plans, A's, praise, and other bribes.** Boston: Houghton Mifflin.

Kravitz, D.A. and Martin, B. 1986. Ringelmann rediscovered: The original article. **Journal of Personality and Social Psychology** 31:936–941.

Latane, B. and Darley, J.M. 1970. **The unresponsive bystander: Why doesn't he help?** New York: Appleton-Century-Crofts.

Latane, B., Williams, K., and Harkins, S. 1979. Many hands make light the work: The causes and consequences of social loafing. **Journal of Personality and Social Psychology** 37:822–832.

Margolis, H. and Freund, L.A. 1991. Implementing cooperative learning with mildly handicapped students in regular classrooms. **International Journal of Disability, Development, and Education** 38:117–133.

Maslow, A.H. 1970. **Motivation and personality.** 2nd ed. New York: Harper and Row.

McDonald, B.A., Dansereau, D.F., Garland, J.C., Holley, C.D., and Collins, K.W. April, 1979. **Pair learning and transfer of text processing skills.** Paper presented at the annual meeting of the American Educational Research Association, San Francisco.

McGagg, E.C. and Dansereau, D.F. 1991. A convergent paradigm for examining knowledge mapping as a learning strategy. **Journal of Educational Research** 84:317–324.

Michaels, J.W. 1977. Classroom reward structures and academic performance. **Review of Educational Research** 47:87–98.

Miller, L.K. and Hamblin, R.L. 1963. Interdependence, differential rewarding, and productivity. **American Sociological Review** 28:768–778.

Miller, N. and Harrington, H.J. 1990. A situational identity perspective on cultural diversity and teamwork in the classroom. In S. Sharan (ed.), **Cooperative learning: Theory and research.** New York: Praeger.

Miller, N. and Harrington, H.J. 1992. Social categorization and intergroup acceptance: Principles for the design and development of cooperative learning teams. In R. Hertz-Lazarowitz and N. Miller (eds.), **Interaction in cooperative groups: The theoretical anatomy of group learning**, 203–27. New York: Cambridge University Press.

Mills, C.J. and Tangherlini, A.E. 1992. Finding the optimal match: Another look at ability grouping and cooperative learning. **Equity and Excellence** 25:205–208.

Moore, D.S. 1991. **Statistics: Concepts and controversies.** 3rd ed. New York: W.H. Freeman and Company.

Moorman, C. and Dishon, D. 1983. **Our classroom: We can learn together.** Portage, MI: Personal Power Press.

Mullen, B. and Cooper, C. 1994. The relation between group cohesiveness and performance: An integration. **Psychological Bulletin** 115:210–227.

Natriello, G. 1989. The impact of evaluation processes on students. In R.E. Slavin (ed.), **School and classroom organization**, Hillsdale, NJ: Lawrence Erlbaum.

Newmann, F. and Thompson, J. 1987. **Effects of cooperative learning on achievement in secondary schools: A summary of research.** Madison, WI: University of Wisconsin, National Center on Effective Secondary Schools.

Nickerson, R., Perkins, D., and Smith, E. 1985. **The teaching of thinking.** Hillsdale, NJ: Lawrence Erlbaum.

Novak, J.D. and Gowin, D.B. 1984. **Learning how to learn.** New York: Cambridge University Press.

Orlick, T.D. 1981. Cooperative play socialization among preschool children. **Journal of Individual Psychology** 37:54–63.

Piaget, J. 1954. **The construction of reality in the child.** New York: Basic Books.

Pradl, G.M. 1991. Collaborative learning and mature dependency. In M. Brubacher, R. Payne, and K. Rickett (eds.), **Perspectives on small group learning.** Oakville, ON: Rubicon.

Reid, J., Forrestal, P., and Cook, J. 1984. **Small group work in the classroom.** Perth, Western Australia: Education Department of Western Australia.

Ringelmann, M. 1913. Research on animate sources of power: The work of man. **Annales de l'Institut National Agronomique.** 2e serie-tome XII, 1–40.

Robinson, A. 1990a. Cooperation or exploitation? The argument against cooperative learning for talented students. **Journal for the Education of the Gifted** 14:9–27.

Robinson, A. 1990b. Response to Slavin: Cooperation, consistency, and challenge for academically talented youth. **Journal for the Education of the Gifted** 14:31–36.

Rosenshine, B. and Stevens, R.J. 1986. Teaching functions. In M.C. Wittrock (ed.), **Handbook of research on teaching**, 3rd. ed., 376–391. New York: Macmillan.

Roy, P. 1990. **Cooperative learning: Students learning together**. Richfield, MN: Patricia Roy.

Rysavy, S.D.M. and Sales, G.C. 1991. Cooperative learning in computer-based instruction. **Educational Technology Research and Development** 39:70–79.

Salomon, G. and Globerson, T. 1989. When teams do not function the way they ought to. **International Journal of Educational Research** 13:89–99.

Schneidewind, N. and Davidson, E. 1983. **Open minds to equality: A sourcebook of learning activities to promote race, sex, class, and age equity**. Englewood Cliffs, NJ: Prentice-Hall.

Sharan, S. 1980. Cooperative learning in small groups.: Recent methods and effects on achievement, attitudes, and ethnic relations. **Review of Educational Research** 50:241–271.

Sharan, S. 1990. **Cooperative learning: Theory and research**. New York: Praeger.

Sharan, S. and Hertz-Lazarowitz, R. 1980. A group-investigation method of cooperative learning in the classroom. In S. Sharan, P. Hare, C.D. Webb, and R. Hertz-Lazarowitz (eds.), **Cooperation in education**. Provo, UT: Brigham Young University Press.

Sharan, S. and Sharan, Y. 1976. **Small-group teaching**. Englewood Cliffs, NJ: Educational Technology Publications.

Sharan, Y., and Sharan, S. 1992. **Expanding cooperative learning through group investigation**. New York: Teachers College Press.

Shaw, M.E. 1964. Communication networks. In L. Berkowitz (ed.), **Advances in experimental social psychology**, vol. I, 111–147. New York: Academic Press.

Shaw, M. 1981. **Group dynamics**. 3rd ed. New York: McGraw-Hill.

Shaw, M.E. 1983. Group composition. In H.H. Blumberg, A.P. Hare, V. Kent, and M.F. Davies (eds.), **Small groups and social interaction,** vol. 1. Chichester, England: John Wiley.

Shepperd, J.A. 1993. Productivity loss in performance groups: A motivation analysis. **Psychological Bulletin** 113:67–81.

Shiffrin, R.M. and Schneider, W. 1977. Controlled and automatic human information processing II: Perceptual learning, automatic attending, and a general theory. **Psychological Review** 84:127–190.

Skinner, B.F. 1953. **Science and human behavior.** New York: Macmillan.

Slavin, R.E. 1977. Classroom reward structure: An analytical and practical review. **Review of Educational Research** 47:633–650.

Slavin, R.E. 1980. **Using student team learning.** rev. ed. Baltimore, MD.: The Johns Hopkins Team Learning Project.

Slavin, R.E. 1983a. When does cooperative learning increase student achievement? **Psychological Bulletin** 94:429–445.

Slavin, R.E. 1983b. **Cooperative learning.** Research on Teaching Monograph Series. New York: Longman.

Slavin, R.E. 1986. **Using student team learning.** 3rd ed. Baltimore, MD: The Johns Hopkins Team Learning Project.

Slavin, R.E. 1989a. Cooperative learning and student achievement. In R.E. Slavin (ed.), **School and classroom organization,** 129–156. Hillsdale, NJ: Erlbaum.

Slavin, R.E. 1989b. Cooperative learning and student achievement: Six theoretical perspectives. In C. Ames and M.L. Maehr (eds.), **Advances in motivation and achievement.** 161–177. Greenwich, CT: JAI Press.

Slavin, R.E. 1990a. Ability grouping, cooperative learning, and the gifted: Point-Counterpoint. **Journal for the Education of the Gifted.** 14:3–8, 28–30.

Slavin, R.E. 1990b. **Cooperative learning: Theory, research, and practice.** Englewood Cliffs, NJ: Prentice-Hall.

Slavin, R.E. April, 1990c. **Cooperative learning and language minority students.** Paper presented at the annual meeting of the American Educational Research Association, Boston, MA.

Slavin, R.E. 1991a. Group rewards make groupwork work: Response to Kohn. **Educational Leadership** 48:89–91.

Slavin, R.E. 1991b. Synthesis of research on cooperative learning. **Educational Leadership** 48:71–82.

Slavin, R.E. 1991c. **Student team learning: A practical guide to cooperative learning.** 3rd. ed. Washington, DC: National Education Association.

Slavin, R.E. 1992. When and why does cooperative learning increase achievement? Theoretical and empirical perspectives. In R. Hertz-Lazarowitz and N. Miller (eds.), **Interaction in cooperative groups: The theoretical anatomy of group learning,** 145–173. Cambridge: Cambridge University Press.

Slavin, R.E., Leavey, M., and Madden, N.A. 1982. **TAI Mathematics: Team Assisted Individualization: Teacher's Manual.** rev. ed. Center for Social Organization of Schools. Baltimore, MD: Johns Hopkins University.

Steiner, I.D. 1972. **Group processes and productivity.** New York: Academic Press.

Stevens, R. and Slavin, R. 1991. When cooperative learning improves the achievement of students with mild disabilities: A response to Tateyama-Sniezek. **Exceptional Children** 57:276–280.

Swisher, K. 1990. Cooperative learning and the education of American Indian/Alaskan native students: A review of the literature and suggestions for implementation. **Journal of American Indian Education** 29:36–43.

Tateyama-Sniezek, K.M. 1990. Cooperative learning: Does it improve the academic achievement of students with handicaps? **Exceptional Children.** 56:426–437.

Triplett, N. 1897. The dynamogenic factors in pacemaking and competition. **American Journal of Psychology** 9:507–533.

Tuckman, B.W. 1965. Developmental sequence in small groups. **Psychological Bulletin** 63:384–399.

Tuckman, B. and Jensen, M.A. 1977. Stages of small group development revisited. **Group and Organization Studies** 2:419–427.

Vygotsky, L.S. 1978. **Mind in society: The development of higher mental processes.** Cambridge, MA: Harvard University Press

Webb, N. 1989. Peer interaction and learning in small groups. **International Journal of Educational Research** 13:21–39.

Webb, N.M. 1992. Testing a theoretical model of student interaction and learning in small groups. In R. Hertz-Lazarowitz and N. Miller (eds.), **Interaction in cooperative groups: The theoretical anatomy of group learning,** 102–119. New York: Cambridge University Press.

Weiner 1986. **An attribution theory of motivation and emotion.** New York: Springer-Verlag.

Wertsch, J.V. 1985. **Vygotsky and the social formation of mind.** Cambridge, MA: Harvard University Press.

Winitsky, N.E. 1991. Classroom organization for social studies. In J.P. Shaver (ed.), **Handbook of research on social studies teaching and learning.** New York: MacMillan.

Wittrock, M.C. 1990. Generative processes of comprehension. **Educational Psychologist.** 24:345–376.

Zajonc, R. 1965. Social facilitation. **Science** 149:269–274.

Index

We are interested in your reaction to **Classroom Connections: Understanding and Using Cooperative Learning** by Philip C. Abrami, Bette Chambers, Catherine Poulsen, Christina De Simone, Sylvia d'Apollonia, and James Howden. You can help us to improve this book in future editions by completing this questionnaire.

1. What was your reason for using this book?

   ☐ university course ☐ college course ☐ continuing education course

   ☐ professional development ☐ personal interest ☐ other (specify) _____

2. If you are a student, please identify your school and the course in which you used this book.

3. Which chapters or parts of this book did you use? Which did you omit?

4. What did you like best about this book? What did you like least?

5. Please identify any topics you think should be added to future editions.

6. Please add any comments or suggestions.

7. May we contact you for further information?

   Name: _____

   Address: _____

   Phone: _____

(fold here and tape shut)

MAIL  **POSTE**

Canada Post Corporation / Société canadienne des postes

Postage paid
If mailed in Canada

Port payé
si posté au Canada

**Business
Reply**

**Réponse
d'affaires**

0116870399   01

0116870399-M8Z4X6-BR01

Heather McWhinney
Publisher, College Division
HARCOURT BRACE & COMPANY, CANADA
55 HORNER AVENUE
TORONTO, ONTARIO
M8Z 9Z9